Asteria Books

Practical Grimoire

Practical Grimoire

© 2025, Asteria Books

ISBN: 978-1-956765-33-5 (paperback)
ISBN: 978-1-956765-34-2 (hardback)
ISBN: 978-1-956765-35-9 (PDF)

This book was written and designed by Laurelei Black for the Asteria Books "Grimoire Project."

No part of this work may be reproduced or distributed to any audience for any purpose without the express written permission of the author.

Information in this book is not intended to replace medical treatment. Please consult with your healthcare provider regarding herbal preparations and recommendations.

laurelei@asteriabooks.com

For more great BOS pages in PDF format, visit our Etsy shop at www.bladeandbroom.etsy.com. Check Amazon and Etsy for our paperback and hardcover grimoire compilations as they become available.

The Grimoire Project

since 2012

Asteria Books

Practical Grimoire

Contents

Basics

How to Write a Spell
Spell Record Sheet
Magical Correspondences
Correspondences
... of the Sun
... of the Moon
... of Mars
... of Mercury
... of Jupiter
... of Venus
... of Saturn
Personal Correspondences
Color Magick
Poppets
Weather Magick
Blood Magick
Substitutions for Blood in Magick
Fiber Magick
Food Magick
Sabbat Wine

Voces Magicae

Voces Magicae (intro)
To Lay the Witch's Compass
To Banish Unwelcome Spirits & Energy
To Evoke a Spirit
To Summon a Person
To Call the WitchMother's Power
To Call the WitchFather's Power
To Command an Unfamiliar Spirit
To Invite a Familiar
To Draw the Spirit's Attention
For Spiritual Enlightenment
To Increase Self-Esteem, Knowledge, and Empowerment
To Travel Tirelessly
To See the Future
To Know Another's Secrets
To Preserve Beauty
To Win the Love of Another
To Attract Love
To Render a Man Impotent
To Provide Wealth in Abundance
To Protect Against Disease and Melancholy
To Protect Against Disease and Evil
For Healing
To Eliminate Pain
To Enhance Healing Magick
For Healing and Protection
To Protect Against All Evils
For Protection Against Evil
For All Manner of Blessings
To Banish Evil & Attract Joy
For Protection & to Enhance Requests
To Enhance Magickal Formulas
To Seal a Working
To Open All Roads
To Ease Childbirth
To Attract Fortune/Luck
To Discover a Liar or Thief
To Escape from Jail
To Pass Unseen
Blank Record

Candle Magick

Candle Magick
Candle Magick Basics
Candle Sizes and Figures
Dressing Candles
Candle Gardens
Candle Magick Tips

Dream Magick

Dream Time
Dream Pillows
Lucid Dreaming
Dream Walking
Dream Casting
DreamWork Herbs
Dream Protection
Insomnia
Night Battles
Dream Lovers
Incubi, Succubi, Night Hags & the Mare
Oneiromancy
Dream Journal

Hearth Magick

Cottage Witchcraft
Cottage Correspondences
Magical House Cleaning
Magical Cleaning Schedule
Cottage Cleansing Rituals
Guardians, Wards & Spirits of Place
House Blessings
Buying, Selling, and Moving
Hospitality
Magic for the Kitchen
Magic for the Bathroom
Magic for the Bedrooms
Magic for the Garage
Sitting Room Magic

Talismanic Magick

Amulets & Talismans
Bellarmine Jars
Cimaruta
Cornicello
Egg Magick
Hag Stones
Hamsa
Witches' Ladders
Lamp Magick
Magickal Pouches
Mano Cornuto
Mano Fico
Milagros
Rope and Feathers
Sator Square
Solomonic Pentacles
... of Saturn
... of Jupiter
... of Mars
... of the Sun
... of Venus
... of Mercury
... of the Moon
Witch Bottles
Witch's Glove
Witch Peg
Witches' Stones
Domination Talismans
Fertility Talismans
Health Talismans
Love Talismans
Luck Talismans
Money Talismans
Protection Talismans
Psychic Power Talismans
Travel Talismans

Sigil Crafting

Sigil Craft: An Overview
Rosy Cross Method
Rose Cross Template (Hebrew)
Rose Cross Template (Latin)
Rose Cross Template (blank)
Kamea Method
Letters to Numbers
Sun Kamea
Moon Kamea
Mercury Kamea
Mars Kamea
Venus Kamea
Jupiter Kamea
Saturn Kamea

AO Spare Method
Spirit Method
Symbolic Method
Planetary Signs and Sigils
Personal Symbol Lexicon

Magickal Alphabets

Theban
Celestial
Alphabet of the Magi
Malachim
Masonic Cipher
Passing the River
Pictish Swirl
Theban

Crystal Magick

Birth Stones
Casting Stones
Cleansing Your Crystals
Charging Your Crystals
Stone Altars
Crystal Balls
Crystal Bowls
Crystal Wands
Getting to Know a Stone
Gemstone Jewelry
Stones in Magick
Stones in Healing
Crystal Grids
Seed of Life
Flower of Life
Hexagram
12-Pointed Star
9-Pointed Star
8-Pointed Star
Gem Elixirs

Crystal Index

Agate
Amber
Amethyst
Ammonites
Apache Tear
Aquamarine
Aventurine
Belemnites
Bloodstone

Boji Stones
Calcite
Carnelian
Cat's Eye
Celestite
Chalcedony
Chrysocolla
Citrine
Clear Quartz
Coal
Coral
Crinoid Columns
Diamond
Echinoids
Emerald
Flint
Fluorite
Garnet
Goldstone
Goshenite
Gryphaea
Heliodor
Hematite
Herkimer Diamond
Jade
Jasper
Jet
Labradorite
Lapis Lazuli
Lava
Libyan Desert Glass
Lodestone
Malachite
Marble
Megalodon Teeth
Moldavite
Moonstone
Morganite
Mother-of-Pearl
Obsidian
Onyx
Opal
Pearl
Peridot
Petrified Wood
Pyrite
Rose Quartz
Ruby
Salt
Sapphire
Selenite
Seraphinite
Shark Teeth
Smoky Quartz
Sodalite
Staurolite
Sugilite

Crystal Index, cont.

Sulfur
Sunstone
Tektites
Tiger's Eye
Topaz
Tourmaline
Trilobites
Turquoise
Zircon

Metal Index

Brass
Bronze
Copper
Gold
Iron
Lead
Mercury
Pewter
Silver
Steel
Tin

Animal Magick

Totemic Animals
Animal Spirit Allies
Shapeshifting
Otherkin
Vulture Culture

Animal Index

Alligator
Bear
Bee
Blackbird
Cat
Cattle
Chicken
Cougar
Coyote
Crane
Crow
Deer
Eagle
Fox
Goat
Goose
Hare
Hawk
Horse
Hound
Hummingbird
Lapwing
Moose
Moth/Butterfly
Owl
Raven
Robin
Salmon
Seal
Sheep
Snake
Spider
Swan
Swine
Toad
Wolf
Wren

Practical Craft

How to Write a Spell

DEFINE THE NEED. What do you need to happen? Will it happen through the natural course of events? Is this need in everyone's best interest? Will something be harmed if you get what you need through magic? Are you okay with that harm? If not, what needs to change?

DETERMINE THE INTENT. This is the final outcome or purpose of the spell. What do you plan to accomplish by doing this spell? What do you want to change? What result do you want? Make sure you understand and describe for yourself how you feel, what you will see/hear/etc when the outcome has been obtained. You want to be able to feel it as a reality when the spell is concluded -- and feel gratitude for it.

PLAN THE BODY OF THE SPELL. What tools do you need? What sacred space do you require? What Deities, Elements, trees, animals, herbs, energies, mythical creatures, etc. do you plan to use to empower the work? What oils, candles, incenses, symbols or other objects can you use? Will you chant? How will you raise and focus energy? Will you make an amulet or a talisman? When should your spell be done for maximum effect? Is the time of day, lunar phase or astrological sign important? All of these things will have some effect on your spell. Is your need strong enough to overcome possible astrological conflicts? Where should you do your spell for greatest effect?

DOCUMENT YOUR SPELL CRAFT. Write down everything you have decided to do. Write down the words of the spell, since variations in wording can change the outcome of the spell.

REFLECT AGAIN ON WHAT YOU HAVE DECIDED TO DO. Look at the whole thing. Are there any troublesome areas? Are your intentions clear? Is this spell in keeping with your personal ethics? Will it achieve the desired outcome? What are all the possible ramifications of this magic? Have you done divinations? What have they told you? What is the price of the magic?

PERFORM THE SPELL. Document any last-minute changes as well as the impressions that you got while performing it. Make note of the outcome in your records and reflect on the overall effectiveness as well as the minutia.

Copyright Asteria Books 2018

Spell Record

Specific purpose:

Moon Phase & Sign: **Sun Sign:**   **Planetary Hour:**

Elementals:

Totemic Animals or Plants:

Deities:

Other Spirits:

Type of Sacrifice:

Materials:

Pre-spell set-up (if needed):

Specific location (if needed):

Steps:

1.

2.

3.

4.

5.

Results
Did the spell work?
How long did it take to manifest?
Is there a time limit on the spell?
Does it need to be repeated?
Describe the specific results and how they manifested:

Magical Correspondences

The practice of magical correspondences has an ancient history, with its origins stretching back to the earliest written magical texts. While the term "correspondence" may be modern, the underlying concept—that objects, colors, plants, and celestial bodies possess specific, interconnected magical properties—is a foundational principle of magic in many ancient civilizations.

The earliest written examples of what we now call correspondences can be found in ancient Mesopotamia and Egypt, dating as far back as the 3rd and 4th millennia BCE.

Ancient Mesopotamia: Ingredients for incantations and rituals were chosen for their symbolic properties. For example, a curse might involve using an effigy of an enemy, while a healing spell might call for herbs with a specific color or shape that "corresponded" to the ailment.

Ancient Egypt: Hieroglyphic amulets and funerary texts like the Book of the Dead are filled with spells and items that corresponded to specific gods, powers, and protective qualities. For example, a scarab amulet corresponded to the god Khepri and was worn for protection and rebirth.

Greco-Roman Texts: Works like the *Cyranides*, a 4th-century grimoire, laid out the magical properties of plants, animals, and stones, linking them to specific remedies and spells. The Hellenistic era also produced texts like the *Greek Magical Papyri* (PGM), which detailed elaborate rituals using objects and symbols that corresponded to Gods, stars, and spirits.

Renaissance Occultism: The concept reached its most complex form during the Renaissance with the work of figures like Heinrich Cornelius Agrippa. His influential book, *Three Books of Occult Philosophy* (1531), provided extensive tables of correspondences that linked planets, angels, colors, metals, herbs, and animals in a vast, interconnected magical system. This work heavily influenced modern Western esotericism and is a direct ancestor of the correspondence tables used today.

Copyright Asteria Books 2025

Correspondences

The magickal associations and correspondences listed on the following pages are based on the work of occult philosophers like Heinrich Corenlius Agrippa.

It should be noted that although these have become somewhat crystallized or standardized in current magickal practice, they are Euro-centric and cannot hope to convey the associations that might be found in he many cultural, indigenous, and folkloric practices that have spanned human history.

Students of folkloric and culture-specific practices would be wise to ignore these pages and instead undertake the task of creating tables that correlate most closely with the magickal practices of their chosen culture within the landscape of its own place and time.

The correspondences shared here might be used most readily as a "lingua franca" or a "common language" of magick for those who have been touched by the colonizing and standardizing expansions of European imperialism.

Correspondences of the Sun

Day of the Week: Sunday

Zodiac Signs: Leo (primary ruler), also associated with Aries

Element: Fire

Metal: Gold

Colors: Gold, yellow, orange, and bright red

Directions: South

Magical Intentions: Success, prosperity, vitality, healing, confidence, power, creativity, joy, and courage

Emotions: Joy, confidence, vitality, pride, and authority

Archetypes: The King, The Father, The Hero, The Leader

Deities: Ra (Egyptian), Apollo (Greek), Helios (Greek), Sol (Roman), Inti (Incan), Lugh (Celtic)

Angels: Archangel Michael

Demons: Bael, Orias, and other powerful Goetic spirits associated with royalty and power (Note: These associations vary widely and are often considered dangerous).

Other Spirits: The Olympic Spirit of the Sun is Och.

Herbs and Plants: Sunflower, Marigold, Frankincense, St. John's Wort, Saffron, Bay Laurel

Stones and Crystals: Citrine, Topaz, Tiger's Eye, Amber, Diamond, Sunstone

Animals: Lion, Eagle, Phoenix, Hawk, Rooster

Tarot Cards: The Sun (XIX), Strength (VIII), The Emperor (IV)

Musical Instruments: Trumpet, Horn, Cymbals

Magickal Tools: Wand, Scepter, Amulets of power

Correspondences of the Moon

Day of the Week: Monday

Zodiac Signs: Cancer (primary ruler)

Element: Water

Metal: Silver

Colors: Silver, white, gray, pearlescent, and opalescent

Directions: West

Magical Intentions: Intuition, psychic abilities, dreams, fertility, healing, cleansing, protection, and emotional balance

Emotions: Intuition, emotions, subconscious, dreams, memory, receptivity

Archetypes: The Mother, The Queen, The Maiden, The Crone, The Priestess

Deities: Selene (Greek), Luna (Roman), Artemis (Greek), Diana (Roman), Isis (Egyptian), Mama Quilla (Incan), Hecate (Greek)

Angels: Archangel Gabriel

Demons: Bune, Murmur

Other Spirits: The Olympic Spirit of the Moon is Phul.

Herbs and Plants: Jasmine, Moonflower, Willow, Poppy, White Rose, Sandalwood

Stones and Crystals: Moonstone, Pearl, Selenite, Opal, Mother of Pearl, Aquamarine

Animals: Crab, Owl, Cat, Frog, Wolf, Hare

Tarot Cards: The Moon (XVIII), The High Priestess (II), The Chariot (VII)

Musical Instruments: Flute, Harp, Bells, Cymbals

Magickal Tools: Chalice, Scrying mirror, Divination tools

Correspondences of Mars

Day of the Week: Tuesday

Zodiac Signs: Aries and Scorpio (primary rulers)

Element: Fire

Metal: Iron and Steel

Colors: Red, scarlet, blood red, and orange-red

Directions: South

Magical Intentions: Protection, courage, strength, defense, conflict, passion, willpower, and physical energy

Emotions: Anger, courage, aggression, passion, willpower, and impulsiveness

Archetypes: The Warrior, The Soldier, The Gladiator, The Rebel

Deities: Mars (Roman), Ares (Greek), Tyr (Norse), Sekhmet (Egyptian), Ogun (Yoruba)

Angels: Archangel Camael

Demons: Agares, Sallos, and other Goetic spirits associated with conflict, war, and aggression

Other Spirits: The Olympic Spirit of Mars is Phaleg.

Herbs and Plants: Basil, Nettles, Thistle, Mustard, Ginger, Garlic, Chili Peppers

Stones and Crystals: Ruby, Garnet, Bloodstone, Red Jasper, Red Tiger's Eye

Animals: Wolf, Bear, Ram, Scorpion, Vulture

Tarot Cards: The Tower (XVI), The Emperor (IV), The Chariot (VII)

Musical Instruments: Drums, Horns, Trumpets, Cymbals

Magickal Tools: Sword, Knife, Athame, Spear, Shield

Copyright Asteria Books 2025

Correspondences of Mercury

Day of the Week: Wednesday

Zodiac Signs: Gemini and Virgo

Element: Air

Metal: Quicksilver (Mercury)

Colors: Yellow, orange, silver, and iridescent

Directions: East

Magical Intentions: Communication, intelligence, travel, business, writing, teaching, and learning

Emotions: Witty, curious, adaptable, nervous, and quick-thinking

Archetypes: The Messenger, The Trickster, The Scholar, The Merchant

Deities: Hermes (Greek), Mercury (Roman), Thoth (Egyptian), Loki (Norse)

Angels: Archangel Raphael

Demons: Bune, Gremory, and other Goetic spirits associated with communication and learning

Other Spirits: The Olympic Spirit of Mercury is Ophiel.

Herbs and Plants: Lavender, Fennel, Dill, Parsley, Anise, Licorice

Stones and Crystals: Agate, Opal, Citrine, Mica, Aventurine

Animals: Fox, Monkey, Magpie, Ibis, Parrot, Swift-moving birds

Tarot Cards: The Magician (I), The Lovers (VI), Judgement (XX)

Musical Instruments: Flute, Whistle, Keyboard, Wind Instruments

Magickal Tools: Wand, Quill, Pen, Books, Communication Devices

Correspondences of Jupiter

Day of the Week: Thursday

Zodiac Signs: Sagittarius and Pisces

Element: Air

Metal: Tin

Colors: Blue, royal blue, purple, and gold

Directions: East (often associated with Jupiter's rising influence)

Magical Intentions: Prosperity, luck, expansion, success, leadership, wisdom, justice, and abundance

Emotions: Optimism, generosity, joy, benevolence, and authority

Archetypes: The King, The Father, The Judge, The Guru, The Benefactor

Deities: Jupiter (Roman), Zeus (Greek), Thor (Norse), Amun-Ra (Egyptian)

Angels: Archangel Sachiel

Demons: Amon, Murmur, and other Goetic spirits associated with knowledge, truth, and leadership

Other Spirits: The Olympic Spirit of Jupiter is Bethor.

Herbs and Plants: Oak, Sage, Dandelion, Hyssop, Star Anise, Cinnamon

Stones and Crystals: Amethyst, Lapis Lazuli, Sapphire, Sugilite, Sodalite

Animals: Eagle, Horse, Elephant, Griffin, Unicorn

Tarot Cards: The Wheel of Fortune (X), Justice (VIII), The Hierophant (V)

Musical Instruments: Organ, Tuba, Drums, and instruments with a deep, resonant sound

Magickal Tools: Scepter, Crown, Ceremonial Robes, Amulets of Success

Copyright Asteria Books 2025

Correspondences of Venus

Day of the Week: Friday

Zodiac Signs: Taurus and Libra

Element: Water and Earth

Metal: Copper

Colors: Green, pink, light blue, and copper

Directions: West

Magical Intentions: Love, beauty, friendship, harmony, pleasure, art, creativity, and money

Emotions: Love, affection, joy, sensuality, appreciation for beauty, and desire

Archetypes: The Lover, The Artist, The Diplomat, The Courtesan

Deities: Venus (Roman), Aphrodite (Greek), Freya (Norse), Hathor (Egyptian), Oshun (Yoruba)

Angels: Archangel Haniel

Demons: Vapula, Sitri, and other spirits associated with lust, love, and passion

Other Spirits: The Olympic Spirit of Venus is Hagith.

Herbs and Plants: Rose, Apple, Myrtle, Cherry, Mint, Passionflower

Stones and Crystals: Rose Quartz, Emerald, Jade, Malachite, Peridot, Copper

Animals: Dove, Swan, Cat, Rabbit, Sparrow

Tarot Cards: The Empress (III), The Lovers (VI), Justice (XI)

Musical Instruments: Lyre, Harp, Flute, Cello, and instruments with a soft, melodic sound

Magickal Tools: Chalice, Mirror, Ribbons, Flowers, Art Supplies

Correspondences of Saturn

Day of the Week: Saturday

Zodiac Signs: Capricorn and Aquarius

Element: Earth

Metal: Lead

Colors: Black, dark blue, indigo, and brown

Directions: North

Magical Intentions: Discipline, boundaries, structure, karma, banishment, protection, wisdom, and time

Emotions: Melancholy, seriousness, responsibility, patience, and concentration

Archetypes: The Father, The Crone, The Hermit, The Architect

Deities: Saturn (Roman), Cronus (Greek), Hel (Norse), Hecate (Greek)

Angels: Archangel Cassiel

Demons: Azazel, Samigina, and other spirits associated with deep knowledge, binding, and structure

Other Spirits: The Olympic Spirit of Saturn is Aratron.

Herbs and Plants: Yew, Cypress, Henbane, Nightshade, Belladonna, Comfrey

Stones and Crystals: Onyx, Obsidian, Jet, Lead, Black Tourmaline, Lapis Niger

Animals: Owl, Goat, Raven, Snake, Bear

Tarot Cards: The World (XXI), The Devil (XV), The Hermit (IX)

Musical Instruments: Bass, Low Drums, and instruments with a low, deep tone

Magickal Tools: Scythe, Hourglass, Anchor, Black Mirror, Binding Cord

Personal Correspondences

In many folkloric traditions of Witchcraft, tables of correspondences are created by the individual Witch and reflect years of study and reflection on one's own dreams, experiences, and symbolic associations. Use the following page as a template to record your own correspondences, making copies as needed for your Book of Arte.

Personal Correspondences

Day of the Week:

Zodiac Signs:

Element:

Metal:

Colors:

Directions:

Magical Intentions:

Emotions:

Archetypes:

Deities:

Angels:

Demons:

Other Spirits:

Herbs and Plants:

Stones and Crystals:

Animals:

Tarot Cards:

Musical Instruments:

Magickal Tools:

Color Magick

Color plays a vital role in the magickal workings of modern Crafters. Whether it was always so vital for our forbears is a matter of debate. Access to dyes and pigments was not always as easy as it is today, so color would have definitely given an extra "kick" to any working the Witch performed. Color, in the past, would have been either costly or arduous to acquire, making its addition something of a sacrifice on the part of the Witch.

One of the least acknowledged aspects of color magick in contemporary times is the fact that different cultures have different associations with the spectrum of colors. Indeed, we've learned that cultural difference can even impact the range of colors we perceive. For this reason, Witches should be distrustful of any source that insists a certain color "means" a certain thing, unless adequate cultural context is provided.

The color associations provided here are taken from the Hermetic tradition, which is one of the foundational pieces of most modern European-derived magick. In the Hermetic tradition, the seven classical planets are each associated with a color, a day of the week, entities and creatures, and a sphere of influence. These associations should be evident in the following list:

Red ~ passion, anger, love, life, vitality, Mars, iron, fire
Yellow ~ sunshine, intellect, joy, wisdom, Sun, gold, fire
Green ~ growth, renewal, hope, love, abundance, Venus, copper, earth
Blue ~ the heavens, divinity, spirit, loyalty, truth, serenity, Jupiter, tin, air
Purple (Indigo, Violet) ~ royalty, spirituality, higher consciousness, sorrow
Black ~ transformation, death, mystery, the unknown, Saturn, lead, earth
White ~ purity, innocence, perfection, divine light, Moon, silver, water

Copyright Asteria Books 2025

Poppets

Dolls have been used in magick all over the world, and the Witch's poppet (as well as the "Voodoo doll") are both iconic symbols of traditional folk magick. Dolls are a common household item, both as a child's toy and as a decorative touch. In terms of sympathetic magic, there is no better representation of the total human body that is so easily within reach.

One can fashion a doll from nearly any material — cloth, clay, wood, paper, leftover plastic sacks, hanks of yarn, bundles of grass. This makes them supremely versatile to the Witch and the Rootworker, both of whom are often using whatever materials are most readily available.

Many people have a preconceived (and incorrect) notion that the poppet is only used for cursing and baneful magicks. To the contrary, Witches just as frequently use dolls in healing, blessing, and protection magick for their target. Like any tool, they can be used for both light and dark work.

To make a simple poppet, cut a roughly human shape from two pieces of fabric. A gingerbread-man shape works very nicely. Decide which piece of fabric is the front and which is the back. On the front, stitch, paint, or draw a face as well as any other identifying markings you which to include. You might consider including scars or birthmarks, gender markers (like a cowrie shell for vulva or a gemstone point for phallus), yarn for hair, astrological signs, names, etc. You can also choose to embellish the outside (front and back) with symbols (runes, sigils), stones, or other magickal bits related to the intention for the target.

Once you have the outside looking the way you want, stitch the front and back together. You can either face the outsides together, stitch (while leaving and opening at the head), and then turn them right-side out so your seams are hidden inside; OR, you can topstitch (still leaving an opening at the head) for a more primitive/rustic look.

Through the opening in the head, you will stuff the poppet with cotton batting (cotton balls work great), herbs, chipped or crushed gemstones, charms, hair or nail clippings of the target, and/or papers with written messages.

When you're finished, name the doll with the target's name and tell it what you want it to do! Use pins to direct energy, if you like.

Copyright Asteria Books 2018

Weather Magick

Some Witches have shown a particular gift with predicting, creating, or controlling the weather. A few can do all three. Weather Witches are sometimes also called *tempestarii*, a title that dates back to at least 815AD. Indeed, weather-witching is one of the earliest documented forms of magick, with attestations of weather magick in the ancient world and nearly all of the Deities of the most ancient civilizations having some control over various aspects of the weather.

Tying Up the Winds

In Scotland, a Witch would tie three knots in a rag for sailors and fishermen to untie at need. If the first knot was untied, wind would fill the sails. With the untying of the second knot, a stronger wind would blow. For the third, a tempest would be unleashed.

Stirring A Storm

In Germany, a young girl during the Witch trials demonstrated her command of the weather with a bowl of water. She called upon the Devil's name as she stirred the water, and rains fell upon the field. With a shift in her focus, hail fell on another field nearby.

Whistling the Wind

You can use the tone, intensity, and pitch of your whistle to command a wind, if you possess the gift to call the Winds. A short, sharp whistle will call a quick gust. A long, light whistle, whistle will call a gentle breeze, etc.

Cutting a Storm

If you are faced with severe weather, you can use your black-handled knife to slice through the storm cell. Face the storm and align with the energy of it until you feel its essence. Hold your knife aloft, blade brandished, and run shrieking into the face of the storm. Stop and thrust your blade into the earth with the blade facing the wind. See the storm sliced open and passing by you to either side. This is said to divert even a tornado.

Copyright Asteria Books 2018

Blood Magick

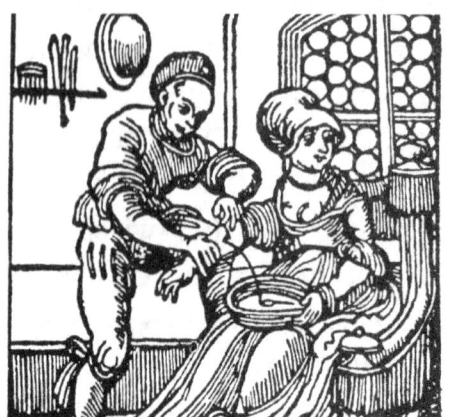

Blood, being the very stuff that nourishes and carries the essence of life, is a powerful magickal substance. Blood-letting in ritual constitutes a sacrifice more dramatic than simply burying coins or pouring libations. Sealing a spell with blood will strengthen almost any working, provided that the blood is shed in accordance with the theme of the spell. (For example, it would be foolish to use your blood in a healing spell when you are ill. However, you could offer a few drops of your healthy blood in a healing spell for a sick friend or covenmate.)

Ethical Considerations

It is the conviction tof many TradCrafters hat shedding any blood other than your own in magick is ethically wrong. Using another individual's blood not only magickally binds them to you, it also can weaken the symbol of blood in the ritual, as the sacrifice made is not your own. Most spells that call for blood can be filled by using only a few drops of personal blood, such as from a finger whose energies correspond to the purpose of the ritual. After all, the life force of a person is transmitted in the blood, and a single drop carries all of the DNA, all of the nutrients, all of the oxygen and life of the person. No more than a drop or two is ever necessary. We often have separate thoughts on sacrificial meals. Blood is definitely spilled when, for instance, a pig is slaughtered for a sacrificial feast. All food dies so that those who consume it might live. Portions of that pig are given to the Godds, and the rest is cooked and eaten by the community as an honoring of the exchange of life and death.

Other Considerations

Always use clean, sterilized pins, blades, or needles when extracting blood for magick. Needles can be sterilized with rubbing alcohol. Never share a needle that you or another person has used to extract blood with. Lancets, like those used by diabetics for pricking fingers before testing blood sugar levels, are convenient, single-use, hygienic alternatives to straight-pins and needles. The "red-handled knife" is used very rarely by most Witches, however it assures that no cross-contamination ever occurs. Each Witch has their own red knife. Keep a supply of bandages and antibiotic ointment handy for after the working.

Copyright Asteria Books 2022

Substitutions for Blood in Magick

Of course, just because a spell calls for blood doesn't mean that blood must be used. Rather, there are many instances where it is preferable not to use blood in a spell, even if it is called for. Squeamish folks may find the thought of pricking themselves with a needle so disturbing that it detracts from the concentration and focus needed to properly cast a spell, or they may choose not to do a great spell at all because they find the call for blood unsettling. Even those comfortable with blood magick may prefer a substitute if more than a drop or two is called for. Here are some common substitutes for blood in magick:

Freshly laid eggs - Fertilized farm fresh eggs from a black hen are thought to be the very best and have long been a charm among the Romani.

Red wine - Even the Catholic Church approves this magickal substitute!

Pomegranate juice - This has the added benefit of looking and smelling vaguely bloody.

Whole pomegranates - Splitting these open with a sturdy boline on the altar can be a memorable and powerful experience, as the fruit is known for "bleeding."

Salt water - One of the reasons salt water is traditionally seen as such a powerful consecration and banishing charm is its taste, which was thought to be similar to that of blood.

Red ink - In place of writing something in actual blood, try using dragon's blood or dove's blood inks.

Menstrual blood - Menstrual cups even make fluid collection easy. (Just beware that using a menstrual cup with an IUD can potentially dislodge your birth control device.)

Iron - considered the menstrual blood of the Earth

Coral - considered the menstrual blood of the Sea

Copyright Asteria Books 2022

Fiber Magick

The term "Fiber Arts" can be used to refer to any type of fiber-related handicraft that is being performed in a traditional way – whether the goal is purely functional, purely artistic, or a mesh of both. Some Crafters prefer this term (over "Fiber Crafts") because it honors the design and skill that is woven into this traditionally female area of work and self-expression.

What types of arts/crafts are included? Practically any that are related to manipulating either natural or synthetic fibers into something useful and/or beautiful. This includes spinning, weaving, knitting, clothing construction, tapestry/wall hanging, dyeing, embroidery, braiding, macrame, rug hooking, lace-making, felting, and more.

Here are a few examples of fiber magick that could be employed by a Witch:

- Spinning fiber to create threads/yarns for ladders, talismans, or embellishment of your robes
- Spinning fiber as a trance-inducing activity for journey work or divination
- Weaving threads to make cloth for robes, putzi bags, or poppets
- Sewing robes, cloaks, and dolls
- Embroidering talismanic or runic designs into robes, cloaks, bags, dolls, and even daily/street clothes
- Piecing and quilting a bed-cover for healing, restful sleep, or passionate intimacy
- Stitching dream pillows
- Creating wall-hangings or banners with magickal intent for home/shrine spaces
- Dyeing a veil for journey work using natural dyes and color symbolism

Copyright Asteria Books 2022

Food Magick

The simple daily rituals of nutrition and hydration are easily available opportunities to infuse your daily life with magickal intention.

Meal-Time Prayer

Though many contemporary Witches and Pagans do not say prayers to bless their meals, there are plenty of examples in ancient Paganism and Polytheism of meal blessings, and we almost all have a blessing of a sacrificial or eucharistic meal within our rituals. I'm not suggesting you perform a full Housle every time you eat, but you might find it meaningful to bring mindfulness and gratitude to your mealtimes as a way to connect more deeply with the cycles of life and sacrifice.

Food-Based Spells

There are LOTS of ways to incorporate food into specific magickal workings. You can use the folkloric associations of ingredients as an inspiration (like working with the "apple pie spices" of cinnamon, nutmeg, allspice, and ginger as prosperity-bringers), or let color and other associations influence the work (like making edible "gold coins" from slices of bananas inscribed with a sigil).

In fact, there are hundreds of traditional spells that are predicated on the notion of you either eating a specially prepared food — or else feeding it to your target.

Ritual(ized) Cooking

The entire practice of kitchen witchery is built on the notion that we can (and do) bake our magick into the food we prepare for ourselves and our loved ones. We have the opportunity to infuse each meal with awareness, love, gratitude, generosity, joy, comfort, etc.

And then there's the cooking we might do for our rites. After all, we have a Red Meal as part of all of our rites. Why not bake a special bread or cake? Or, when it feels appropriate, we could prepare a whole meal — a feast, even. The harvest rituals of Lammas, Fall Equinox, and Samhain, as well as the Midwinter holiday all rather beg for food. These are times when we are celebrating bounty, and even the traditions in popular culture tend to revolve around eating treats and feasts from the first whiff of harvest through the gaiety of Yule.

Copyright Asteria Books 2022

Sabbat Wine

"Entheogen" is a Greek-derived word that means "generating the divine within." An entheogen, therefore, is a psychoactive substance that is used in a religious, spiritual or shamanic context. Traditional Witches have used entheogens of several types for centuries, as recorded in the lore of mythology, in the records of the trials and persecutions, and in the regional indigenous shamanic practices that have been assimilated into the Craft in various locales. Among the most commonly used and widely known entheogens in European and American Witchcraft practice are Sabbat Wine and Flying Ointment.

Sabbat Wine

Wine, just as it is, constitutes a powerful entheogen. The Dying and Resurrected God is embodied in the wine in the form of Dionysos -- and in Jesus, for that matter, whose symbolism and mythology associates him with the wine. Dionysos, though, is the "Twice Born" God of the Vine, and his cup is the offering of ecstasy and madness. "I am the vine," he says, and he offers insight into death and rebirth, despair and joy.

Many Witches drink wine -- either a little or a lot -- as a part of their Sabbat rites no matter what. In American Folkloric Witchcraft, we include Sabbat Wine for two separate and distinct purposes -- and the wine is different depending on that purpose.

If we are celebrating the Housle as we usually do within the regular course of ritual, we will sacrifice a cup of red wine. It is the shed blood of the Red Meal that is the Housle. In this instance, we don't add anything to the wine because we don't need any additional entheogenic effect.

If, however, we are doing trance work, flying out, seething, or otherwise seeking an altered state of consciousness, we might prepare our special Sabbat Wine (vinum sabbati). We also prepare this Sabbat Wine for initiations. The vinum sabbati is a sweet red wine in which mugwort and lemongrass have been mulled. After straining the herbs, we add honey to sweeten the mix and cut the bitterness of the mugwort. Both mugwort and lemongrass have gentle psychoactive properties.

It's interesting to note that the term "vinum sabbati" has actually been associated with flying ointment, or the witches' salve, which is the other major entheogen of witchcraft. In fact, Nigel Jackson said flying ointment was "the black wine of owls."

Copyright Asteria Publishing 2012

Voces Magicae

Voces Magicae

Voces magicae, Latin for "magical words," are the powerful, often nonsensical, and rhythmic utterances found in ancient magical texts and spells. These words were not meant to be understood in a conventional language but were believed to be the secret names of spirits, fragments of a divine language, or even the language of the Gods themselves.

The purpose of these words was to provide a direct source of power in a spell. Reciting them was thought to be a way of bypassing the limitations of human language to directly communicate with and command supernatural entities. They were a key component of ancient rituals for protection, commanding demons, and achieving various magical effects.

These words were an essential part of ancient magic, representing a belief that true power lay not in understandable commands, but in the secret, divine, and often incomprehensible language of the Cosmos.

The words of power on the following pages are shared with my own understanding of their use. Some are "barbarous words" while others are known Latin and Greek ritual phrases.

My own teacher shared the belief that Words of Power could be simple and common phrases in one's own language, as well — without losing their power simply due to their familiarity. "NO!" said in the right tone and with full authority and presence can stop anyone (Seen or Unseen) in their tracks.

Copyright Asteria Books 2025

To Lay the Witch's Compass

ZETA TSEDA ZYIDA SZYADA

Outcome/Intention:

To honor and activate the Witch's Compass.

How/When to Use:

Intone the words while walking around the space. I like to alternate between whispering them, singing them, and "vibrating" them. As you do this, visualize the Spirits of the Compass appearing before you in the directions where you know them.

Origin: Spirit-Derived, given to Laurelei Black

To Banish Unwelcome Spirits and Energy

APO PANTOS KAKADAIMONOS

Outcome/Intention:

To banish negativity, evil Spirits, and all unwanted energies and beings from a space. These Greek words mean: "Away (from here) every evil Spirit."

How/When to Use:

Place your right finger to lips in the "call to silence" gesture. Take a breath to steady yourself and gather authority. Then sweep your arm down and behind you while forcefully saying (or shouting) these words. It is worth pointing out that you are not speaking TO the Spirits, but rather ABOUT them. You are declaring to all that they cannot be present.

Origin: Liber XXV: The Star Ruby

To Evoke a Spirit

IAŌBAPHRENEMOUN IARBATHA

Outcome/Intention:

To seal an invocation or evocation to a Spirit whom you desired to appear within your Pyramid of Arte.

How/When to Use:

After speaking whatever words and performing whatever actions you want, wish, or are instructed to say to call upon the Spirit to be present, you may finalize the invocation or evocation by saying these words.

Origin: The Greek Magical Papyri (Papyri Graecae Magicae, PGM)

To Summon a Person

ACOTOS   EXFETEN   CANABO

Outcome/Intention:

To summon a person so they appear before you.

How/When to Use:

Can be used to summon the Spirit of a deceased person to appear before you. Is also able to summon a living target to come to you (though this application is not as instantaneous). Pronounce the words three times. After the first pronouncement, say the person's full name. After the second, say their name again along with any nicknames or aliases. After the third, say their name and their relation to yourself. Finish by burning a chime candle inscribed with their name.

Origin: Reinhold Werner (via Claude Lecouteux)

To Call the Witch Mother's Power

PHORBA PHORBOBAR BARO
PHORPHOR PHORBAI

Outcome/Intention:

To raise and channel the Power of the WitchMother toward the goal for which you are working.

How/When to Use:

Chant these words without ceasing until the energy is raised or the WitchMother is present. Note that "PH" is pronounced like "P" (not like "F").

I find this chant exceptional at calling her to the space for oracular work, divination, and healing.

Origin: The Greek Magical Papyri (Papyri Graecae Magicae, PGM)

Copyright Asteria Books 2025

To Call the Witch Father's Power

ABRAT ABRASAX
SESENGENBARPHARANGES

Outcome/Intention:

To raise and channel the Power of the WitchFather toward the goal for which you are working.

How/When to Use:

Chant these words without ceasing until the energy is raised or the Witch-Father is present. Note that "PH" is pronounced like "P" (not like "F").

I find this chant exceptional at calling him to the space for oracular work, protection, and flight.

Origin: The Greek Magical Papyri (Papyri Graecae Magicae, PGM)

Copyright Asteria Books 2025

To Command an Unfamiliar Spirit

SHEMHAMPHORASH

Outcome/Intention:

To gain mastery over oneself and influence with others (Seen and Unseen). Wisdom is the key that unlocks this mastery and influence. This word translates to "the explicit name" or "the separated name" which references the 72-fold name of God. In some tales of Solomon's magic ring, this name was inscribed on the band. When Solomon looked at the ring, he found the wisdom needed to answer any question and handle any situation.

How/When to Use:

Inscribe the word around the edges of a circular black mirror. When you have need of wisdom and reflection, gaze into the mirror encircled by the word. In stillness and connection to the All, the wisdom will come.

Origin: Sefer Raziel HaMalakh, Key of Solomon, Sefer HaBahir

To Invite a Familiar

CHACHACH   CHACHACH   CHARCHARACHACH

Outcome/Intention:

To call for and invite a "holy assistant" (Familiar) Spirit to be your guide and aide. This phrase is part of a larger spell, but this phrase may be used as part of your own ritual to invite and attract a Familiar.

How/When to Use:

Chant this phrase without ceasing in groups of seven (7, 14, 21, etc) while you raise energy and wait for a Spirit to appear in your Pyramid of Arte. When the Spirit appears, you may ask them questions to determine whether they right as your "holy assistant."

Origin: The Greek Magical Papyri (Papyri Graecae Magicae, PGM)

To Draw the Spirit's Attention

OTHO

Outcome/Intention:

To draw the attention of a Spirit assisting in your spell to the next words you speak or actions your perform. This is a name sometimes associated with both Apollo and Thoth (who were sometimes conflated or syncretized during this time period).

How/When to Use:

This word (another magickal palindrome) is both a Deity's name and also a command to "take heed."

Say this word with authority just before you perform an action or speak a phrase that is the power of your spell. (Pronounced: O-TOH)

Origin: The Greek Magical Papyri (Papyri Graecae Magicae, PGM)

For Spiritual Enlightenment

ABERAMENTHO

Outcome/Intention:

To call upon a "Great Enlightened Master" Spirit (sometimes viewed as Jesus, Thoth, or Hermes) for the purpose of enlightenment and merging with the Divine.

To know oneself as a Divine Being.

How/When to Use:

Speak this holy name alone, in a solitary and wild place. Commune with the Spirit of the Master Teacher before you and within you.

(Note on pronunciation: "TH" here is pronounced "T")

Origin: Pistis Sophia

To Increase Self-Esteem, Knowledge, and Empowerment

TETRAGRAMMATON

Outcome/Intention:

To know oneself, wholly and clearly. Tetragrammaton translates to the "four letters" which is a reference to the name of God, commonly written YHVH. Both those letters and the reference-word Tetragrammaton are ascribed magickal power. YHVH roughly means "I Am That I Am."

How/When to Use:

Self-knowledge and self-acceptance are the ultimate goal in the quest for enlightenment. To know and accept oneself fully and honestly is to step into one's full power.

There are many ways to use both Tetragrammaton and YHVH. One way is to write a goal on a piece of paper and writing the magick word in a circle around it. Fold and carry the paper with you until it comes apart or disappears.

Origin: Mesha Stele, Jewish magical papyri

To Travel Tirelessly

VERINIEL AND JURIMIEL

Outcome/Intention:

To travel great distances without becoming tired.

How/When to Use:

Write these words on the insides of your shoes to give you stamina, strength, and lightness of limb as you travel. These words are particularly useful for runners and hikers, but may also be used very effectively by those travelling internationally by any mode of transport. Write VERINIEL inside the left shoe, and JURIMIEL inside the right shoe.

Origin: Popular, unknown

To See the Future

URIEL SERAPH JOSATA ABLATI AGLA CAILA

Outcome/Intention:

This spell evokes the Angel Uriel to show true visions of the future to the speaker.

How/When to Use:

This formula can be spoken before divination by scrying in water, flame, clouds, smoke, or crystal. It may also be repeated as a chant before lucid dreaming.

Origin: Grimorum Verum

To Know Another's Secrets

NITRAC RADOU SUNANDAM

Outcome/Intention:

To discover the secrets kept by another person. This formula is especially useful when you suspect that person of intentionally withholding the full truth from you.

How/When to Use:

Inscribe the three words on in the inside of a ring. Hold the ring to your ear and speak the words. You will then hear voices from Unseen Spirits and Guides telling you the secrets you would know.

Beware, though! Sometimes the truth is more terrible than you suppose it to be. And what is revealed will stay with you, perhaps to your great regret. After all, ignorance is bliss.

Origin: Tresor

Copyright Asteria Books 2025

To Preserve Beauty

HORMALZA

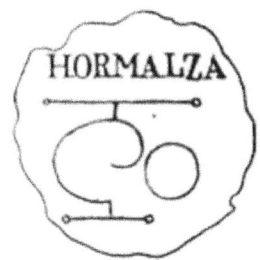

Outcome/Intention:

To preserve both inner and outer beauty. This talisman is said to be of Hebrew origin. According to 19th Century scholar and theologian JJ Bellermann, HORMALZA is a contraction of two words (horma and elza) and means something like "honor to beauty."

How/When to Use:

The word and its accompanying sigil are typically inscribed on jewelry worn close to the skin. Golden pendants are often preferred, since gold is associated with unfading and unassailable beauty in many cultures. (Gold doesn't rust or tarnish.) It can also be written in gold ink or paint upon cosmetics cases, the backs of mirrors, or other items associated with beauty.

Origin: Erfurt manuscript of 1349

To Win the Love of Another

ELØNE ELØNE ELONARUM

Outcome/Intention:

To cause another person to fall in love with you. To enhance and magnify the love they already feel for you.

How/When to Use:

Carve these words onto the skin of an apple and give to your Beloved to eat. By ingesting the words (on a fruit long associated with love), your Beloved will deeply absorb the love magic. For an added boost, you can bite the apple together!

Origin: Norske Hexeformularer og Magiske Opskrifter

To Attract Love

TOOGRAS

Outcome/Intention:

To awaken love in oneself. This is a broad and encompassing sense of love, not simply desire or affection for another person.

How/When to Use:

After waking, but before the sunrise, write the word TOOGRAS on one of your hands.

Origin: Svenske Trollformler, recorded by Bengt af Klintberg

To Render a Man Impotent

RIBALD NOBAL VANARBI

Outcome/Intention:

To afflict a man (particularly a bridegroom) with erectile dysfunction so that he many not consummate his love with his bride/lover.

How/When to Use:

Tie three knots in a length of cord or string in the presence of the target. The original source for this spell says to do this work during the wedding ceremony. Tie each knot tighter than the previous knot. And as each knot is tied, breathe the words: RIBALD on the first knot; NOBAL on the second and tighter knot; VANARBI on the final and tightest knot. If you are able to attach this ligature to the dress of the bride/beloved, or secret into the boudoir, all the better.

Origin: Jean Bodin is credited with recording these words and corresponding spell (according to John Davenport in Aphrodisiacs and Anti-Aphrodisiacs). Note: This spell is currently being promulgated on the Internet as one that "consolidates" love, when in fact it does quite the opposite.

To Provide Wealth in Abundance

SEMZO

Outcome/Intention:

To provide wealth in abundance and attract fortune in its broadest sense. The origin of this talisman is the same as HORMALZA. This is a solar talisman.

How/When to Use:

Draw or engrave this talisman on items associated with money and finance. This might include a money clip or wallet, a cash box, or a safe. If you own a business, you might also display the talisman as a piece of art near the place where transactions are conducted. For online entrepreneurs, you might embed the talisman on your website or use it as a wallpaper on your computer's desktop.

Origin: Erfurt manuscript of 1349

To Protect Against Disease and Melancholy

MONASCHIM

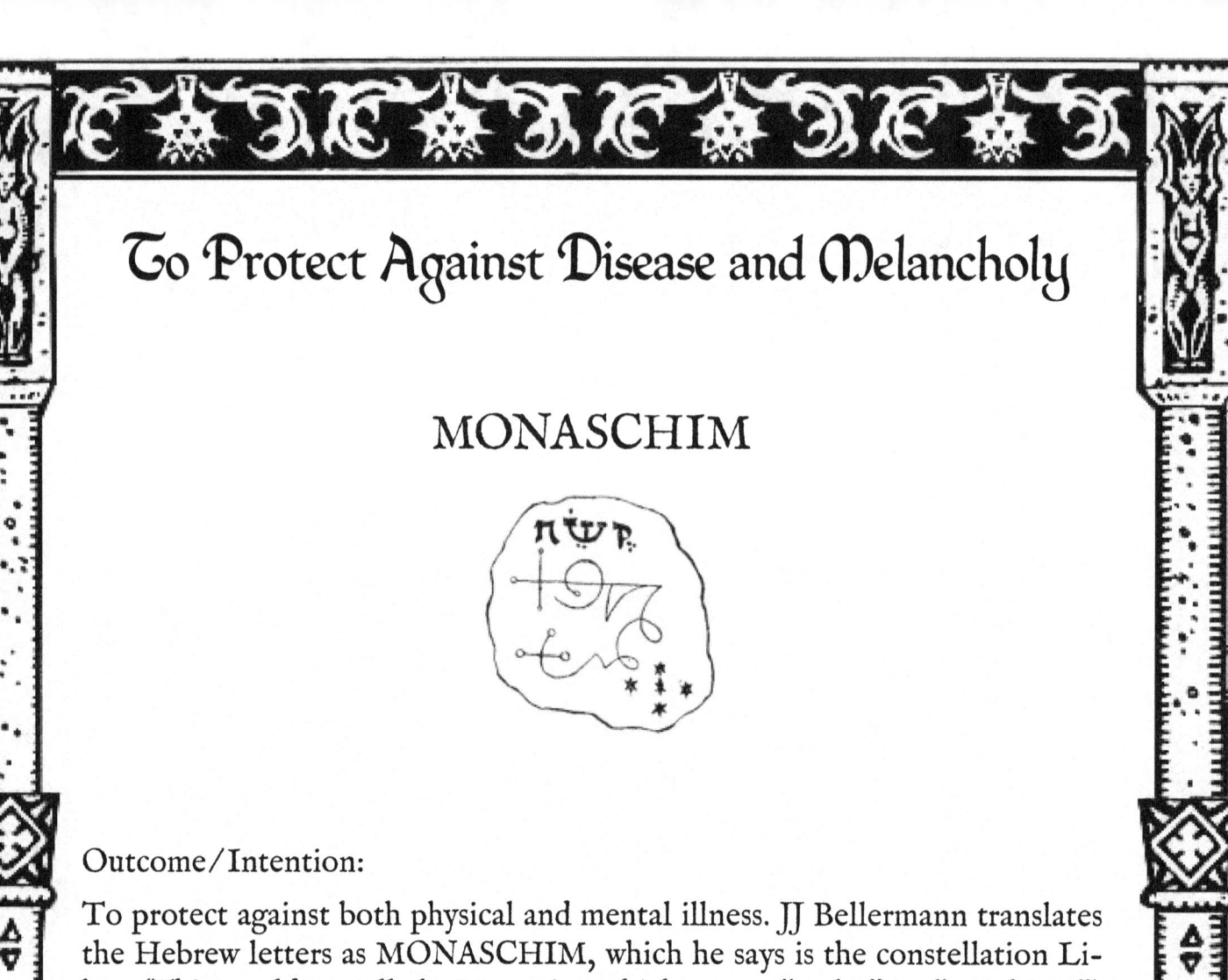

Outcome/Intention:

To protect against both physical and mental illness. JJ Bellermann translates the Hebrew letters as MONASCHIM, which he says is the constellation Libra. (This would actually be Moznaim, which means "scales" or "weighing.") Classical occultists such as Agrippa have attributed Libra with protecting against disease and melancholy while promoting harmony and balance.

How/When to Use:

Chant the word while making this talisman. It could take many forms, such as a wall-hanging in the home of family, a piece of jewelry, etc.

Origin: Erfurt manuscript of 1349

Copyright Asteria Books 2025

To Protect Against Disease & Evil

ABRACADABRA

Outcome/Intention:

To protect against illness or affliction and protect against any evil. This phrase is associated with the Aramaic phrase "abra ke-dabra" which means "I create as I speak" making it a powerful charm of manifestation, invoke the generative powers of the Word.

How/When to Use:

This powerful charm can be worn or displayed to ensure vibrant good health and to attract good luck while repelling negativity. Additionally, it can be spoken aloud before and after stating the intention of a spell.

Origin: Liber Medicinalis

For Healing

EDOAE VEOAFP BEOAEV

Outcome/Intention:

To eliminate pain, especially from a cramp. This spell can be used for both physical and emotional pain with any origin.

How/When to Use:

Write these three word on a small piece of paper and affix to the area of the body affected—under a compress or with a bandage. Then chant the words three times — or until you begin to feel relief.

Origin: Albertus Magnus, Secrets of Egypt

To Eliminate Pain

ANASAGES   ANASAGES   ANASAGES

Outcome/Intention:

To soothe and eliminate intense, focused pain.

How/When to Use:

Speak the words aloud (or repeat them clearly in your mind) until the pain subsides. This should be performed by the person who is in pain. ANASAGES sounds like AH-NAH-SAH-GAYS.

Origin: Treatise on Superstitions

To Enhance Healing Magick

HIM BIT SONA SEL

Outcome/Intention:

To seal a healing working and give it additional power. These words mean "You'll be better soon."

How/When to Use:

Speak the words to the target of your healing magick, as you wrap up the working. The person does not need to be present.

Origin: Leechbook, also Lacnunga

For Healing and Protection

ASKI   KATASKI   LIX   TETRAX
DAMNAMENEUS   AISIA

Outcome/Intention:

To wrap oneself in powerful protection and healing. This combination of words is called the Ephesia Grammata – or the Ephesian Letters.

How/When to Use:

This powerful formula is essentially invoking the fourfold power of light, darkness, sun, and earth to bless and protect the speaker. It is to be spoken aloud as well as inscribed in metal and given to either the water or the earth.

Origin: The Greek Magical Papyri (Papyri Graecae Magicae, PGM)

To Protect Against All Evils

ABLANATHANALBA

Outcome/Intention:

To invoke powerful protection of body, mind, and spirit. This is one of the more well-known magickal palindromes of the PGM.

How/When to Use:

The palindrome can be spoken aloud, while the speaker visualizes their spiritual father. (For many reading this, that will be the WitchFather, the bringer of enlightenment.) It can also be written in a diminishing triangular form (like ABRACADABRA so often is done) in order to enhance its power. This palindrome is often found on talismans, jewelry, and other objects. It is a powerful protection again evil, fear, disease, and attack.

Origin: The Greek Magical Papyri (Papyri Graecae Magicae, PGM)

Copyright Asteria Books 2025

For Protection Against Evil

ANANIZAPTA

Outcome/Intention:

To protect or ward against evil Spirits and other evil-doers.

How/When to Use:

Inscribe as a protective talisman on a ring or pendant. When empowering it, chant the word 9 times. Anytime you need to activate its protection — especially when you are feeling fearful or panic-ridden — hold the ring before you as a shield and chant the word again, in groupings of 3.

Origin: Erfurt manuscript of 1349, Enchiridion of Pope Leo

Copyright Asteria Books 2025

For All Manner of Blessings

ERCE, ERCE, ERCE, Mother of the Earth

Outcome/Intention:

To invoke the blessing of Nature/Mother Earth in any task. This Anglo Saxon invocation calls upon the Ancient Mother of the Earth to lend powerful blessings to requests for healing, protection, abundance, and more.

How/When to Use:

Best when used outdoors and accompanied with an offering given directly to the Earth by burying it. You can speak, sing, or intone the words ERCE ERCE ERCE with or without adding "Mother of the Earth" — so long as you understand that ERCE references the Earth Mother herself and was also understood to mean "true" or "holy" in its original context. You are calling upon the true, holy, and life-sustaining Earth Mother to imbue your desired outcome with her truth, holiness, and life.

Origin: Bald's Leechbook, Cotton Caligula collection

Copyright Asteria Books 2025

To Banish Evil & Attract Joy

ELO ELLEAM FAGIAM GRANTEM

Outcome/Intention:

To attract joy and to banish evil and negativity through this joy. These words are derivative from other languages, and so they can't be translated directly. This formula was specifically created to make people dance.

How/When to Use:

Pronounce these words upon the threshold of a home where tension and sadness currently prevail. You can also write the words on a leaf during a moment of your own joy and give it as a gift to someone who needs it.

Origin: Danmarks Trylleformler (Spells of Denmark) Ferdinand Ohrt

For Protection and to Enhance Requests

AGLA

Outcome/Intention:

To add power and protection to all magickal workings. This word is essentially a kabbalistic acronym of the Hebrew words: Aieth Gadol Leolam Adonai — which means "Thou, O Lord, art mighty forever."

How/When to Use:

As a talismanic feature, this word is often added to other talismans to add power and protection. It can also be chanted when performing a spell or other magickal operation to draw more power to the outcome and to protect both the work and the Witch.

Origin: Kabbalistic — appearing on charms as early as the 12th Century

To Enhance Magickal Formulas

PROBATUM EST

Outcome/Intention:

To enhance and seal a spell or other magickal working. "Probatum est" is a Latin phrase meaning "It is proved" which affirms the speaker's faith in the outcome – because it has already been assured through tried and tested measures.

How/When to Use:

Speak these words aloud at the conclusion of a spell or magickal ritual to seal and assure the outcome you desire.

Origin: Leechbook, Lacnunga

To Seal a Working

IARBATHA

Outcome/Intention:

To finalize a spell and seal the working.

How/When to Use:

As the final word spoken in the ritual space, before making offerings and farewells to any Spirits who helped you, speak this word forcefully. This seals the working and confirms that which you have spoken is indeed so. (I use this phrase instead of the more contemporarily common phrase "So Mote It Be" – particularly when working with Spirits.)

Origin: The Greek Magical Papyri (Papyri Graecae Magicae, PGM)

To Open All Roads

EFFATA   EFFATA   EFFATA

Outcome/Intention:

To open roads, both physical and metaphorical. EFFATA is an Aramaic word meaning "Be opened" and has been used in healing applications as well as spells and workings to create opportunity or remove barriers.

How/When to Use:

Speak these words when performing any type of healing or "road opening" work. This could be during times when you are feeling blocked by circumstances, need an opportunity to appear, notice stagnant energy in your life, or want an abundance of luck. In healing work, these words open the energy flow of the body and mind to move freely for vibrant mental and physical health.

Origin: Albertus Magnus, Secrets of Egypt

To Ease Childbirth

EXI FORAS, SOL TE VOCAT

Outcome/Intention:

To ensure an easy labor and delivery. The words are Latin and mean "Come out, the Sun is calling you."

These words can also be used during periods of initiation or when enlightenment is sought after the "dark night of the soul."

How/When to Use:

For childbirth, any time after a mother has started labor, speak the words to the baby.

For formal initiation, an initiator would say these words following the final trial and before a vow is made. For personal initiation, recognize and honor the process you are undergoing by gazing at your reflection in a mirror and speaking these words to your higher self.

Origin: Oribasius of Pergamon, Medical Synagogues

To Attract Fortune/Luck

FILIBUM STRIT MASO FRANKO

Outcome/Intention:

To win a lottery drawing or other games of chance. Can be used for manifestation and "double fast luck" in general. (These words are derivative from other languages, and so they can't be translated directly.)

How/When to Use:

On the day of the drawing, write these four words on your lottery or raffle ticket. (If there is no ticket for the game you are playing, write the words on a small strip of paper.) I suggest lightly anointing the corners of the paper/ticket with a luck or money drawing oil, and then placing it in your wallet.

Origin: Danmarks Trylleformler (Spells of Denmark) Ferdinand Ohrt

To Discover a Liar or Thief

FOR FROE NOBALUTZ EST

Outcome/Intention:

To reveal if someone has lied to you or stolen from you.

How/When to Use:

Another ingestion spell from the Norske Hexeformularer, but this time we are writing the words on a piece of cheese and offering the cheese to the suspected culprit. If they are unable to eat the cheese, they are guilty of the deed you suspect them of. A similar test existed in which a blessed piece of cheese and a piece of dry bread was offered to a person suspected of lying. If guilty, they would choke on the food and be unable to swallow.

Origin: Norske Hexeformularer og Magiske Opskrifter

To Escape from Jail

ADRA   ADRATA   ADRATTA

Outcome/Intention:

To escape from jail, literally. Can also be used to escape a situation in which you feel mentally or emotionally imprisoned.

How/When to Use:

To the lock (either the one on the literal door or else on a lock you have purchased to represent the situation), say ADRA ADRATA ADRATTA. Speak the words aloud to the lock. Then write: "F. AKO qt" – upon the lock. After this has been done, watch for and TAKE your opportunity to flee your prison.

Origin: German University Library of Heidelberg (Cpg 369, folio 168)

To Pass Unseen

ACHA ACHACHA CHACH
CHARCHARA CHACH

Outcome/Intention:

To become invisible (unseen/unnoticed).

How/When to Use:

On a Sunday, inscribe the words on an amulet or gemstone as you chant them aloud. Hold in your mind the image of a lion-faced Sun God/Spirit. Place this talisman on a string and wear close to your body. Wear this talisman any time you wish your presence to go unnoticed.

Pronunciation note: "CH" here is pronounced like a breathy "K" (as it is a derivative of the Greek letter chi (X).

Origin: The Greek Magical Papyri (Papyri Graecae Magicae, PGM)

Copyright Asteria Books 2025

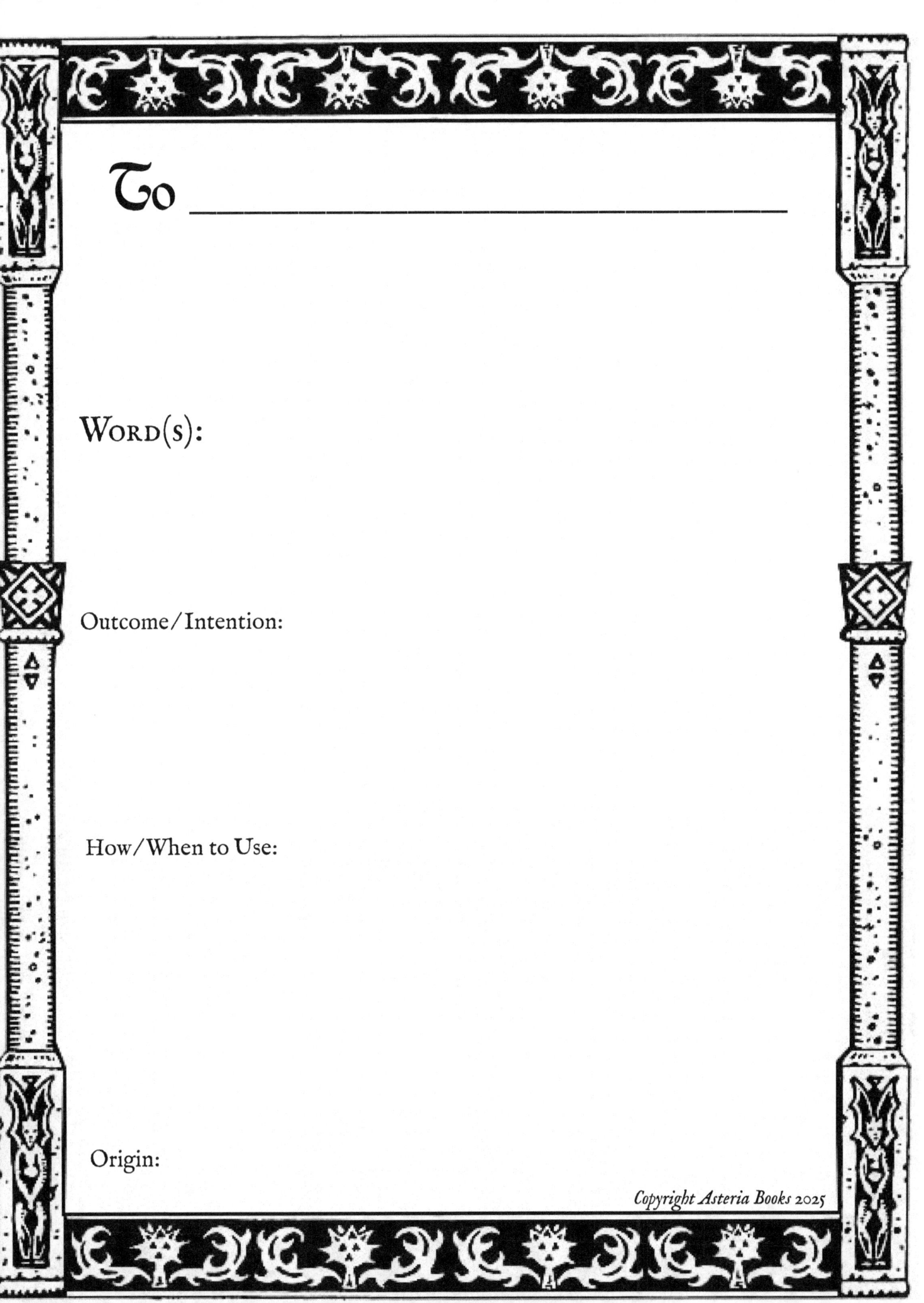

To _____

Word(s):

Outcome/Intention:

How/When to Use:

Origin:

Candle Magick

Candle Magick

Candles and oil lamps have lit the homes of people since time immemorial. In many parts of the world, candles are no longer necessary tools for illumination, but they still maintain an air of mystery, romance, danger, and magick. Most people still keep candles in order to set a mood, have emergency lighting, or even cast spells.

Candle magick is among the earliest magicks that we learn as children – when we are taught to blow out the candles of our birthday cakes while making wishes that we must keep secret.

Some of the most common themes within candle magick include:
- Inscribing intentions, names of targets, or symbols into the wax prior to burning
- Using color correspondences to add oomph to one's intention
- "Dressing" candles with oils, roots, herbs, and other substances prior to burning
- Placing candles in proximity to other spell items to "fuel" them (such as placing a utility, tea, chime, or votive candle atop a jar spell)

There are also some customs that have developed regarding candle usage within magick, including:
- Using a snuffer or finger-pinch to extinguish candles, rather than blowing them out with one's own breath
- Inscribing taper and chime candles from the middle to the ends, rather than from tip to tail (or vice versa)

Never leave candles burning unattended, and be sure to use fire-proof containers for all candle magick.

Copyright Asteria Books 2023

Candle Magick Basics

Candles have an interesting and perennial association with the Craft. In the pre-electric era, every home would have had a supply of either candles or lamp oil to provide basic illumination during the dim hours of the clock, making candles a relatively accessible and common resource that wouldn't have drawn undue suspicion from prying eyes looking for evidence of maleficia. These days, candles are available in a dizzying array of shapes, sizes, and colors — all of which can play a role in your magick.

Candle magick is fairly simple, but it involves much more than simply lighting a wick and walking away. Consider these factors when planning your candle magick:

Intention ~ Before you perform any act of magick, you should be very clear about what you are hoping to achieve. Be specific — for your own benefit as well as for any partners (Seen or Unseen) aiding you in the work.

Personalization ~ Magick benefits from connection to the target of the spell. This can include carving a name into the wax or embedding a small amount of hair or nail clippings.

Correspondences ~ "Dress" your candle using oils, small stones, herbs, and other materials that further connect it to your spell's target and/or intention.

Power ~ Raise energy or call on a Spirit to empower your work.

Safety ~ Take proper precautions to prevent fire. Don't leave candles burning unattended, and don't overload candles with too many highly flammable additions.

Copyright Asteria Books 2025

Candle Sizes and Figures

Candles come in every size and color these days, which can give a Witch lots of options when choosing which candle to use in a spell or ritual. Here are some options, ranging from traditional to creative:

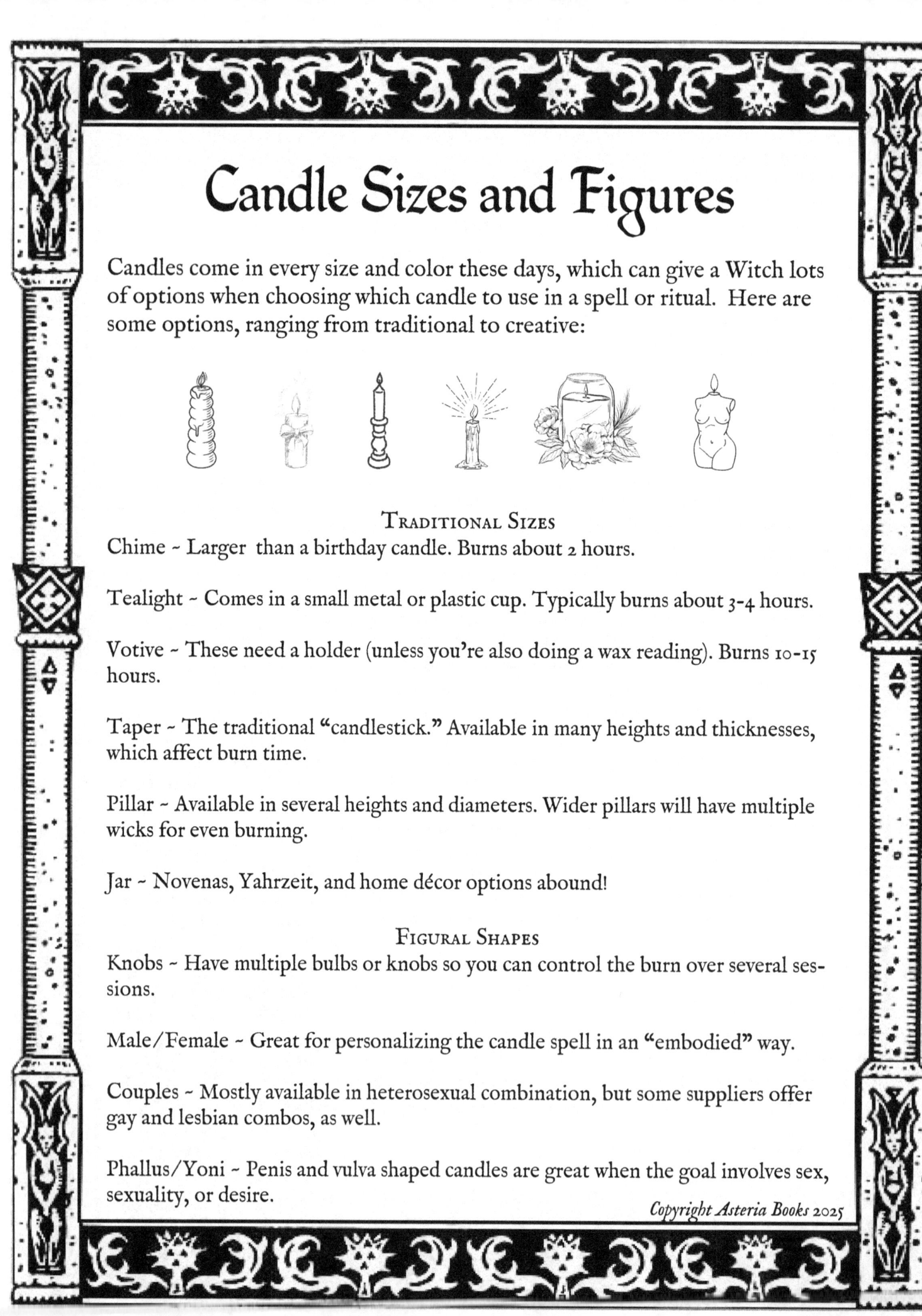

Traditional Sizes

Chime ~ Larger than a birthday candle. Burns about 2 hours.

Tealight ~ Comes in a small metal or plastic cup. Typically burns about 3-4 hours.

Votive ~ These need a holder (unless you're also doing a wax reading). Burns 10-15 hours.

Taper ~ The traditional "candlestick." Available in many heights and thicknesses, which affect burn time.

Pillar ~ Available in several heights and diameters. Wider pillars will have multiple wicks for even burning.

Jar ~ Novenas, Yahrzeit, and home décor options abound!

Figural Shapes

Knobs ~ Have multiple bulbs or knobs so you can control the burn over several sessions.

Male/Female ~ Great for personalizing the candle spell in an "embodied" way.

Couples ~ Mostly available in heterosexual combination, but some suppliers offer gay and lesbian combos, as well.

Phallus/Yoni ~ Penis and vulva shaped candles are great when the goal involves sex, sexuality, or desire.

Copyright Asteria Books 2025

Dressing Candles

All types of candles can be enhanced in their magickal purpose by processes that are sometimes called loading, dressing, fixing, or consecrating. (Some traditions have specific ways of using these terms, so check with your own elders or teachers for clarity. "Consecrating" is a safe term that isn't associated with any specific or closed practice.)

All sorts of items can be included in this process:
- Essential oils, infused oils, and oil blends
- Crystal and gemstone powders and chips
- Powdered or crushed botanicals (flowers, leaves, woods, roots, resins, etc)
- Taglocks (sometimes called "personal concerns") like hair, nail clippings, names, handwriting, etc from/of the target

And many actions, as well:
- Inscribing the candle with words and symbols
- Empowering it with a stream of your own energy
- Awakening it by knocking on it, kissing it, or blowing on it

The process I like to use for a small taper candle is this:
>Inscribe the name of the target from the middle of the candle toward its top.
>Inscribe the intention of the spell from the middle toward the base.
>Coat the candle in an oil blend aligned with the intention.
>Roll the candle in an incense blend aligned with the same.
>Tap the candle's base 3 time on the altar/work table.
>Whisper my desired outcome to the candle.
>Light the candle.
>Meditate while it burns.
>(Snuff it and ignite its astral flame between sessions.)

Candle Gardens

In a Candle Garden, we're grouping "like items" together to amplify the effect. In this case, the items are candles. The grouping usually happens on or inside a container of some sort. I've usually done this on a tray or mirror, but I've also seen them done in a hearth, inside an empty aquarium, in a bowl with floating candles, etc.

There are two basic concepts around which we build a Candle Garden.

In the first, all of the candles are burning for different (possibly even unconnected) individuals who share similar needs or goals. For instance, maybe they all need healing work done. These people don't have to know each other. They don't have to be dealing with the same health problems. They are just people that you are doing healing magick for.

In the other version, the people are connected in some way, but maybe their goals aren't. So for instance, this might be a family, coven, or learning circle doing a Full Moon candle ritual. Each person has their own goals and outcomes, and the point of connection is the bond they share as a group.

In both of these scenarios, the grouping of the candles helps to "boost the signal" of each individual candle.

With any kind of candle magick, you have the opportunity to include lots of other considerations. These candles can be color-coded to align with the associations you have for color magick. You can inscribe them with words, sigils, runes, or other symbols. You can dress and load them with herbs and crystals and other bits. You can write or draw on glass-encased candles with Sharpies or glass paint.

Copyright Asteria Books 2025

Candle Magick Tips

There are a few practical considerations that will make your candle magick really glow!

Don't place candles in a draft. This can cause them to burn unevenly and can pose a fire hazard.

Use a hurricane glass to protect candles when you can't control the draftiness of a space — for instance, when you are outside.

Votive candles are typically made in a way that they require a votive cup to burn properly. If you place a votive on a plate or atop a jar (like you might do to enliven a jar spell), the candle will burn quickly and leave a puddle of un-melted wax.

The wax is the fuel for your candle flame. Be sure to let the entire top layer melt before snuffing the candle so you don't bore a hole in the middle of the candle and bury the wick.

Pillar candles are made with a harder wax layer to keep the melted wax from spilling out. When you are ready to snuff the candle, you can press the softened shell around the candle's lip so it hardens in an even way.

Engraving words or symbols on a pillar's shell will weaken the wax in that spot, which will likely result in melted wax spilling through.

Don't leave candles burning unattended! If you have to leave your candle spell, you can snuff the physical flame and "ignite" an astral flame instead.

Be aware of curtains an other flammable materials in the vicinity of your candle flame. A draft or gust could cause a blaze.

Copyright Asteria Books 2025

Dream Magick

Copyright Asteria Books 2025

Dream Time

The Dreaming, also known as Dream Time, is not merely the absence of waking reality, but a vibrant and complex dimension that exists parallel to our own. It's the ever-shifting landscape where our minds wander during sleep, a place where the laws of physics are pliable and the subconscious speaks in a language of symbols and metaphors. While some believe it to be an ephemeral void, experienced dreamwalkers know it to be a real, traversable realm with its own unique flora, fauna, and governing principles.

Navigating the Dreaming
The Dreaming is vast, encompassing both the collective unconscious and the personal dreamscapes of every living being. It's often divided into three primary layers, though these boundaries are fluid and permeable.

The Somnolent Shore: The outermost layer, where the newly asleep first arrive. This is the land of half-conscious thoughts and hypnagogic imagery. It is a transitional space, filled with echoes of the waking world: distorted memories, stray thoughts, and the familiar faces of those we know. For novice dreamwalkers, this is the safest place to practice, as it's the easiest to return from.

The Deep Sea: The heart of the Dreaming, a churning ocean of archetypes and raw emotion. This is where the true power and danger of the Dreaming lies. Here, dreams are more vivid, the symbols more potent, and the emotional currents run strong. This layer is home to both beautiful, illuminating dreamscapes and terrifying, nightmarish realms. Navigating the Deep Sea requires a strong sense of self and a clear intention, as it's easy to get lost in its depths.

The Astral Expanse: The furthest reaches of the Dreaming, a space of pure consciousness and cosmic connection. This is where the truly ancient dreams reside—the collective myths and timeless stories of humanity. Reaching this layer is rare and requires immense skill. Those who do often return with profound insights, but the experience can be disorienting and even dangerous for the unprepared mind.

Copyright Asteria Books 2025

Dream Pillows

A dream pillow is more than just a cushion; it is a talismanic vessel, intentionally crafted to draw specific energies into your sleep. By placing it beneath your head, you invite its concentrated power to guide your journey through the Dream Time, enhancing recall, inviting prophecy, or ensuring a night free from fear. The act of creating it is a ritual in itself, imbuing it with your will and intent.

Design and Embellishments

Begin with a small pillow or sachet made from natural fibers like linen, cotton, or silk. The fabric color can correspond to your intention: indigo for psychic vision, violet for spiritual connection, or silver for lunar magic and intuition. Stitch a personal sigil of protection or clarity into the fabric, or draw it on a slip of paper to be placed inside. Consider adding a small, cleansed crystal such as amethyst for its calming and intuitive properties, or lapis lazuli to aid in dream recall. You might also embroider sigils or symbols on the pillow or pouch to further aid in your goal.

The Herbal Fillings

The heart of the dream pillow lies in its blend of herbs, each chosen for its unique oneiric properties. For prophetic dreams and vivid recall, use mugwort. For peaceful slumber and protection against nightmares, include lavender or dried rose petals. A touch of chamomile can soothe the mind, inviting gentle and restful dreams. For a more advanced practice, a pinch of Calea zacatechichi, known as the "dream herb," can be added to encourage lucidity and a greater awareness within the dream state.

As you craft, embellish, and fill the pillow, focus your intention on the desired outcome. Once sewn shut, your dream pillow becomes a powerful anchor, a physical manifestation of your will in the metaphysical seas of the Dreaming.

Copyright Asteria Books 2025

Lucid Dreaming

Lucid Dreaming is the pinnacle of the Dream Witch's craft: the act of becoming aware you are in the Dream Time while the dream is still unfolding. It is the moment the veil thins and the dreamer becomes the director, the wanderer becomes the architect. This conscious awakening within the Dreaming transforms a passive journey into an active, Will-full exploration.

The path to lucidity is paved with Reality Checks. These are small, deliberate rituals performed in the waking world to train the mind to question its state. Common checks include counting your fingers (they often appear distorted in dreams), trying to push a finger through your palm (it will usually pass right through in the Dreaming), or examining text (it frequently changes or dissolves). By performing these checks throughout the day, you instill a habit that may one day echo in a dream, triggering the moment of realization.

The power of lucid dreaming is not for idle play; it is a tool of immense spiritual and psychological significance. The lucid state allows you to directly confront your subconscious fears, symbolized by the monsters or shadows in your dreams. You can speak to these manifestations, ask them questions, and learn their purpose. It is also a powerful conduit for creative inspiration and problem-solving, as you can command the Dream Time to present solutions or guide you to new ideas.

Maintaining lucidity requires focus. Upon awakening in the dream, resist the urge to get excited, which can cause you to wake up prematurely. Instead, anchor yourself by spinning in place or rubbing your hands together. With practice, you can learn to stabilize the dreamscape and fully harness this profound state of conscious magic.

Copyright Asteria Books 2025

Dream Walking

Dream walking is an advanced art, distinct from mere lucid dreaming. While lucidity grants you mastery over your personal dreamscape, dream walking is the intentional act of traveling from your own mind to the shared fabric of the Dreaming—and from there, to the dream of another. It is the practice of becoming a conscious traveler in a landscape of pure consciousness, a way to connect with others on a profound, non-physical level.

The Portal & The Destination

The first step of dream walking is to achieve full lucidity within your own dream. Once awake within the Dreaming, you must abandon the urge to control your surroundings and instead, focus on an exit. This is done by visualizing a portal or door. The destination must be clear and specific in your mind: a person's name, a specific place, or even a particular memory you wish to revisit. With focused intent, you open this doorway and step through. The journey is often disorienting, a blur of color and emotion as you pass through the collective unconscious. You must hold fast to your intention, or you may find yourself lost in the chaotic currents of the Deep Sea.

The Ethic of the Dream Walker

Adept Witches and Mages have used dreamwalking for both good and ill. In positive contexts, a Dream Walker can be an invited guest into another person's psyche, which can result in greater bonding between the two or even assistance and insight. However, it is also possible to use dreamwalking to invade another person's most private and uncontrolled desires and fears. Use this technique with caution.

The most potent tools are a strong anchor and a clear mind. A personal sigil can be used as a return key, and a consecrated dream pillow can help set your intention and ground your return. Ultimately, dream walking is a journey of the spirit, a test of will and focus that only the most dedicated dreamers should attempt.

Dream Casting

Dream Casting is the intentional act of weaving a specific dream narrative and projecting it into the subconscious of another. This is not a casual or lighthearted practice; it is a powerful form of psychic influence that requires immense focus, ethical clarity, and a strong sense of purpose.

The Ritual of Projection

The practice of dream casting begins not with sleep, but with focused intent. The caster must first determine the precise nature of the dream to be sent. Is it a dream of comfort for a grieving friend? A message of encouragement? Or a prophetic vision of a shared future? Once the intent is clear, the caster creates a strong mental image or a symbolic talismanic anchor—an item that represents the dream or the recipient. This could be a photograph, a lock of hair, or a simple object that holds personal meaning.

Before falling asleep, the caster enters a deep meditative state, holding the anchor and visualizing the dream in vivid detail. They must feel the emotions of the dream, see the colors, and hear the sounds. As sleep approaches, this meticulously crafted dream is not simply experienced; it is willed outward, like a radio signal broadcast on the etheric waves of the Dreaming. The caster's conscious mind becomes the projector, and the anchor serves as the focus for the transmission.

The Ethical Anchor & The Warning

Dream casting is, at its core, a form of psychic entry. Most modern Witches find it crucial to have the recipient's consent, or at the very least, a clear and benevolent purpose. However, there are those who will cast a dream with malicious or manipulative intent, in much the same way they might engage in baneful or blasting magick against an enemy. Be warned, therefore, that this can cause psychic backlash, disrupting the caster's own mental equilibrium and attracting malevolent entities from the Dream Time. In all acts of witchcraft, hold to your ethical code, perform divination prior to casting, gird yourself with protection, and be accountable for your actions (no matter your intentions).

Copyright Asteria Books 2025

Dream Work Herbs

By ingesting, burning, or incorporating these herbs into a dream pillow, you can attune your mind to the frequency of the Dreaming, unlocking doorways to prophecy, healing, and conscious awareness.

Mugwort (Artemisia vulgaris): A cornerstone of oneiromancy. Known as the herb of prophecy, mugwort is a potent tool for increasing dream vividness and recall. It's a key ingredient for those seeking to remember the details of their nocturnal journeys or to receive clear, prophetic visions.

Calea zacatechichi (Calea ternifolia): A bitter leaf revered as the dream herb. For those seeking to master lucid dreaming, Calea is an invaluable ally. It doesn't guarantee lucidity, but it significantly enhances the awareness and clarity needed to recognize you are in the Dreaming, making it easier to take conscious control.

Lavender (Lavandula angustifolia): A soothing and protective herb. While many herbs pull you deeper into the Dreaming, lavender's purpose is to purify. It is essential for warding off nightmares and banishing psychic static, ensuring your journey is one of peace and restful magic.

Rose (Rosa spp.): The flower of emotional healing and heart magic. Adding dried rose petals to your dream work can invite dreams of comfort, self-love, and healing. It is especially useful for those working through grief or emotional turmoil, allowing the subconscious to process and mend in a gentle, supportive space.

Chamomile (Matricaria recutita): The gentle soother. Chamomile works by quieting the noise of the day, calming the nervous system, and allowing for a smooth and peaceful transition into sleep. It helps to prevent the chaotic, scattered dreams that come from a restless mind, preparing the way for more focused dream work.

Copyright Asteria Books 2025

Dream Protection

The Dreaming, while a source of profound wisdom, is not always a tranquil space. As you venture into its ethereal currents, you may encounter chaotic thought-forms or psychic static. True mastery of dream magic requires a clear intention of protection, a practice that safeguards your mind on its nightly voyages. The first and most vital step is the creation of a Sleep Circle.

The Sleep Circle: A Sanctuary

The Sleep Circle is a sacred space created and consecrated prior to sleep, a protective boundary between your physical self and the vastness of the Dreaming. To cast a circle, stand in your bedroom and, with a clear voice, state your intention to create a secure space for rest and magic. Walk the perimeter of your room, physically or with your mind's eye, visualizing a shimmering, impenetrable wall of light. As you do this, affirm: "This space is mine. Only energies of peace, clarity, and healing may enter. All others are barred."

Guardians and Wards

Within the confines of your newly created circle, you can further fortify your defenses.

- Sentinels – Call on your spiritual guardians, ancestral spirits, or a personal deity to stand watch over your sleep and defend your sacred space.
- Herbal wards – Lavender or dried rose petals tucked into a sachet will banish nightmares.
- Shield sigil – Drawn and charged with your intent for safety, can be placed beneath your pillow to act as a personal anchor, a constant reminder to your subconscious that it is shielded.

Copyright Asteria Books 2025

Insomnia

Insomnia is more than a simple restlessness of the body; it is a disconnection from the Dreaming, a state where the mind, unable to surrender to the nocturnal currents, remains tethered to the mundane world. It is a form of psychic static, preventing the soul from its necessary journey of rest and rejuvenation. Try adopting these sacred practices for quieting the mind, calming the spirit, and reclaiming the night.

The Cleansing of the Chamber

Before any ritual for sleep can begin, the space itself must be consecrated. The bedroom is a sanctuary, not a repository for the day's lingering anxieties and chaotic energies. Begin by opening a window to allow fresh air to cleanse the space. Then, with a smudge stick of lavender or sage, move clockwise through the room, allowing the smoke to purify the corners, the bed, and any areas that feel heavy or stale. As you do so, state your intention aloud: "This space is a sanctuary of peace. All discord and chaos are banished. Only rest and tranquility remain."

The Rune of Slumber

Create a simple sleep sigil, a personal rune that symbolizes peaceful rest. On a small square of paper, draw a circular symbol that feels calming to you. As you draw, pour all your intention for deep and dreamless sleep into the lines and curves. Charge this sigil in one of your preferred ways.

Herbal Elixirs

Beyond the physical space, seek the aid of herbal allies. A warm infusion of chamomile and lavender (or a stronger decoction of valerian and skullcap) an hour before bed can soothe the nervous system, while a small sachet of dried hops placed near your head can ease a restless mind and invite profound calm. These restorative herbs are your guides, preparing your physical vessel for its journey into the Dreaming.

Copyright Asteria Books 2025

Night Battles

In the folklore of Friuli, Italy, a remarkable form of dream magic was practiced by the Benandanti, or "good walkers." These were people born with a caul, a sign of their supernatural destiny. During the four Ember Days of the year, their spirits would leave their bodies and descend into the Dreaming to fight against the Malendanti, or "evil walkers."

The Battle for the Harvest

The benandanti's purpose was to ensure the fertility of the crops and the well-being of the community. They rode into battle on a variety of animals, armed with fennel stalks, which served as both weapon and magical staff. The malendanti, in turn, rode on goats and cats, wielding sorghum stalks to cast curses and bring blight. The fate of the harvest, and indeed the entire village, was decided in these ethereal skirmishes. If the benandanti were victorious, the year would be one of abundance. If they lost, the land would suffer from famine and disease.

The Modern Benandante

To the modern practitioner, the "night battles" take on new meaning. The malendanti now represent the oppressive forces that seek to drain us: the personal demons of anxiety, self-doubt, and addiction, as well as the oppressive political and social forces that bring decay to our communities. The benandante's struggle for the harvest is the fight for our own inner peace and for a more just world. By consciously entering the Dreaming with protective intent, we become a warrior in this eternal struggle, defending not just ourselves, but the collective future.

Copyright Asteria Books 2025

Dream Lovers

Within the vast landscape of the Dreaming, there exist spirits of profound connection known as Dream Lovers. Unlike the predatory and malevolent incubi and succubae that drain life force, these entities are often benevolent, compassionate, and inspiring. They are not physical beings but rather conscious thought-forms that arise from a deep-seated longing for intimacy, guidance, and companionship. To the modern practitioner, a dream lover can be a powerful psychic ally, a muse, or a source of profound emotional healing.

Known Archetypes & Guides

The form a dream lover takes is often a reflection of a deeper psychic truth. They may appear as a personification of the Anima or Animus, the subconscious inner feminine or masculine aspects of the self, offering balance and integration. Other times, they present as figures from ancient folklore, such as the Arabic Qarinah, a spiritual double or companion tied to one's destiny, who may offer counsel or guidance in dreams. The presence of these beings is marked by a dream of deep, soulful connection, not just physical intimacy. Upon waking, the feeling is one of peace, inspiration, and renewed emotional clarity, as if your deepest desires have been honored.

Setting Boundaries and Intention

Working with a dream lover requires a clear and intentional practice. Before sleep, it is crucial to set boundaries. Cast a Sleep Circle and declare your intentions aloud: "I invite my Dream Lover — who comforts, delights, guides, and protects me in both the Seen and Unseen realms — to commune with me in the Dreaming. None else may enter." To deepen the connection, you can create a specific sigil for spiritual partnership or use a dream pillow infused with rose petals to open your heart to the experience. By consciously engaging with these spirits, you turn your dreams into a sacred space for personal growth, insight, and magical partnership.

Copyright Asteria Books 2025

Incubi, Succubae, Night Hags & the Mare

Disturbing as it is to acknowledge, there are conscious, predatory spirits that actively seek out vulnerable sleepers for their own sustenance, feeding on life force, sexual energy, and fear. To a magical practitioner, knowing their nature is the first step toward effective defense.

The Seductive and the Oppressive

Incubi and succubae are seductive spirits, male and female respectively, that drain a person's vital energy through nocturnal encounters. They often appear as figures of irresistible beauty, drawing their victims into vivid, alluring dreams only to leave them feeling exhausted and depleted upon waking.

The Night Hag is a more viscerally terrifying entity, often associated with sleep paralysis. This spirit is said to sit upon the chest of the sleeper, creating a suffocating pressure and a feeling of dread that paralyzes the body and silences any scream. Similarly, the Germanic spirit known simply as the Mare is a malicious entity believed to "ride" the sleeper, causing suffocating nightmares and a profound sense of exhaustion.

Wards Against the Intruder

These spirits thrive on vulnerability. To combat their influence, the sacred space of sleep must be guarded.

- A well-cast Sleep Circle is the most potent defense, creating an impenetrable barrier.
- Placing a simple protection sigil beneath your bed and ensuring your bedroom is cleansed of stale, chaotic energy are also essential practices.

Copyright Asteria Books 2025

Oneiromancy

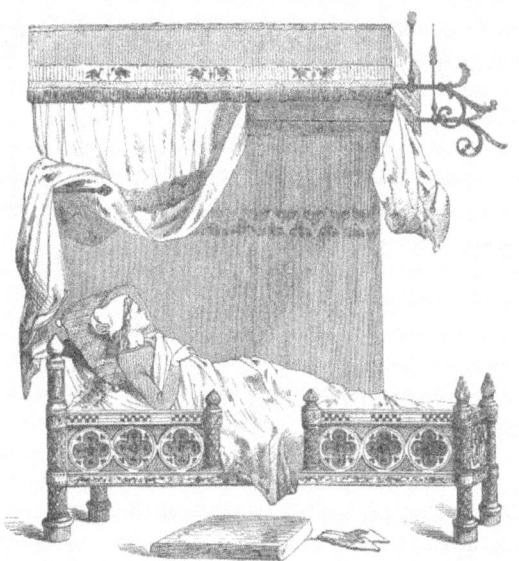

Oneiromancy is the arcane practice of deciphering dreams to gain insight, foresight, or a deeper understanding of the self. It is not simply remembering what you dreamt, but actively engaging with the symbolic language of the Dream Time. The oneiromancer understands that the waking mind and the dreaming mind are two halves of a whole, and that dreams are not random neurological firings, but carefully coded messages from our deepest self.

The primary tool of the oneiromancer is the dream journal, which serves as an ever-growing lexicon of personal symbols. While a book of generic dream meanings can be a starting point, true oneiromancy relies on a highly personal dictionary. A dream of a snake for one person might signify a (possibly terrifying) transition or transformation, while for another, it might simply be a memory of a childhood pet. The journal, meticulously maintained, allows you to track these unique connections and build your own internal glossary.

The practice begins before sleep. Meditate on a specific question or problem, intentionally inviting the Dream Time to provide clarity. You might create a sigil related to this question and draw it on your body before falling asleep. Upon waking, the ritual of immediate journaling is critical. Once the dream is recorded, the process of divination begins. Look for recurring motifs, emotional echoes, and unexpected shifts. Cross-reference new dreams with old ones, searching for a narrative thread that spans days, weeks, or even months. The meaning is rarely literal; it is found in the relationships between symbols, the feeling-tone of the dream, and its ultimate reflection in your waking life.

Copyright Asteria Books 2025

Dream Journal

Many Witches and Mages who choose to work inside the Dreaming find their Dream Journal is their most valuable tool for this branch of magic. The journal itself can be anything that feels right to you: a worn leather-bound book, a simple spiral notebook, or even a digital file. What matters is the consistent act of recording.

The true power of a dream journal lies in the ritual. When you awaken, try not to move any more than you must. Stay in that liminal space between worlds. The details of a dream are like smoke; they vanish with the slightest distraction. Before you even open your eyes fully, reach for your journal. Record everything you can recall, no matter how small or insignificant it may seem.

> Be Immediate: The first few moments upon waking are the most crucial. Capture the feelings, colors, and fragments before they dissipate.
>
> Be Honest: Don't try to make sense of the dream as you write. Record it exactly as it occurred, with all its bizarre transitions and illogical twists.
>
> Be Detailed: Note the emotions you felt, the setting, the people, and any strange objects. Was a cat speaking? Did you fly through a red sky? These details are the sigils of your inner world.

Over time, your dream journal will reveal patterns. You'll begin to notice recurring symbols, places, and characters. This is where the real work begins.

Recurring Symbols: A specific animal, a certain house, or a repeating color isn't a coincidence. It's a message. Use your journal to track these symbols and their context. Do they appear during times of stress or joy?

Emotional Echoes: Pay attention to how a dream makes you feel, both in the dream and upon waking. A recurring feeling of being lost may point to a sense of directionlessness in your waking life.

Personal Archetypes: The figures that populate your dreams—a wise elder, a mischievous child, a frightening shadow—are often parts of yourself. By observing their actions in your dreams, you can gain insight into your own psyche.

A dream journal is more than just a record; it's a dialogue with your deeper self. By honoring your dreams with attention, you begin to understand the hidden currents that shape your reality.

Copyright Asteria Books 2025

Hearth Magic

Cottage Witchcraft

What we might call Cottage Witchery (or Hearth or House Craft) is a form of practical magic that focuses on the cleansing, protection, and blessing of the dwelling or domicile. It is not necessarily its own Tradition of Craft, which would be associated with its own lineage, tools, etc. Indeed, as a study of practical magic under the greater umbrella of Craft lore, it is accessible to all students of the Craft, regardless of Tradition.

Forms of this type of folk magic are present in every religion and date to pre-historic times. Cottage Witchery is part of our ancestral heritage. It is natural to have a desire to cleanse, protect, and bless the space that provides our shelter – and thereby the people with whom we share this most fundamental of human needs.

Much of what we think of as "old wives tales" or backwoods superstitions are actually the Old Ways that have been preserved through generations – handed down to us in the memory of our elders. Very often, these folk-ways are based on even older long-forgotten customs of Spirit-veneration (or in some cases, Spirit-appeasement – or even banishment).

Home is an outward reflection of the Self in many ways. We have basic shelter here, yes; but we also choose tools, comforts, and decorations that reflect our tastes and aspirations. It's where we're our most vulnerable – when sleeping, sick, or otherwise in need of recovery. It is our sanctuary. It is also our Temple, housing our tools of Arte.

Whenever possible, choose natural materials and fibers (wood, stone, metal, jute, cotton, wool, silk, etc) and incorporate living plants into the home. Derivatives like ceramic potter and glass are also preferable to plastics and other synthetics. Energy simply moves better through and around natural materials.

Copyright Asteria Books 2020

Cottage Correspondences

SUNDAY

Planet: Sun

Energy: Growth, Success, Achievement

Spaces: Kitchen, Garden, Porch

Tasks: Meal-prep, baking, tending house-plants

MONDAY

Planet: Moon

Energy: Intuition, Prophecy

Spaces: Bathroom, Laundry Room

Tasks: Laundry

TUESDAY

Planet: Mars

Energy: Protection, Ambition, Courage

Spaces: Weight/Rec Room

Tasks: Maintenance checks, security system checks

WEDNESDAY

Planet: Mercury

Energy: Communication, Luck, Travel

Spaces: Garage, Craft Rooms

Tasks: Organizing, filing, planning

THURSDAY

Planet: Jupiter

Energy: Authority, Power, Wealth

Spaces: Parlor

Tasks: Bill paying

FRIDAY

Planet: Venus

Energy: Romance, Beauty, Sensuality

Spaces: Bedrooms

Tasks: Decorating, hosting

SATURDAY

Planet: Saturn

Energy: Endings

Spaces: Basement, Cellar, Storage

Tasks: Chore review & rewards, culling donation items, canning/storing food

Copyright Asteria Books 2020

Magical House Cleaning

Doing chores and housework may not seem very magical, but the tasks associated with housework are linked with so much mystical lore that it's impossible to deny the connection between a clean house and a healthy mind-body-spirit.

Here are just a few tips to infuse your cleaning routines with sorcerous potency to bring more awareness and enchantment to your daily activities.

- Approach even basic chores as acts of magical cleansing and blessing. Bringing active visualization and energetic intent to these processes transforms removing dirt and rubbish into banishing negativity, harm, and illness, while the finishing touches (lighting candles, sweetening the air, etc) become general blessings and offerings to the Wards.

- Lore says to use clockwise motions while cleaning and scrubbing – and to move in a clockwise pattern through rooms and through the house at large.

- Sweep/vacuum toward the hearth (if you have one). You can substitute the kitchen stove for this, as it serves at the modern cookfire. Never sweep your luck out the front door!

Copyright Asteria Books 2020

Each Morning

∴ Declutter for 10 minutes
∴ Unload dishwasher
∴ Make beds

Each Evening

∴ Declutter for 10 minutes
∴ Load and start dishwasher
∴ Clean kitchen (spot clean floor, wipe counters, organize food)
∴ Task of the Day (from list)
∴ 2-4 chores from "Lunar List"

Task of the Day

Monday: Clean Toilets/Sinks
Tuesday: Dust/Clean Surfaces
Wednesday: Vacuum/Mop
Thursday: Clean Fridge/Pantry
Friday: Organize Outside Areas
Weekend: Laundry/Garden

Lunar List

New Moon Wk: Bedrooms/Outside

∴ Dust tops of furniture
∴ Clean and organize end tables
∴ Wash comforters
∴ Wipe down baseboards
∴ Clean walls and cobwebs
∴ Clean windows and blinds
∴ Wipe doors/disinfect handles
∴ Organize garage
∴ Maintain flower beds
∴ Organize backyard and porch
∴ Edge yard

Full Moon Wk: Kitchen/Dining Rm

∴ Wipe down baseboards
∴ Take things off counters & clean
∴ Clean oven and microwave
∴ Organize cabinets and clean
∴ Wipe cabinet doors
∴ Deep clean refrigerator
∴ Deep clean sink
∴ Clean windows
∴ Clean trash can
∴ Clean light fixtures
∴ Clean all ceiling fans in house (tops, too)

Waxing Moon Wk: Sitting Rm & Etc

∴ Vacuum furniture
∴ Organize TV areas
∴ Wipe down baseboards
∴ Clean washer, dryer, deep freezer
∴ Organize cleaning supplies
∴ Wipe doors/ disinfect handles
∴ Clean walls and cobwebs
∴ Clean windows and blinds
∴ Organize playroom toys
∴ Clean and organize garage
∴ Deep clean cars

Waning Moon Wk: Baths/Closets

∴ Deep clean sinks
∴ Clean windows
∴ Clean showers/tubs
∴ Wash all linens (towels, mats, etc)
∴ Wipe down baseboards
∴ Clean walls and cobwebs
∴ Clean trash cans
∴ Wipe doors/disinfect handles
∴ Organize linen closets/under sinks/ bath drawers
∴ Organize clothes
∴ Organize shoes

Copyright Asteria Books 2020

Cottage Cleansing Rituals

Cleaning and housework are chores that we tackle on routine schedules (from daily tasks like doing dishes to semiannual ones like removing and sanitizing the AC vents). But sometimes the home needs a spiritual cleansing that goes deeper and extends further than the routines.

House Cleansing rituals are absolutely called for before moving into a new home (to remove the energy of the previous residents). It is best to cleanse, bless , and make offerings to the guardians of the home, family, and land before moving any personal belongings into the home.

According to lore, you shouldn't move a broom from one home to another (nor use a broom left by a former resident). Instead, thank and burn or throw away the old broom, and buy a new one. On this fresh new broom, inscribe (by carving or inking) "I sweep in good fortune and abundance" from tip to brush on one side of the handle. One the other side of the handle, going the other direction (brush to tip), inscribe "I sweep out misfortune and evil."

Spring and Fall are also impactful times for deep house cleansing (because they help move energy that may have become stagnant), as are periods of family transition, celebration, and mourning (which are metaphysical magnets due to the big emotions experiences by the home's residents).

When engaging in cleansing rites, make physically cleaning the space part of the ritual. Amp up the magical cleaning by adding herbal infusions (or a few drops of essential oils) to the wash water, cleaning windows with white vinegar (to brighten the "wind's eye"), opening the windows to bring in fresh air, and sprinkling powdered cleansing herbs or a dash of salt before vacuuming.

The cleansing ritual can also include burning dressed and blessed candles or oil lamps (with herbs, etc in the basin) in each room, asperging with living water (spring, rain, river, ocean, etc) or holy/blessed water, and censing with incense. Cleansing herbs like rosemary, thyme, dill, and sage are great for inclusion.

Ring a bell to make a change to vibrational energy, as well, especially to seal the rite.

Copyright Asteria Books 2020

Guardians, Wards & Spirits of Place

Cultures from all over the world, throughout the ages, have recognized two major categories of Spirits that have direct impacts on Cottage Witchcraft. The first is the class of Spirit that we might call the Family Guardian (who is attached to a family line or cluster and goes where they go to safeguard both well-being and good fortune), and the other is the Spirit of Place (which is found upon arrival in a new location, and will remain to care for either the land or a specific feature of it long after specific inhabitants have moved on).

Among the Family Guardians, we see examples like the Lares in ancient Rome, the Agathos Daemon in ancient Greece, and the Dís and Fylgjia of Scandinavia.

Spirits of Place include a wide variety of Spirits, including landwights, devas, tree and water Spirits (for which both the Greeks and the Celts had a dizzying array of nymphs/faerie names), and the Genius Locii of a given area of the landscape – or feature thereof. Every lovely boulder, bubbling spring, laughing grove had its Spirit.

These Spirits of Place also included manmade places like houses, roads, and temples – and most especially the liminal (between) places like bridges, thresholds, crossroads, windows, mirrors, chimneys. The places that were neither here nor there, out nor in. Those places are full of power (and therefore, in need of extra guardianship).

Other potent places of Spirit within and around the home are the well (now the faucet) and the cookfire/hearth (now the stove/oven). These are the life-blood and heartbeat of the home. Love and honor them.

Affix talismans of blessing and protection at these notable places and make offerings to the Spirits of Place & Family. A pentagram or hand (Witch Glove) at the front door. Green glass fishing float hung in the windows. A little food buried under the porch.

Copyright Asteria Books 2020

House Blessings

House Blessing rituals or spells should ideally be performed after a thorough round of cleaning and cleansing, and they should be followed by either setting fresh wards and protections or making offerings to the Spirits of Place, Family Guardians, and Ancestors who are already watching over you, your home, and its residents.

Warming the House – The custom of housewarming (yes, as in the parties and visits) is a way for friends and extended family to offer their blessings to you and your new home. Extend your hosting hospitality by offering food, drink, and the warmth of your hearth to those whose companionship you value, and in return, their presence will warm your halls and walls. This act introduces the Spirits of your new Place to your favorite people. If they bring gifts, they should be for the care or maintenance of the house.

Lunar Blessing Ritual – You'll either need a helper for this, or you'll move through your house multiple times. Either way is fine. Both are great energy! Use a white, silver, or clear bowl to catch the Full Moon's rays in living water (spring, rain, ocean, etc – not tap water). Asperge each room with the water using a spring of thyme. As you do so, your helper will carry a white pillar candle on a mirror into each room. Finish the blessing by sharing white grapes, cheese, and white wine under the moonlight – offering the first tastes to the Land Spirits and Guardians.

Incense Blessings – Sweet blessings of ancient origin can be added at any time by simply burning a blend of myrrh and golbanum resins in every room.

Copyright Asteria Books 2020

Buying, Selling, and Moving

Leaving one home and entering a new one can be a time of hope and promise, but it is also a time of upheaval and turmoil. As a liminal time/experience, it is full of power, but also chaos. This is a great time to call on Witchy resources to traditional lore to help.

∴ You may not have much choice in your moving day, but if you do, consider the planetary influences (or lunar phase) at work. The day and hour you bring the first items into your new home will set the tone for your years there.

∴ Make offerings to your Family Guardians and to this new home's Spirits of Place before you bring in personal items. Bread, salt, wine, and silver/gold coins are traditional. A basket overflowing with fruits, meats, nuts, cheeses, and veggies to be shares with he Spirits and the family and friends helping you move also has a nice symbolic message.

∴ Perform a House Cleansing before moving in personal items.

∴ The first personal item to come into the home should be something solid that can't be blown away — like a wooden piece of furniture.

∴ Cleanse the old house before you go.

∴ Leave a little bit of money (even just coins) at the old house for luck and as a final thanks to the Spirits of Place there.

∴ To sell a house: pass a picture of the house through the smoke of a smoldering money-drawing herb (like basil or cinnamon). Write SOLD and your asking price in red letters on the picture. Place the picture & a pinch of the herbs under the doormat.

∴ To find the right house: decorate a small paper box to look like a house, with doors, windows, etc. Into the box, add charms that represent the desired qualities and . In a pinch, you can write your needs on slips of paper and add them individually. Or make sigils.

Copyright Asteria Books 2020

Hospitality

Hospitality was considered an important virtue in the traditional cultures of our ancestors, when life and well-being were often held in the balance of the guest-host relationship. In many parts of the world now, hospitality is no longer a matter of life and death, but it will always remain an important part of maintaining relationships with family, friends, community, and even with Ancestors.

Hospitality rituals are best performed in either the sitting room or the dining room — the two rooms where we entertain guests. As for timing of the rituals, choosing a day and hour that are ruled by Venus and Mercury (so that elements of comfort, joy, companionship, conversation, and both emotional intellectual connection are imbued into the magic) work best. So, Wednesday (Mercury) in the 2nd hour after sunset (Venus), OR Friday (Venus) in the 2nd hour after sunset (Mercury) would both be excellent choices for hospitality spellwork.

Hallways, foyers/entryways, and sitting rooms (depending on your floorplan) are the first impression that most guests will have of your home. Make it welcoming and pleasant by sweetening the air with a wax warmer, oil diffuser, or pot-pourri bowl; keeping live plants to boost the energy in these areas; and keeping things tidy. Hyacinths grow well indoors, and they are ruled by Venus — therefore promoting friendship.

Consider the symbols you have made visible in guest space — and symbolic messages you are giving your guests through the pictures, art, and decorations.

Guests will feel more secure with a wall at their back and a view of the exit. Consider this when thinking of seating at the dinner table and sitting room.

Copyright Asteria Books 2020

Magic for the Kitchen

The kitchen is often revered as the heart and soul of the home. In modern homes, it is the location of powerful Spirits (even Gods) of Water, Fire, and Home Blessings, if we recognize the "hearth" to be the place where we cook (as opposed to a *fireplace* that may now be a luxury addition in most homes these days), and the "well" as the place from which we draw water for cooking, cleaning, etc. Food and drink sustain us and have the power to bring joy and pleasure. So much magic, indeed, that whole books of kitchen lore exist!

Here are just a few simple things you can do to honor the Kitchen Spirits and work the magic of blessing and protection from your own hearth and well.

- Be mindful as you cook, and let intuition guide you.
- Treat your kitchen like a temple and make offerings to the Fire Spirit & Water Spirit who dwell there — as well as any others who you honor there.
- Place symbolic magnets on your fridge (or even word magnets) to create visual spells.
- Prepare magical meals for birthdays, feast days (Sabbats), etc. Similarly, be mindful of each meal and make it a magical act.
- Add seasonal centerpieces to the dining table.
- Grow aloe vera in a kitchen window to protect the cook (which can also be used to treat burns, if needed). Conversely, hang a rope of garlic for protection, but DON'T eat the bulbs — as they are absorbing misfortune.
- Paint blessing symbols (solar crosses, hearts, runes, sigils, etc) on cookware, appliances, storage containers, dishes, etc using essential oils.
- Offer the first tastes to Ancestors and Guardians. Don't fully clean your plate in recognition that those first morsels were theirs. Lore says that poverty haunts the person who always cleans their plate (most likely from not leaving a share for their Beloved Dead.).
- Use clockwise motions when stirring food and passing food around the table, and swish a cup (or stir a bowl) clockwise three time before the first taste.

Copyright Asteria Books 2020

Magic for the Bathroom

Life on Earth began in the Sea, and much lore exists about the rejuvenating power of the bath. A ritual bath is often part of workings or rites, and there are several Spirits and Deities whose mythos is tied up with bathing. Baptismal and lustral rites, both of which are bathing rituals, are a common thread throughout spiritual practice. The first is a watery initiation/rebirth that acts as a formal induction into a practice or group, while the second is a touchstone of cleansing that we can repeat on either a schedule or as needed. It's usually encouraged to fully submerge oneself in the magical bath (often three times), but that practice can be altered to accommodate special needs or circumstances. For instance, pouring ritually prepared water over one's head, heart, and hands will typically satisfy the requirements of the ritual bath (provided that the body is physically clean — ie, freshly showered).

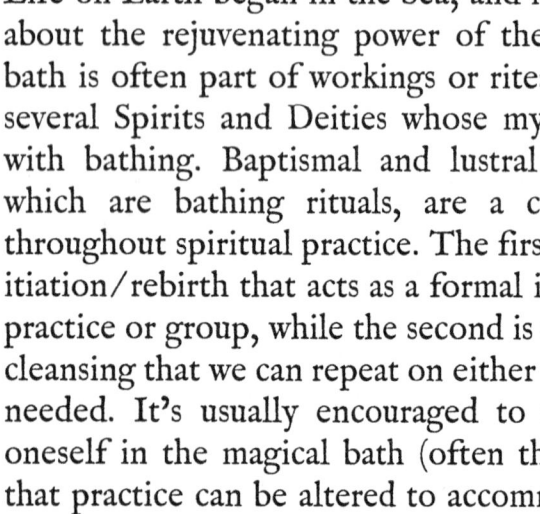

Here are other considerations for bringing magic to your bath and bathroom:

∴ Add a sachet of herbs (or an herbal infusion) to the water to bring the properties of those herbs into your working. You can also add loose herbs and flowers to the bath and use a drain-strainer to sift them out at the end.

∴ Fire and water are a powerful alchemical combination. Catch firelight in the tub by placing candles nearby to reflect on the water.

∴ Salt is a powerful purifier of both body and spirit. Add it to the water to boost your cleansing work. Or mix it with essential oils to make magical bath salts.

∴ Adding silver pendants or silver coins to the bath beckons prosperity.

∴ Cosmetics (so often applied in this room) have their origin in magic and mysticism. According to Enoch, Azazel (one of the names of the WitchFather) taught the art of applying kohl to the eyes to the daughters of men (along with Witchcraft, itself). If and when you apply cosmetics, do so with intent, with power, and with the knowledge of a lineage of sorcery in this deceptively simple act.

Copyright Asteria Books 2020

Magic for Bedrooms

Bedrooms are interesting, magically, because we expect a lot double-duty from them. A child's bedroom is often their playroom and their sleeping sanctuary. A guest room needs to have a broad appeal of hospitality and safety. A teen's bedroom should be able to transition with them, while an adult's bedroom needs to be a place of rest and recovery, possibly a magical meditation space, and (in most cases) the center for pleasure-filled delights. It can be tricky to  create an atmosphere that is both restful and stimulating in the ways we need out each of these bedrooms. Here are a few thoughts on weaving magic in to these spaces:

- Use color and texture to create the primary environment you need most in this most intimate sanctuary for each intended occupant, always keeping an eye on comfort for sleep. Cool tones will relax the mind, while warm ones will excite it (and the body). In children's rooms, try to create some division so that toys aren't easily visible (and therefore overstimulating) from bed.
- Place a broom or a knife under the bed (or mattress) to protect the occupants.
- Empower a doll or stuffie to act as a n enchanted sentinel to guard sleeping dreamers.
- Hang dreamcatchers over beds or suncatchers in windows.
- Hang thin cotton bags stuffed with protective herbs in closets as sachets. Lavender, vervain, sage, anise, mint, and thyme are lovely for this.
- Create space in children's rooms for their own altar with wall shelves or cabinets that hold their own pocket-sized Deity figures, talismans, and special items.

Copyright Asteria Books 2020

Magic for the Garage

Most people don't seem to think of including the garage in their Cottage Witchcraft, although most of us have reflexively engaged in folk customs to protect our cars — such as naming them, choosing colors for them we feel make them more (or us) powerful (or attractive, savvy, fast, etc) in some way, and hanging good luck charms from the rearview mirror, placing saint/Deity statues on the dash, affixing stickers to the bumper, getting specialized (almost talismanic) license plates, etc. Many of these customs are the folkloric descendants of protective traditions we would have given to the horse, ox, donkey, or goat and cart we would have used in bygone days. And their livery or stable had its own charms, too.

Contemporarily, the garage is a space that may be doing more than just housing your vehicle. It may also be a workshop, storage space, laundry room, home gym, or even a temple. The suggestions given here can be applied in this multi-use space.

- Design and hang a hex sign either inside or outside the garage. These colorful, six-pointed symbols are meant for the protection of buildings and their contents, and are often seen on barns, stables, and houses — and are traditionally used inside, as well.
- Chalk protective sigils or bindrunes under the place where your vehicle sits.
- Place a witch bottle with rusty nails, screws, and other hardware, as well as the garage floor sweepings in a secret place within the garage.
- Add an infusion of rosemary or dill to the rinsewater (or a spray bottle) when you wash your vehicle.
- Hang a talisman of bells, wheels, red/white roses, and/or eyes tied with red cord from the rearview mirror of the vehicle.
- Place a charge quartz crystal in the glove box.

Copyright Asteria Books 2020

Sitting Room Magic

Since the sitting room (living room, parlor) is so heavily associated with entertaining guests, it is wise to do magic to increase the hospitality of the home and this room, in particular. A Venus hour on Wednesday (2nd hr after sunset) or a Mercury hour on Friday (same timing) will blend the charm, love, friendliness, playfulness, communication, and understanding that these two planetary bodies bring us. Whether your focus is more on entertaining guests or keeping the family happy, these are great energies to promote!

Light and color are both important for setting mood and changing the energy of a room. Use LED dimmable, color-changing bulbs to soften, brighten, and infuse the room in a wash of color magic at a moment's notice.

Hearth Bowl Blessing — Whether or not your home is graced with w a fireplace, you can bring (or bless) the magic and blessing of this ancient, potent liminal space. In an earthenware bowl, place one or more large red stones. Choose different types, if you like, to represent the different types of fire that bless a home — sun, candlelight, hearth, cookfire. Place a red candle in the East at sunrise, and hold your bowl of stones aloft to "catch" both fires here, asking for their blessings. Light a fire in the hearth and a burner on the stove and "catch" both fires there — and their blessings, as well. Give offerings to the Fire Spirits before extinguishing their flames (or turning away from the Sun), and place the bowl on the mantle or a coffee table keep the room warm and filled with spark of joy and life.

Copyright Asteria Books 2020

Talismanic Magick

Copyright Asteria Books 2025

Amulets & Talismans

"Amulet" and "talisman" are often used as interchangeable terms by those who don't practice magick. Even those within the Craft can sometimes confuse the meanings of the two words. However, careful study and consideration of historical talismans and amulets will reveal their differences. While both are magical objects purported to bestow protection or certain forms of good fortune upon their bearer, they are different in their creation.

More specifically:

An AMULET is a naturally occurring object whose physical properties give it inherently protective or magical energies. For example, a stone with a natural hole (a "hag stone," as pictured above), the fur or feathers of your totem animal, and the parts of sacred tree are all amulets. An amulet doesn't necessarily need to be embellished or empowered — just claimed, recognized, and honored (and used). It can be cleansed and empowered, if desired, but this isn't always necessary.

A TALISMAN is a man-made object designed and produced for a specific magical purpose. It may incorporate natural materials or it may not. It can be inscribed or drawn on a piece of paper or other surface or be an object that includes braiding and knotting, color associations, beads, magical alphabets, sigils, numbers, sacred geometry, metal- or woodworking, textiles, angelic/demonic names, Gods, etc. The possibilities are almost endless in terms of both construction and application. It must be prepared and charged by a Witch or Magician to have power. All aspects of the talisman's design should work together to achieve its goal. (The talisman to the right is a Solomonic device called the 4th pentacle of Venus.)

Amulets and talismans are usually (but not always) small enough objects to be portable, and they are very frequently worn or carried in a pocket or pouch to convey their properties to their target.

Copyright Asteria Books 2018

Bellarmine Jars

A Bellarmine jar is, by strictest definition, a brown ceramic bottle or jug with a face depicted on its side, used by Witches for housing spirits, hexing targets and removing curses or hexes. These jars were very durable, and they were very, very popular among the west county Witches of England because they would last, literally, for centuries -- protecting both their contents and the magic contained therein.

They weren't always known as Bellarmine jars, though. "Bellarmine" is a reference to an unpopular 16th Century Cardinal whose face appeared on the jars. Originally, though, these jars were manufactured in Frechen, near Cologne, in Germany. Here, they were called Bartmann jars -- "bearded man" jars, in reference to the bearded face who always appeared on the side.

Today, they are commonly called Witch Bottles, and the availability of a variety of materials used for bottling, canning and preservation means that contemporary Witches needn't use only brown crockery. Of course, the more durable and longer-lasting, the better. Glass might be the most popular of today's choices, but standard glass may not be your sturdiest alternative.

When creating a Bellarmine jar as a spirit house, the old, customary face can be a useful depiction of the spirit to whom you've provided a vessel. You can find potters and artisans who make contemporary versions of the old jars, or you can paint/carve/engrave your own.

Common contents of Bellarmine jars, for both spirit houses and curse/protection bottles, are hair, nail clippings, and charms/figurines. A spirit jar might also contain a few drops of blood and offerings related to the spirit housed within. A jar with the aim of both cursing and protecting might contain pins, broken glass, and urine. Sometimes the jar is buried in the yard with a warding chant such as follows:

Into the ground go without fear
To guard me now both far and near
Throw back all evil from whence it came
By Aradia's holy name

Cimaruta

The Cimaruta is an ancient and intricate folk amulet from Italy, deeply entwined with the traditions of Stregheria, or Italian witchcraft. Its name, meaning "sprig of rue," perfectly describes its form.

The base of the charm is a branch of the rue plant, an herb historically sacred to the goddess Diana and renowned for its potent protective properties in European folklore. Traditionally cast in silver — a metal associated with the moon, intuition, and purification — the amulet's primary purpose is to defend the wearer against the malevolent force of the evil eye, known in Italian as the *malocchio*.

What makes the Cimaruta so powerful is the collection of smaller apotropaic symbols that branch from the central sprig. Each element adds a specific layer of magical defense. Common symbols include a crescent moon, representing cyclical magic and goddesses like Diana; a key, symbolizing access to hidden wisdom and spiritual gateways; a serpent for cunning and transformation; and a dagger to sever negative energy.

Other frequent additions are a fish for abundance and a protective hand gesture like the mano cornuta ("horned hand"). Worn as a personal pendant or pinned over a child's crib, the Cimaruta is a complex talisman where every symbol works in synergy, creating a formidable shield.

Copyright Asteria Books 2025

Cornicello

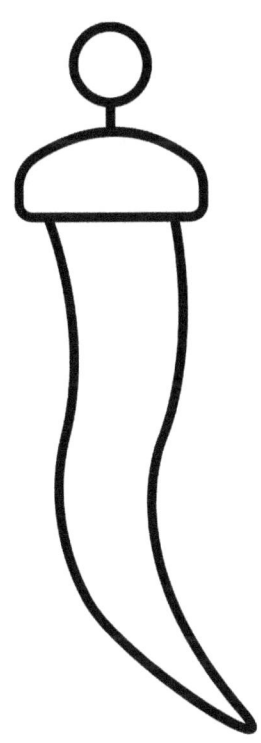

The cornicello, or "little horn," is one of Italy's most recognized and cherished amulets. This twisted, horn-shaped charm is a powerful talisman worn to protect against the malocchio, the dreaded evil eye. Its presence is ubiquitous throughout Italy and its diaspora, a testament to its enduring role in folk tradition and magick, often worn alongside other protective symbols like the Christian cross or a saint's medal.

The cornicello's origins are ancient, likely predating Roman times and tracing back to Neolithic veneration of horned animals, which represented strength, fertility, and virility. The horn was a sacred symbol associated with the Moon Goddess and the life-giving force of nature. While the phallic shape itself is potent, the material traditionally held great significance. Red coral was the preferred medium, believed to possess its own protective magic against illness, infertility, and malevolent spirits. The color red was also associated with blood and life, amplifying its power. Today, cornicelli are crafted from many materials, including gold, silver, bone, and terracotta.

This potent amulet is most commonly worn as a pendant on a necklace, kept close to the body for personal protection. It is also frequently hung from rearview mirrors in cars, attached to keychains, or placed in homes to safeguard the space and its inhabitants from envy and ill will. For many, especially within Italian-American culture, wearing a corno is more than just superstition; it is a proud emblem of heritage, a powerful symbol that has transcended millennia to provide a tangible shield against negativity.

Copyright Asteria Books 2025

Egg Magick

From ancient paganism to modern folk magic, eggs are a powerful and versatile symbol in spiritual practices. Here are 10 ways they are used across different times and cultures:

Fertility Rituals: As a universal symbol of life and creation, eggs have been used for millennia to promote fertility. In ancient Iran, brides and grooms exchanged eggs, and in ancient Egypt, eggs were hung in temples to encourage new life. This symbolism is also found in modern pagan practices.

Offerings to Deities: Eggs have been offered to gods and goddesses across history. They were a key part of the ancient Greek "Deipnon," or suppers for the goddess Hekate, often left at crossroads for purification and protection.

Protection Spells: The egg's shell represents a powerful barrier. In folk magic, especially with the use of powdered eggshells known as cascarilla, a protective circle can be drawn to ward off negative energy, evil spirits, and psychic attacks.

Cleansing and Purification: A raw egg can be used in a spiritual cleanse (a *limpia con huevos*), a practice popular in many Latin American traditions. The egg is rolled over a person's body to absorb negative energy, illness, and the evil eye. The egg is then cracked into a glass of water for a reading of the absorbed energies.

Funerary Rites: In ancient Roman and Germanic tombs, eggs were placed as offerings to the deceased, symbolizing rebirth and the hope of an afterlife.

Modern Easter Traditions: The tradition of decorating and exchanging eggs at Easter has its roots in ancient springtime festivals celebrating fertility and the return of new life after winter.

Home and Land Blessings: Eggs are used to bless homes, fields, and gardens. In medieval Europe, farmers would smear eggs on their tools to ensure the fertility of the soil. Some modern practices involve burying eggs on a property to bring prosperity and abundance.

The Four Elements: The egg is considered a perfect microcosm of the universe, containing all four classical elements. The shell represents Earth, the inner membrane is Air, the yolk is Fire, and the white is Water, making it a powerful and balanced tool in magical workings.

Copyright Asteria Books 2025

Hag Stones

Hag stones, also known as adder stones, witch stones, or holey stones, are naturally occurring rocks with a hole bored clean through them by water and time. The term "hag stone" likely comes from their use in warding off hags, witches, and the malevolent entities of the night that were believed to ride horses and cause nightmares by "hag-riding" them. By hanging a hag stone in the stable or over the bed, a person could prevent these nocturnal attacks. The hole, a magical doorway, was thought to be a one-way portal for energy, allowing benign spirits in while blocking malevolent forces.

In modern practice, hag stones are prized for several key uses:

Scrying and Divination: Looking through the hole of a hag stone is said to allow one to see beyond the veil. The hole acts as a lens, focusing the user's sight into the ethereal world. It can be used to peer into the past, glimpse the future, or observe the auras of people and places.

Offerings and Messages: The hag stone's hole can be used as a passage for sending messages or offerings to the Otherworld.

Protection and Wardings: Hung on a string in a window or above a doorway, a hag stone serves as a powerful ward against negative energy, the evil eye, and unwanted spirits. Its protective qualities are a direct result of its ability to filter and redirect energy.

Healing and Spellwork: In spellwork, a hag stone can be used to focus healing energy, with the healer visualizing the patient's ailment passing through the hole and being neutralized. In binding magic, a thread can be passed through the hole and knotted to symbolically "bind" a negative influence.

I like to activate a hag stone by anointing it with dew from one of the liminal times of year (like Samhain or Beltaine).

Copyright Asteria

Hamsa

The Hamsa is a palm-shaped amulet recognized across the Middle East and North Africa as a powerful symbol of divine protection. It appears as a stylized open right hand, an image that has been used for millennia to ward off the evil eye.

Its name derives from the Hebrew and Arabic words for "five," alluding to the five fingers of the hand. While its design can be symmetrical (with two thumbs), the asymmetrical open palm is most common.

With roots stretching back to ancient Mesopotamia as the Hand of Ishtar, the symbol has been adopted by numerous faiths and is used in non-religious contexts, as well. In Judaism, it is the Hand of Miriam, sister of Moses, with the fingers representing the five books of the Torah. In Islam, it is the Hand of Fatima, daughter of the Prophet Muhammad, symbolizing the Five Pillars of Islam. Often, an eye is depicted in the center of the palm, directly confronting and neutralizing malicious gazes.

The orientation of the hand alters its specific function. When facing up, it is a universal sign against evil—a protective ward that repels negativity and hatred. When facing down, it bestows blessings, abundance, and good fortune upon the owner.

Commonly crafted from silver and adorned with blue stones like turquoise, lapis lazuli, kyanite, blue topaz, and sapphire, the Hamsa is worn as jewelry or hung in homes to invoke divine protection and welcome benevolent energy.

Copyright Asteria Books 2025

Witches' Ladders

String/cord and knot magick have been used for both spell-working and meditation within traditional forms of Witchcraft all over Europe. The tools made from this method are known in various locales as Witches' Ladders, Garlands, or Girdles or simply as "rope and feathers" due to the predominant use of the those particular materials in the ladders' construction.

In Robert Cochrane's article "On Cords," he describes the use of both devotional and magickal ladders:

"When worked up properly they should contain many different parts --herbs, feathers and impedimenta of the particular charm. They are generally referred to in the trade as "ladders," or in some cases as "garlands," and have much the same meaning as the three crosses. That is they can contain three blessings, three curses, or three wishes. A witch also possesses a devotional ladder, by which she may climb to meditational heights, knotted to similar pattern as the Catholic rosary."

Historically, the oldest sets of preserved ladders seem to have been used for cursing and included either gander feathers or black hen feathers. The cord contained usually three, nine, or thirteen knots; but more contemporary versions base the number of knots on a variety of factors, including alignment with a particular magickal intention or system. Ladders used for cursing could only be thwarted by finding the rope and untying the knots, sometimes followed by special purification baths.

Contemporary ladders are just as frequently (maybe even more frequently) made for meditational purposes like a rosary or for beneficent spellwork. The "rope and feathers" of traditional ladders are more commonly replaced by braided or knotted string or cord and beads, charms, and other trinkets. Initiation cords, for covens who use them, are a variation of witches' ladders.

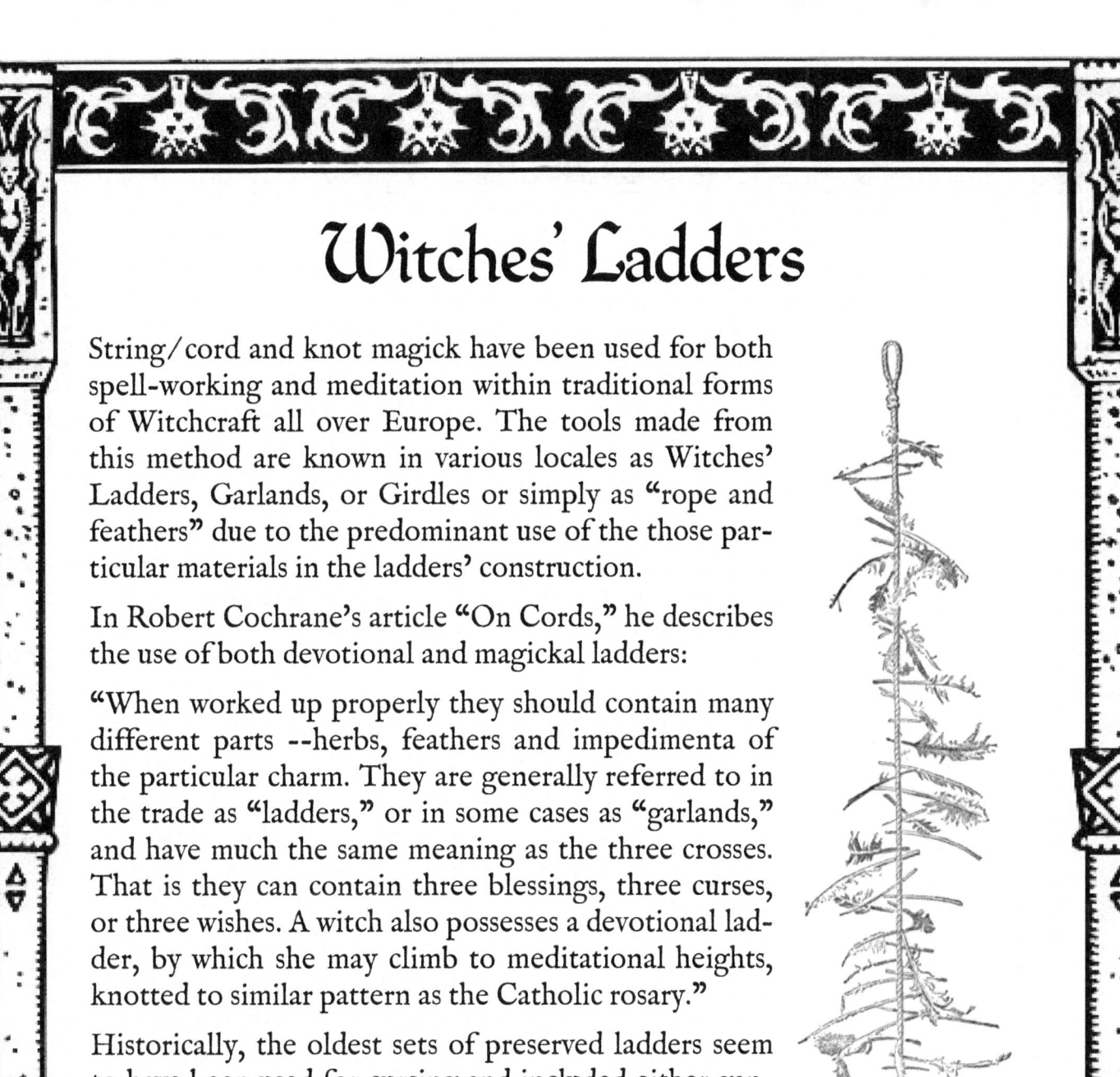

Copyright Asteria Books 2018

Lamp Magick

The oil lamp, a humble vessel of light, is a powerful tool in the contemporary witch's arsenal. Beyond its practical use, it serves as a focal point for intention, a conduit for communication, and a beacon of sustained magical energy. Unlike the ephemeral candle flame, the lamp's steady glow is a symbol of endurance, representing long-term workings and the patient cultivation of one's craft.

One of the most potent applications of the oil lamp is in anointing. The base oil—be it olive, sunflower, or grapeseed—becomes a canvas for magical intent. To empower a working for prosperity, infuse the oil with herbs like cinnamon, basil, or a few drops of patchouli essential oil. For protection, add black pepper, rosemary, or a sprinkle of sea salt. As you prepare the lamp, visualize your intention soaking into the liquid, charging it with your will. When the wick is lit, the energy is released steadily into your space, a constant stream of your desired outcome.

Divination is another key use. The flickering flame, the smoke's dance, and the oil's surface all hold messages. Gaze into the flame, letting your mind soften, and ask a question. The way

Copyright Asteria Books 2025

Magickal Pouches

The humble pouch, whether a simple sachet, a complex mojo hand, or a protective putzi bag, is a cornerstone of folk magic traditions worldwide. These tools are far more than just containers; they are living spells, charged with intention and carried on the body or placed in specific locations to work their magic continuously. They are coded items, their contents speaking a magical language understood by the witch and the spirits.

The Anatomy of a Pouch

At its core, a magical pouch is built around a specific purpose. There are three key components:

The Container: This is the vessel itself. A drawstring bag is common for its ease of use. The material is often chosen for its magical properties: red flannel for love, green cotton for prosperity, or black leather for protection. The container holds the spell's components and keeps them discreetly together.

The Contents: These are the heart of the working. They are carefully selected ingredients that correspond to the spell's purpose. This could include herbs, roots, stones, curios, and personal items like hair or a piece of a loved one's clothing. Each item is chosen to act as a magical "word" in the spell, its properties contributing to the overall intention. For example, a money mojo might contain a lodestone to draw wealth, a piece of cinnamon for speed, and a silver coin for a physical representation of money.

The Consecration: This is the moment the pouch is imbued with life. After the contents are assembled, the pouch is typically "fed" or "dressed" with a magical oil or liquid, often corresponding to the pouch's purpose. This feeding ritual activates the spell. From that point on, the pouch must be fed regularly to keep its power strong. This can be done by adding a few drops of oil or even by speaking to it, thanking it for its work and reminding it of its purpose.

Modern Applications

In contemporary practice, these pouches are incredibly versatile. A mojo hand is a powerful spell for a single, focused purpose like attracting love or luck. A sachet is a lighter version, often used for things like sweetening a space or bringing peaceful sleep. A putzi bag, a term originating in some Eastern European traditions, is a potent protective charm, often carried to ward off the evil eye or negative energy.

The beauty of the magical pouch is its portability and subtlety. It allows you to carry your magic with you, a constant source of support and a tangible connection to your intention.

Copyright Asteria Books 2025

Mano Cornuto

The mano cornuto, or "horned hand," is a potent symbol in Italian folk tradition, used both as a physical gesture and a protective amulet. Formed by extending the index and pinky fingers while holding the middle and ring fingers down with the thumb, its primary purpose is to ward off the malocchio (evil eye) and deflect bad luck. This gesture is one of the most immediate and personal forms of apotropaic magic still in active use today.

The gesture's orientation is critically important. For protection, the fingers must point downwards, symbolically directing any negative energy or curse into the earth to be neutralized. Pointing the mano cornuto upwards at someone is a grave insult in Italy and other Mediterranean regions, insinuating that the person is a cornuto — a cuckold, a term for a man whose partner is unfaithful. This crucial distinction separates the protective gesture from similar-looking signs.

Like the cornicello amulet, the horned hand's power is rooted in ancient beliefs that associated horns with the strength, virility, and power to pierce and destroy evil. To serve as a constant ward, the gesture is also crafted into physical charms. These amulets are often made from traditional materials like red coral, silver, or gold and worn as pendants.

Copyright Asteria Books 2025

Mano Fico

The Mano Fico, or Fig Hand, is an ancient and widely recognized amulet, though its meaning varies dramatically by region. It is a gesture made by forming a fist and tucking the thumb between the index and middle fingers. While considered obscene in some cultures, its true power lies in its protective qualities as a potent ward against the evil eye.

Its origins trace back to the Roman era, where it was known as the manu fica and associated with fertility rites and the goddess Venus. The gesture was believed to represent female genitalia, a powerful symbol of life and creation used to mock and neutralize sterile, destructive forces like envy and malice. It embodies the principle of overwhelming darkness with a potent, life-affirming vulgarity.

Typically carved from materials like silver, jet, or red coral, the Mano Fico is worn as a personal charm on a necklace or bracelet. It serves as a constant guardian, deflecting curses, repelling bad luck, and absorbing the negative energy of a malicious gaze before it can harm the wearer. It is said that if an amulet breaks, it has successfully intercepted a powerful curse meant for its owner, sacrificing itself in the process. The Fig Hand remains a popular form of folk magic, especially in Italy and Brazil, a testament to its enduring power to protect.

Copyright Asteria Books 2025

Milagros

The word "Milagro" translates to "miracle," and these small metal charms are precisely that: the humble seeds from which miracles may sprout. Forged of tin, silver, or gold, they are petitions given physical form, tangible prayers offered to the spirit world in hope of succor, healing, or favor. They are a potent and ancient form of sympathetic magic, rooted in the belief that "like attracts like."

Each charm is a symbol representing a specific need. An arm or a leg is offered for the mending of a limb, an eye for clarity of sight or spirit, a heart for matters of love or to heal a broken spirit. One might offer the charm of a cow for the health of their livestock, a house for the protection of their home, or a book for success in their studies. The variety of forms is nearly endless, for human need is a vast and varied landscape.

To work their magic, the practitioner must first charge the Milagro with their focused intention. Hold it tightly within your palm until it is warm with your energy, whispering your plea or prayer into the metal. Visualize your desire as a brilliant light flowing from your core and into the charm, sealing your will within it.

The final act is one of offering. Traditionally, the charged Milagro is pinned to the raiment of a saint's statue or left upon a dedicated altar or shrine. This act of release is crucial; it is a trade, an offering of faith in exchange for intervention. The charm remains as a constant, silent prayer long after you have departed. One may also carry a charged Milagro as a personal talisman, keeping the intention close until the desired miracle has manifested.

Copyright Asteria Books 2025

Rope and Feathers

Materials

- 9 yd of ribbon or cording
- 9 feathers or charms
- White handled knife or scissors
- Timing

Gather the materials and perform your spell on a Wednesday night during the Full Moon. If possible, time your Laying the Compass to coincide with "Jupiter hour," which will begin approximately 3 hours after sunset.

Process

1. Lay the Compass in your usual fashion, or use the method provided in this grimoire.

2. Say the following aloud three times as you hold the cording and feathers in your hands: "I call upon the Ancient Powers. By the might of three times three, let harm and hurt pass over me."

3. Say one of the following strings of barbarous words that come to us from the Greek Magical Papyri: (to call the Witch Mother's power) PHORBA PHORBOBAR BARO PHORPHOR PHORBAI; (to call the Witch Father's power) ABRAT ABRASAX SESENGENBARPHARANGES

4. Cut the cording into three equal lengths, knotting them together at one end.

5. Braid the cording as you rock and sway, braiding in your feathers and charms as you go. While you do this, hold an image in your mind of either the Witch Mother who is the Queen of Heaven and Hell, Mis-tress of the Crossroads, Lady of Elphame; or the Witch Father who is the Lord of Misrule, Auld Hornie, the Pukha. Feel free to chant, sing, or intone the barbarous words associated with the One whose protection you are invoking as you work.

6. When you come to the end of your cordage, tie an end knot to bind the rope.

7. Tie knots at or over each of your nine feathers or charms, starting in the middle and moving out, alternating sides. You may have to work carefully to keep from damaging the feathers as you pull them through the loops. Don't, however, take the shortcut of knotting as you work your way down the braid. That approach, while faster and easier, short circuits the power of the working because it disrupts the flow of energy into the braid as you work, and places the knots out of order.

8. When the knotting is completed, drape the rope and feathers around your neck and make an offering to the Witch Mother or Witch Father. (The Housle Rite works well for this.)

Wear the rope and feathers each time you approach Spirits, especially when meeting or working with a Spirit who is unfamiliar to you. If you ever have need to unleash the power in your rope, you will need to make a new one.

Copyright Asteria Books 2022

Sator Square

The Sator Square is a well-known and powerful symbol used for protection. It consists of a five-by-five grid of letters that form a unique palindrome, which can be read forwards, backwards, upwards, and downwards. This clever word puzzle is believed to hold magical properties.

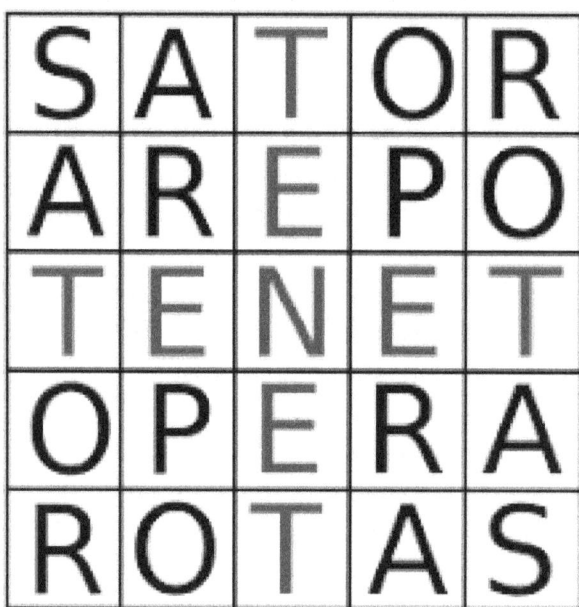

It is often used as a protective ward. When inscribed on a doorway, it is said to block negative energy or evil influences from entering. When carried as an amulet, it is thought to shield the owner from curses and bad luck. The central word, "TENET," which forms a cross, is seen as the core of its power, holding the other words in balance. The square's strength comes from its perfect, self-contained structure—an unbroken loop of words.

Copyright Asteria Books 2025

Solomonic Pentacles

Where the Milagro is a quiet prayer given form, the Pentacles of King Solomon are commands etched in metal, instruments of celestial power designed to compel the spirits and bend the currents of fate. These are not mere symbols of hope, but complex diagrams of power, cosmic circuits that draw down the specific influences of the seven ancient planets. They are an inheritance of high ceremonial magic, a key to unlocking the authority of the heavens.

Each pentacle is a microcosm, a map of divine forces. At its heart lies the influence of a planet—the martial fire of Mars, the loving grace of Venus, the wise authority of Jupiter, or the dark discipline of Saturn. This primary influence is focused and amplified through a matrix of Hebrew names of God and His angels, potent sigils, and verses from holy scripture, all inscribed within the perfect geometry of a circle. It is this combination of divine word, angelic sigil, and planetary correspondence that gives the pentacle its formidable power.

To wield a pentacle is to align oneself with a specific cosmic current. The Second Pentacle of Venus, for instance, is employed to gain favor and love, while the Fourth Pentacle of Jupiter is used to acquire wealth and honor. The practitioner does not simply ask for a boon; they consecrate the pentacle through ritual, charging it under the proper astrological conditions and with the correct incantations. This act awakens the talisman, turning it from a simple disc of silver or parchment into a potent magical engine.

These are not tools for the unprepared. Their use demands precise knowledge of planetary hours, angelic hierarchies, and divine names. To misuse a pentacle is to risk discord, for the powers they command are vast and impartial. They are a testament to the belief that through wisdom, discipline, and divine invocation, the magus can become a conduit for the very power that orders the cosmos.

Copyright Asteria Books 2025

Solomonic Pentacles of Saturn

Solomonic Pentacles of Saturn

The seven Pentacles of Saturn are generally concerned with protection, binding enemies, compelling spirits of the earth, and bringing about destruction or ruin to others' plans.

Metal: Lead

Incense: Asafoetida, Sulphur, Scammony, and powders of Lodestone. For general workings, Myrrh or Civet are also acceptable.

Primary Divine & Angelic Names: YHVH, Agiel, Zazel, Aralim, Omeliel.

1st Pentacle of Saturn: Used to compel obedience and submission from others, and to draw on Saturn's powers for protection, justice, and knowledge.

2nd Pentacle of Saturn: Said to be of great value when facing adversaries, especially in business or competitions. It's also recommended for those seeking employment or negotiating financial contracts.

3rd Pentacle of Saturn: Designed for protection against plots and evil spirits.

4th Pentacle of Saturn: Used to execute destructive actions and can be employed when seeking news from the south.

5th Pentacle of Saturn: Provides protection for the home and possessions, and is said to chase away spirits guarding treasures.

6th Pentacle of Saturn: Can be used to invoke demons to possess an enemy when their name is pronounced.

7th Pentacle of Saturn: Associated with making others listen and tremble before the wearer's words.

Copyright Asteria Books 2025

Solomonic Pentacles of Jupiter

Solomonic Pentacles of Jupiter

The seven Pentacles of Jupiter are invoked for the acquisition of glory, honors, riches, and peace of mind. They are also used for discovering treasures and charming those in positions of power.

Metal: Tin

Incense: Saffron, Nutmeg, Lignum Aloes, Storax.

Primary Divine & Angelic Names: Eheieh, Iophiel, Hismael, Seraphim.

1st Pentacle of Jupiter: Attracts wealth, business success, and treasure, featuring angelic names associated with fame, balance, riches, and vast treasures.

2nd Pentacle of Jupiter: Brings glory, honor, wealth, fortune, success, and peace of mind. It is also said to help discover treasures and dispel spirits guarding them.

3rd Pentacle of Jupiter: Provides protection against enemies and evil spirits.

4th Pentacle of Jupiter: Attracts wealth, honor, and lasting respect, with the names of angels Adoniel and Bariel associated with divine blessings and spiritual transformation.

5th Pentacle of Jupiter: Grants spiritual and psychic vision.

6th Pentacle of Jupiter: Offers protection against all earthly dangers, with the names of four elemental rulers: Seraph, Kerub, Ariel, and Tharsis, according to the Key of Solomon.

7th Pentacle of Jupiter: Protects against poverty.

Copyright Asteria Books 2025

Solomonic Pentacles of Mars

Solomonic Pentacles of Mars

The seven Pentacles of Mars are of a martial nature. They are used to invoke courage, ambition, and victory in battle or conflict. They can also be used to bring judgment upon one's enemies and to resist hostile forces.

Metal: Iron

Incense: Dragon's Blood, Euphorbium, and any pungent, fiery resin.

Primary Divine & Angelic Names: Elohim Gibor, Graphiel, Bartzabel, Seraphim.

1st Pentacle of Mars: This pentacle is associated with courage and ambition, potentially assisting in overcoming obstacles and achieving goals.

2nd Pentacle of Mars: It is believed to offer protection against diseases and bodily pains, with a focus on healing and preserving life.

3rd Pentacle of Mars: This pentacle is used for repelling enemies and resisting negativity.

4th Pentacle of Mars: It is said to be powerful in arguments and disputes, helping one to win and persuade.

5th Pentacle of Mars: This pentacle is believed to offer protection against negative energies and entities.

6th Pentacle of Mars: It is associated with protection against physical harm, with the belief that it can cause an attacker's weapons to turn against them.

7th Pentacle of Mars: This pentacle is thought to provide protection and weaken enemies.

Copyright Asteria Books 2025

Solomonic Pentacles of the Sun

Solomonic Pentacles of the Sun

The seven Pentacles of the Sun deal with acquiring renown, glory, and wealth. They are said to render the possessor gracious in the eyes of the powerful, grant clarity of mind, and make one invisible at will.

Metal: Gold

Incense: Frankincense, Lignum Aloes, Cloves, Cinnamon, or any fine Solar gums.

Primary Divine & Angelic Names: YHVH Eloah Vedaath, Michael, Nachiel, Sorath.

1st Pentacle of the Sun: This pentacle is believed to grant the power to compel obedience from creatures, angels, and solar spirits. It is associated with gaining respect, authority, and overall power. Some believe it can help in fulfilling one's desires.

2nd Pentacle of the Sun: This pentacle is used for protection against aggression and potential harm. It is considered a powerful talisman for general protection.

3rd Pentacle of the Sun: This pentacle is used for acquiring kingdom and empire, as well as for inflicting loss and acquiring renown and glory. It is associated with achieving recognition and fame, particularly through divine influence. It is believed to be especially potent due to the repeated use of the Tetragrammaton, one of the names of God.

4th Pentacle of the Sun: This pentacle is used to reveal spirits that may be invisible to those who invoke them. It is used to prevent one's enemies from prevailing.

5th Pentacle of the Sun: This pentacle is used to invoke spirits that can transport the user from one place to another over long distances.

6th Pentacle of the Sun: This pentacle is used for invisibility when properly made.

7th Pentacle of the Sun: This pentacle is used to grant release from prison.

Solomonic Pentacles of Venus

Solomonic Pentacles of Venus

The five Pentacles of Venus are used to obtain grace and honor, to attract love, and to compel the desired person to come to the practitioner. They are also used for inciting passion and finding friendship.

Metal: Copper

Incense: Sandalwood, Myrtle, Lignum Aloes, or any fragrant, pleasing floral incense.

Primary Divine & Angelic Names: YHVH Tzabaoth, Hagiel, Kedemel, Seraphim.

1st Pentacle: Used to attract friends and dispel enchantments, particularly those associated with false prophets and false gods.

2nd Pentacle: Used to obtain grace and honor and to help fulfill heart's desires related to Venus.

3rd Pentacle: Used to attract love, respect, and admiration.

4th Pentacle: Used to attract love and can be used to mend broken relationships or reunite loved ones.

5th Pentacle: Said to arouse passion and desire in others.

Solomonic Pentacles of Mercury

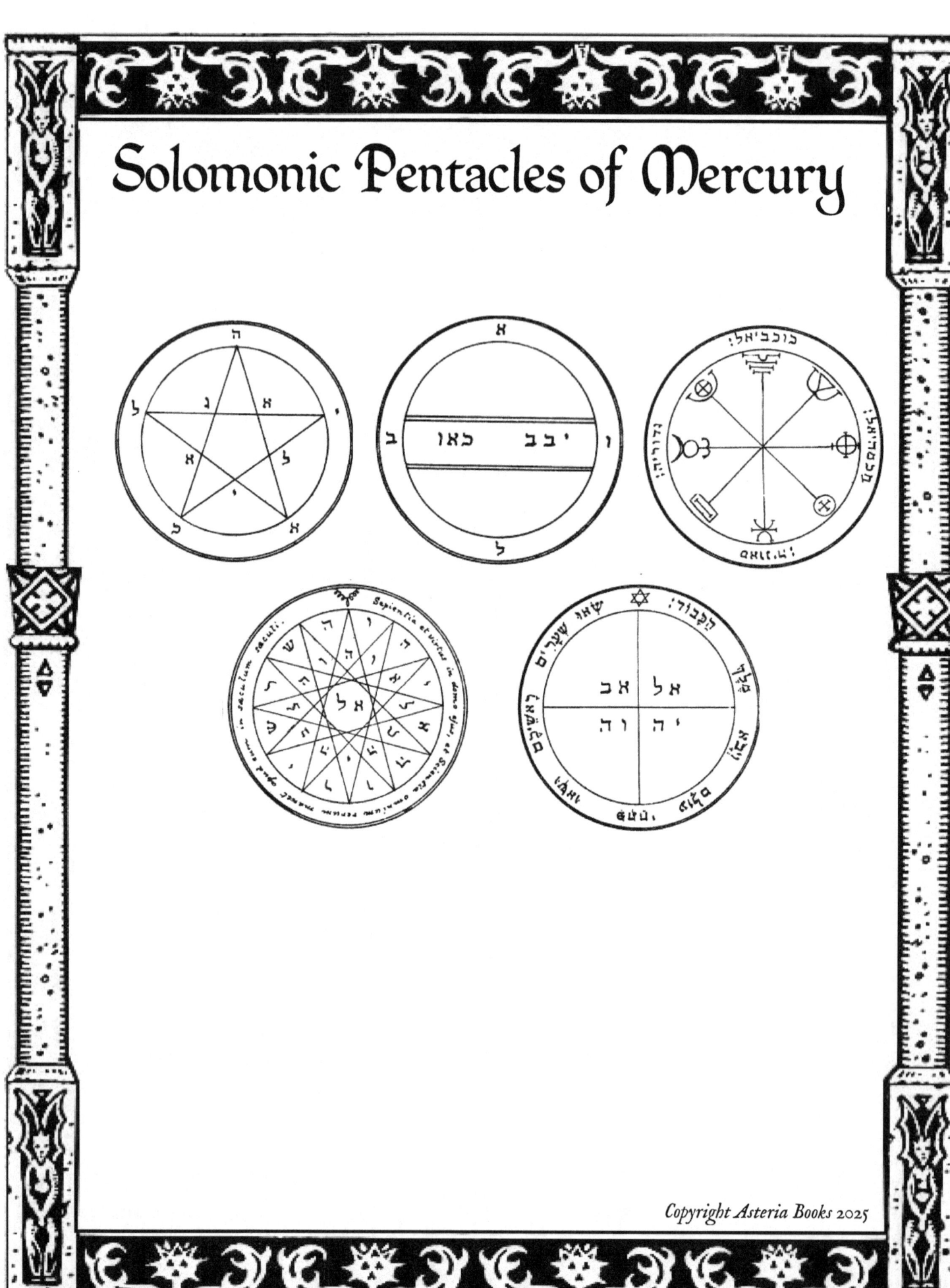

Solomonic Pentacles of Mercury

The five Pentacles of Mercury serve to quicken the intellect and memory, enhance eloquence, and open doors that are closed. They are used to understand the sciences and to compel spirits to serve the magus's will.

Metal: Mercury (or alloys such as Zinc or Brass)

Incense: Mastic, Storax, or any gums of a mixed, subtle scent.

Primary Divine & Angelic Names: Elohim Tzabaoth, Raphael, Taphthartharath.

1st Pentacle of Mercury: Grants personal magnetism and is used to invoke Spirits under the Firmament.

2nd Pentacle of Mercury: Used to achieve the impossible, fulfill wishes, and relax stress.

3rd Pentacle of Mercury: Used to acquire spiritual powers and invoke Spirits.

4th Pentacle of Mercury: Fosters understanding, wisdom, and reveals hidden knowledge.

5th Pentacle of Mercury: Opens pathways and doors, removing obstacles.

Solomonic Pentacles of the Moon

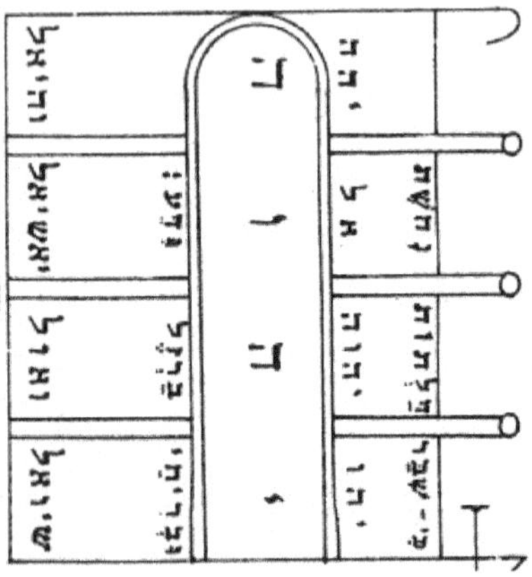

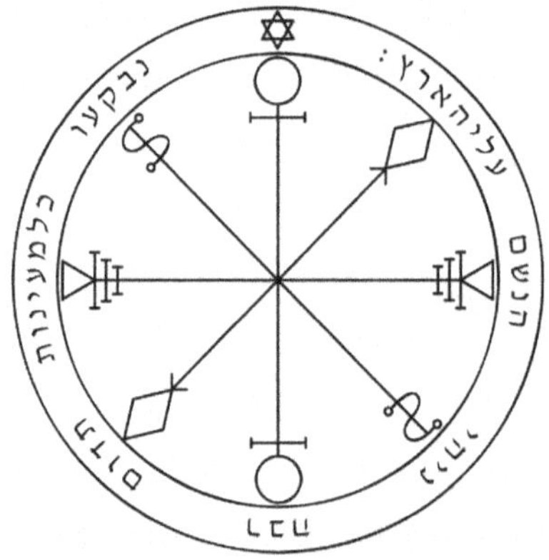

Solomonic Pentacles of the Moon

The six Pentacles of the Moon are used to protect against all dangers by night, to cause storms, to open locks, and to invoke the spirits of the Moon to obtain answers through dreams and divination.

Metal: Silver

Incense: White Sandalwood, Camphor, Amber, or any fresh, watery scent like Willow bark or Cucumber seeds.

Primary Divine & Angelic Names: Shaddai El Chai, Gabriel, Elim, Chasmodai

1st Pentacle: Invokes lunar spirits and open doors, both material and metaphysical.

2nd Pentacle: Protects from danger, particularly when traveling.

3rd Pentacle: Protects from both bodily and spiritual harm.

4th Pentacle: Provides protection and wisdom.

5th Pentacle: Helps in sleep and provides answers in dreams.

6th Pentacle: A "seal of wonders," potentially used for various magical operations.

Witch Bottles

The witch bottle is a powerful piece of folk magic, primarily from the British Isles and Colonial America, designed to trap and neutralize malevolent spells or curses sent by a witch or sorcerer. The principle behind it is a form of sympathetic magic, where the contents of the bottle act as a lure and a trap for the negative energy.

The traditional recipe for a witch bottle calls for a glass bottle to be filled with personal items from the person being targeted, such as hair, fingernail clippings, or urine. These items serve as a magical "bait," drawing the spell's energy into the bottle. The bottle is then armed with sharp, defensive objects like bent nails, pins, or thorns, which are meant to pierce and "imprison" the curse. A common addition is red wine or vinegar, which is believed to both sour the magic and make it unpalatable to the sender.

Once sealed, the witch bottle is typically buried near the threshold of the home -- under a hearth, a doorstep, or a window (or inside a wall) -- to create a permanent magical barrier. The spell is considered complete once the bottle is hidden, its contents actively working to deflect and contain any harmful magic sent toward the household. Modern practitioners may use a witch bottle to ward off general negativity or malicious gossip, filling it with symbolic ingredients and burying it on their property to create a protective ward. The goal remains the same: to turn a curse back on itself and safeguard the home and its inhabitants.

Copyright Asteria Books 2025

Witch's Glove

The Witch's Glove is an uncommon tool or symbol among Witches. It is not used or even known by many. My own teacher didn't use this name for it, in fact. She simply called it a "Hand." However, it has its roots in the dim past, possibly as far back as the Hand of Ishtar.

The Witch's Glove is a hand-shaped set of symbols that acts as something of a personal heraldic device. It is both a banner and a shield for the Witch.

In order to prepare this talisman, you should engage in a series of personal meditations and reflections to discover a set of symbols that speak very deeply to your core nature, as well as to your aspirations. These can be almost any type of symbol — from animals to trees, ruses, alchemical symbols, etc.

Consider the colors and textures you will use to convey those symbols, as well.

The Glove can be fashioned out of an actual glove, an artist's posable hand, a hand-shaped ring-folder, or other three-dimensional hand-shaped object. Alternatively, it can be painted, etched, or sewn onto a two-dimensional surface of wood, glass, fabric, leather, metal, etc.

Some Witches who employ the Glove place it outside the door of their dwelling. Others keep it inside their bedroom or upon their working altar.

Copyright Asteria Books 2025

Witch Peg

The witch peg, also known as a witch pin or a nowl, is a powerful but often misunderstood tool in the modern witch's practice. While not as historically prominent as witch bottles or poppets, its use is rooted in a deep folk tradition of sympathetic magic and focused intent. It is a simple tool, often nothing more than a large nail, a railroad spike, or a piece of a sturdy, sharp branch. Its power lies not in its complexity, but in its ability to anchor and direct energy with singular purpose.

The use of sharp objects in magical practice is ancient, with pins, needles, and thorns appearing in folklore and ritual across many cultures. While the specific term "witch peg" is more contemporary, its function echoes practices documented for centuries. Pins were used in poppets for both healing and cursing, and nails were a key component of protective witch bottles. The folklore surrounding witches often connects them to sharp objects, either as tools for harm or as items to be used against them—for example, the belief that a witch could be identified by the prick of a pin, or that a silver bullet or button was needed to defeat a witch in animal form. The witch peg synthesizes these ideas into a single, intentional tool.

The witch peg is primarily a tool for pinning down, anchoring, and directing energy. Its sharp point is a physical representation of focused will.

For Protection: A common use is to drive a witch peg into the ground at the four corners of a property to create a protective barrier. As you hammer it into the earth, you can visualize it anchoring a powerful shield, keeping unwanted energies from crossing your boundaries. It can also be placed in the doorway or windowsill to "pin" negative energy and prevent it from entering.

For Binding and Containing: The witch peg can be used in binding spells to "pin down" a harmful person or a negative situation. It is often driven into a piece of paper with the name of the person or the description of the problem, symbolically halting its progress.

For Grounding and Attunement: For many practitioners, a witch peg is a tool for connecting with the land. Driving it into the earth can serve as an act of grounding, helping you to absorb the raw, wild energy of the land. It can also be used to collect energy from a sacred site or a powerful natural location, acting as a magical battery that can be taken home and used later.

For Cursing (or Uncrossing): The witch peg can be a powerful instrument for inflicting focused spiritual harm on a target; however, it can also be used in "uncrossing" or "unhexing" rituals, where it is used to "pin down" the energy of the curse itself, effectively neutralizing it.

Copyright Asteria Books 2025

Witches' Stones

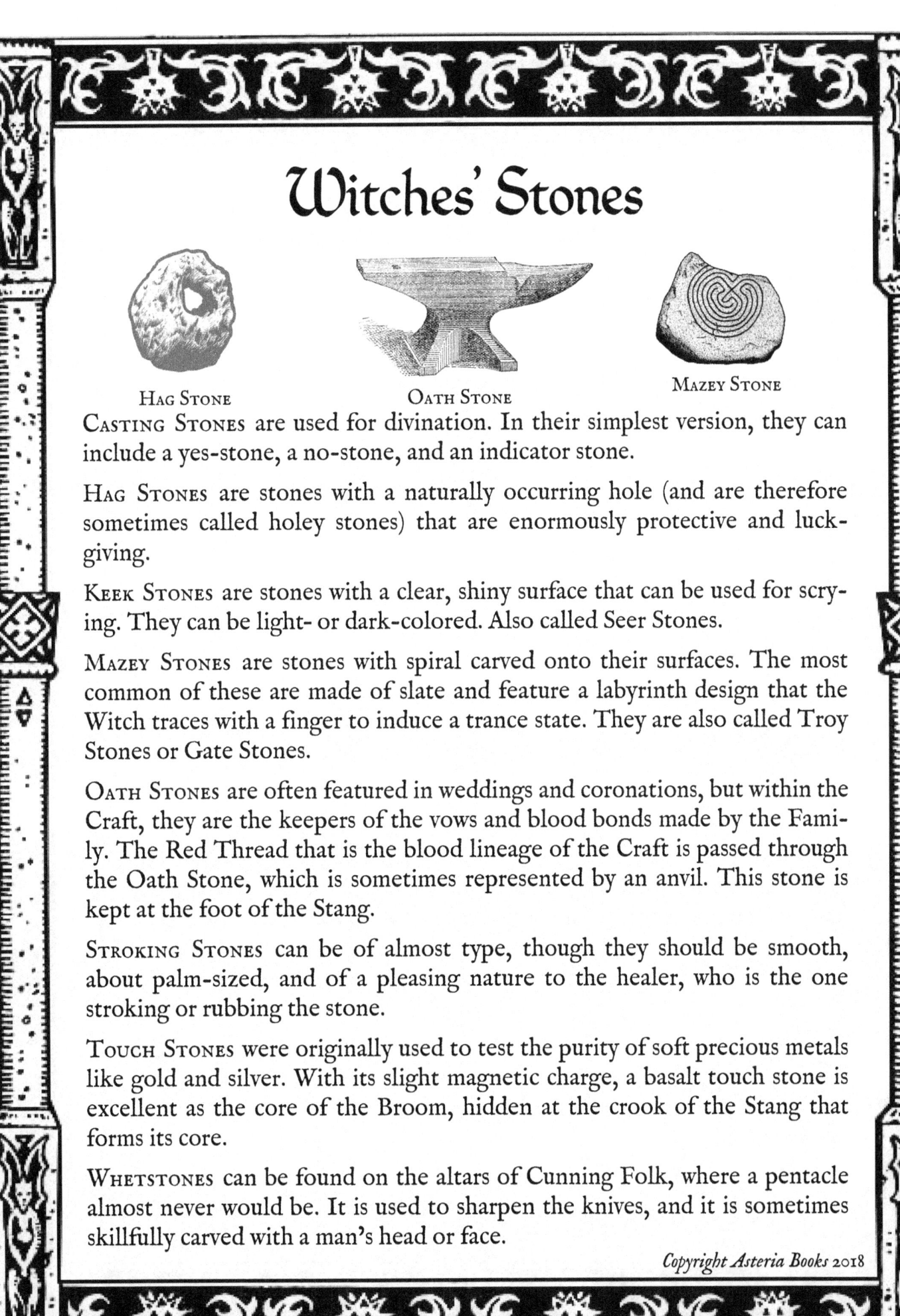

Hag Stone — Oath Stone — Mazey Stone

Casting Stones are used for divination. In their simplest version, they can include a yes-stone, a no-stone, and an indicator stone.

Hag Stones are stones with a naturally occurring hole (and are therefore sometimes called holey stones) that are enormously protective and luck-giving.

Keek Stones are stones with a clear, shiny surface that can be used for scrying. They can be light- or dark-colored. Also called Seer Stones.

Mazey Stones are stones with spiral carved onto their surfaces. The most common of these are made of slate and feature a labyrinth design that the Witch traces with a finger to induce a trance state. They are also called Troy Stones or Gate Stones.

Oath Stones are often featured in weddings and coronations, but within the Craft, they are the keepers of the vows and blood bonds made by the Family. The Red Thread that is the blood lineage of the Craft is passed through the Oath Stone, which is sometimes represented by an anvil. This stone is kept at the foot of the Stang.

Stroking Stones can be of almost type, though they should be smooth, about palm-sized, and of a pleasing nature to the healer, who is the one stroking or rubbing the stone.

Touch Stones were originally used to test the purity of soft precious metals like gold and silver. With its slight magnetic charge, a basalt touch stone is excellent as the core of the Broom, hidden at the crook of the Stang that forms its core.

Whetstones can be found on the altars of Cunning Folk, where a pentacle almost never would be. It is used to sharpen the knives, and it is sometimes skillfully carved with a man's head or face.

Copyright Asteria Books 2018

Domination Talismans

Mirror: Used in various cultures, a mirror can symbolize reflection and the ability to mirror back energy or intentions towards others.

Binding Knots: Knots tied with specific intentions to bind or control situations or individuals. These knots can be physical or represented symbolically.

Serpent Symbol: In some traditions, serpents symbolize wisdom, transformation, and control over hidden forces. Snake motifs or imagery can be used as talismans.

Dagger or Athame: A ritual knife used in ceremonial magic, often symbolizing power, authority, and the ability to direct energy.

Powerful Animals: Symbols or images of powerful animals, such as lions, eagles, or wolves, can be used as talismans for dominance and control.

Copyright Asteria Books 2024

Fertility Talismans

Fertility Goddess Statues: Statues or figurines of fertility goddesses from different cultures, such as Venus (Roman), Aphrodite (Greek), or Freyja (Norse), are believed to promote fertility and conception.

Acorns: In Celtic traditions, acorns symbolize fertility, growth, and potential. Carrying an acorn is believed to bring fertility blessings.

Cowrie Shells: Used in African and Caribbean cultures, cowrie shells are believed to symbolize fertility and femininity. They are worn as amulets or carried for fertility blessings.

Circles and Spirals: Symbols such as the spiral (representing the womb and fertility) or the circle (representing the cycle of life) are used as talismans for fertility and conception.

Fish: In many cultures, fish symbolize fertility and abundance. Images or figurines of fish are used as talismans for fertility blessings.

Lotus Flower: In Eastern cultures, the lotus flower symbolizes purity, enlightenment, and fertility. It is worn or kept as a talisman for fertility and spiritual growth.

Egg: The egg is a universal symbol of fertility and new life. Decorated eggs or egg-shaped talismans are used to promote fertility and conception.

Phallus (representing male fertility) and **Yoni Symbols** (representing female fertility) from ancient cultures are used as talismans for fertility blessings.

Copyright Asteria Books 2024

Health Talismans

 Celtic Cross: A symbol of protection and balance, the Celtic Cross is believed to ward off illness and promote overall health

Scarab Beetle: In ancient Egyptian culture, the scarab beetle symbolizes rebirth and regeneration, and it was often worn as a talisman for good health and protection.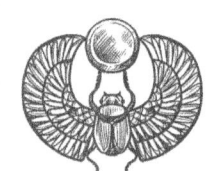

 Ankh: An ancient Egyptian symbol representing life and immortality, the Ankh is sometimes carried or worn for protection and physical health.

Sun Symbol: Symbols associated with the sun, such as the Sun Wheel or Sun Cross, are believed to bring vitality, energy, and good health.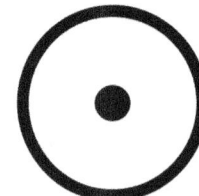

 Tree of Life: A symbol of growth, strength, and connection to nature, the Tree of Life is often used as a talisman for health and vitality.

Om Symbol: In Hinduism and Buddhism, the Om symbol represents the essence of the universe and divine energy. It is used as a talisman for spiritual and physical well-being.

 Caduceus: A symbol of healing and medicine, the caduceus is often used as a talisman by medical professionals and those seeking health and healing.

Copyright Asteria Books 2024

Love Talismans

Rose Quartz: Known as the stone of unconditional love, rose quartz is believed to promote love, compassion, and harmony. It's often used in jewelry or kept as a polished stone to attract love into one's life.

Love Knot: A traditional symbol of everlasting love, the love knot (also known as a true lover's knot) is often depicted as intertwined or braided loops, symbolizing an unbreakable bond.

Cupid's Arrow: In Greek and Roman mythology, Cupid's arrow is a symbol of love and desire. A talisman in the form of an arrowhead or arrow motif is believed to invoke feelings of attraction and passion.

Red String or Ribbon: In various cultures, a red string or ribbon tied around the wrist or worn as a bracelet is believed to attract love and protect relationships. It symbolizes the connection between two people and wards off negative energies.

Lovebirds: Representing monogamous and affectionate relationships, images or figurines of lovebirds are often used as talismans to strengthen love bonds and attract romantic partners.

Heart-shaped Amulets: Heart-shaped amulets or pendants are worn as symbols of love and affection. They are believed to radiate loving energy and attract romantic connections.

Aphrodite or Venus Symbols: Symbols associated with the goddesses of loveare used as talismans to invoke their blessings and attract love and beauty.

Copyright Asteria Books 2024

Luck Talismans

Four-leaf Clover: Found in nature, the four-leaf clover is a universal symbol of good luck. Each leaf represents faith, hope, love, and luck.

Lucky Rabbit's Foot: A traditional talisman in European and American folklore, believed to bring luck and protect against evil spirits.

Horseshoe: Hung above doorways with the ends pointing upwards to catch luck and prevent it from spilling out. It is a symbol of good fortune and protection in many cultures.

Acorns: In Celtic traditions, acorns symbolize potential, growth, and luck. Carrying an acorn is believed to attract prosperity and good fortune.

Elephant: In Asian cultures, elephants symbolize strength, wisdom, and good luck. A figurine or image of an elephant with its trunk raised is considered especially auspicious.

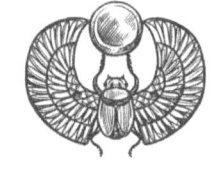

Scarab Beetle: In ancient Egypt, scarab beetles symbolize rebirth and protection. They are believed to bring good luck and ward off negative energies.

Lucky Cat (Maneki-Neko): A Japanese talisman believed to bring good luck and prosperity. The raised paw is said to beckon good fortune.

Fish: Fish are symbols of abundance and good luck in many cultures. In Feng Shui, a fish tank with live fish is believed to attract luck and prosperity.

Sun Symbol: Symbols associated with the sun, such as the Sun Wheel or Sun Cross, are believed to bring vitality, energy, and good luck.

Copyright Asteria Books 2024

Money Talismans

Lucky Cat (Maneki-Neko): A Japanese talisman believed to bring good luck and prosperity to its owner, especially in business. The raised paw is said to beckon wealth and fortune.

Money Tree (Jade Plant): In Feng Shui, the Jade Plant is considered a symbol of prosperity and good fortune. Keeping a healthy Jade Plant in the home or office is believed to attract wealth.

Four-leaf Clover: Considered lucky in many cultures, finding a four-leaf clover is believed to bring financial luck and prosperity.

Goldfish: In Feng Shui, goldfish are symbols of wealth and abundance. Keeping live goldfish in a tank or a painting of goldfish is believed to attract financial success.

Dragon: In Chinese culture, dragons are symbols of power, strength, and good luck. Dragon statues or images are used as talismans for prosperity and financial success.

Money Frog (Three-legged Toad: A Feng Shui symbol believed to attract wealth and prosperity. The money frog is often depicted with a coin in its mouth and is placed near entrances or wealth corners.

Abundance Symbol: Symbols such as the infinity symbol (∞) or the dollar sign ($) are used as talismans to attract financial abundance and prosperity.

Prosperity Coins: Ancient coins with auspicious symbols or inscriptions are kept as talismans for wealth and prosperity.

Copyright Asteria Books 2024

Protections Talismans

Evil Eye Amulet: Found in many cultures around the world, the evil eye amulet is believed to protect against malevolent glances and negative energies that may cause harm.

Hamsa Hand: Also known as the Hand of Fatima, the Hamsa Hand is a Middle Eastern symbol of protection against the evil eye and negative energies.

Pentacle: A five-pointed star enclosed within a circle, the pentacle is used in Wiccan and pagan traditions as a protective symbol against negative influences and harm.

Cross: In Christianity, the cross is a symbol of divine protection and faith. It is worn as a pendant or carried as a talisman for spiritual and physical protection.

Runes: Ancient Norse symbols used for divination and magical purposes, runes such as Algiz (ᛉ) are used as talismans for protection and warding off danger.

Triskele: A Celtic symbol consisting of three interconnected spirals, the triskele represents protection, strength, and progress.

Eye of Horus: An ancient Egyptian symbol of protection, royal power, and good health, the Eye of Horus is worn as an amulet to ward off evil and promote healing.

Dragon: In Chinese culture, dragons are symbols of protection, power, and good fortune. Dragon statues, charms, or images are used as talismans for protection.

Copyright Asteria Books 2024

Psychic Power Talismans

Tarot Cards: Carry the High Priestess, Moon, Queen of Cups, Ace of Cups, or Ace of Swords card to boost your psychic ability.

Runes: Carry the Laguz rune - or add it to other spellwork - to boost your intuition and tap into spiritual energy.

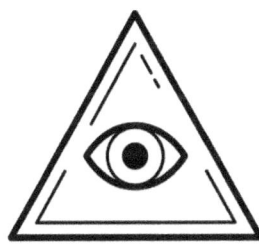
Third Eye Symbol: The third eye symbol, often depicted as an eye in the center of the forehead, represents inner vision and spiritual insight. It can be worn as a pendant or kept as a symbol to awaken psychic awareness.

Feather: Feathers are symbols of spiritual ascension and connection to higher realms. They can be worn or kept as talismans to enhance psychic sensitivity and intuition.

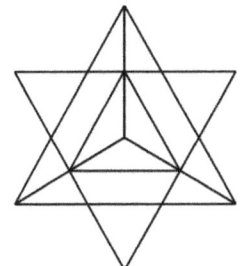
Merkaba Symbol: A sacred geometry symbol representing the energy field around the body, the Merkaba is believed to enhance psychic abilities and spiritual protection. It can be visualized or worn as a pendant for spiritual alignment.

Copyright Asteria Books 2024

Travel Talismans

St. Christopher Medal: A widely recognized Christian talisman, St. Christopher is the patron saint of travelers. His medal is worn or carried for protection during journeys.

Ganesha Statue: In Hinduism, Ganesha is the remover of obstacles and the god of new beginnings. A small statue or image of Ganesha is carried by travelers to ensure a smooth journey.

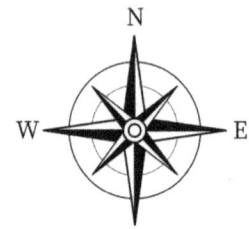
Compass: A practical travel talisman, a compass symbolizes direction and guidance, ensuring travelers find their way safely to their destination.

Labyrinth Symbol: A labyrinth symbolizes the journey of life and can be carried or worn as a talisman to guide travelers through their personal journeys.

Turtle Figurine: In some cultures, turtles are symbols of protection, longevity, and safe travel. Small turtle figurines or charms are carried by travelers for luck.

Lucky Coin: A coin, especially one with a hole in the center, is sometimes carried by travelers as a charm for good luck and financial security during trips.

Copyright Asteria Books 2024

Sigil Crafting

Copyright Asteria Books 2025

Sigil Craft: An Overview

The word "sigil" comes from the Latin *sigillum*, meaning "seal," a mark of both authority and a container for secrets. In modern witchcraft, a sigil is a symbol charged with a specific magical intention, acting as a direct conduit for focused will. Its power comes not just from its design but from the act of its creation, which imbues it with the caster's personal energy and desire. Sigils are both keys that unlock magical potential and locks that contain and direct it. The beauty of this practice is its flexibility; there are numerous ways to create a sigil, and the best method is the one that resonates most deeply with you.

Methods of Sigil Creation

1. Spirit- and Trance-Derived: The oldest method, involving receiving the sigil's design from a spiritual entity or during a visionary trance state.
2. Kamea Method: A classical approach that uses planetary magic squares to turn a phrase or word into a geometric design by connecting numbers.
3. Rosy Cross Method: A method from the Golden Dawn that plots letters onto a specific cross-and-rose diagram to form a sigil.
4. Austin Osman Spare Method: A popular chaos magic technique where you write out your intention, eliminate all vowels and duplicate letters, then creatively combine the remaining letters into a single, abstract design.
5. Symbolic Method: A more intuitive, artistic method where you compose a sigil by combining personal, meaningful symbols—like runes, planetary icons, or other pictograms—into a unique design that represents your intention.

Empowerment and Use

To empower a sigil, you must bring it to life with focused energy. This can be done by meditating on the sigil until you feel it "light up," using a moment of intense emotion or spiritual ecstasy, or by dedicating it in a ritual. Once charged, the sigil can be used on its own as a charm, drawn on your body, or integrated into a larger spell, serving as a powerful and compact representation of your magic.

Copyright Asteria Books 2025

Sigil Craft: Rosy Cross Method

The Rose Cross (or Rosy Cross) Method comes to us from the Hermetic Order of the Golden Dawn and is based on the symbol to the left. Embedded within it are mathematical, kabbalistic, planetary, and elemental alignments and references.

Traditionally, folks work with this using Hebrew letters, which (like Norse Runes) are whole and complete symbols unto themselves, aside from being phonemes. (Phonemes are units of sound in a language, and they are the basis of "phonics" which used to be a standard way of teaching reading in English.)

While it is traditional to work with Hebrew letters, you can put the characters of any phonemic alphabet on petals of the Rose Cross and get a similar (if not precisely identical) result. You just want to match them up as closely as you can with their Hebrew counterparts.

If you want to use a language whose graphemes/symbols represent something other than a single sound/phoneme -- maybe a whole syllable, a word, or a concept -- you can probably still find a way, if you get creative. You just might have a LOT of petals.

You then plot their course across from number to number across the rose. A couple of notes: It is traditional to use a small circle to indicate the starting point and a perpendicular line to indicate the end. You can make little bumps or zigzags to denote repeated numbers, and you can curve the lines for visibility.

Copyright Asteria Books 2025

Rose Cross Template

This Rose Cross template features the Hebrew letters that are traditional for students of the Golden Dawn's methods.

Rose Cross Template

This Rose Cross template features Latin characters for easy use by speakers of languages that use this alphabet.

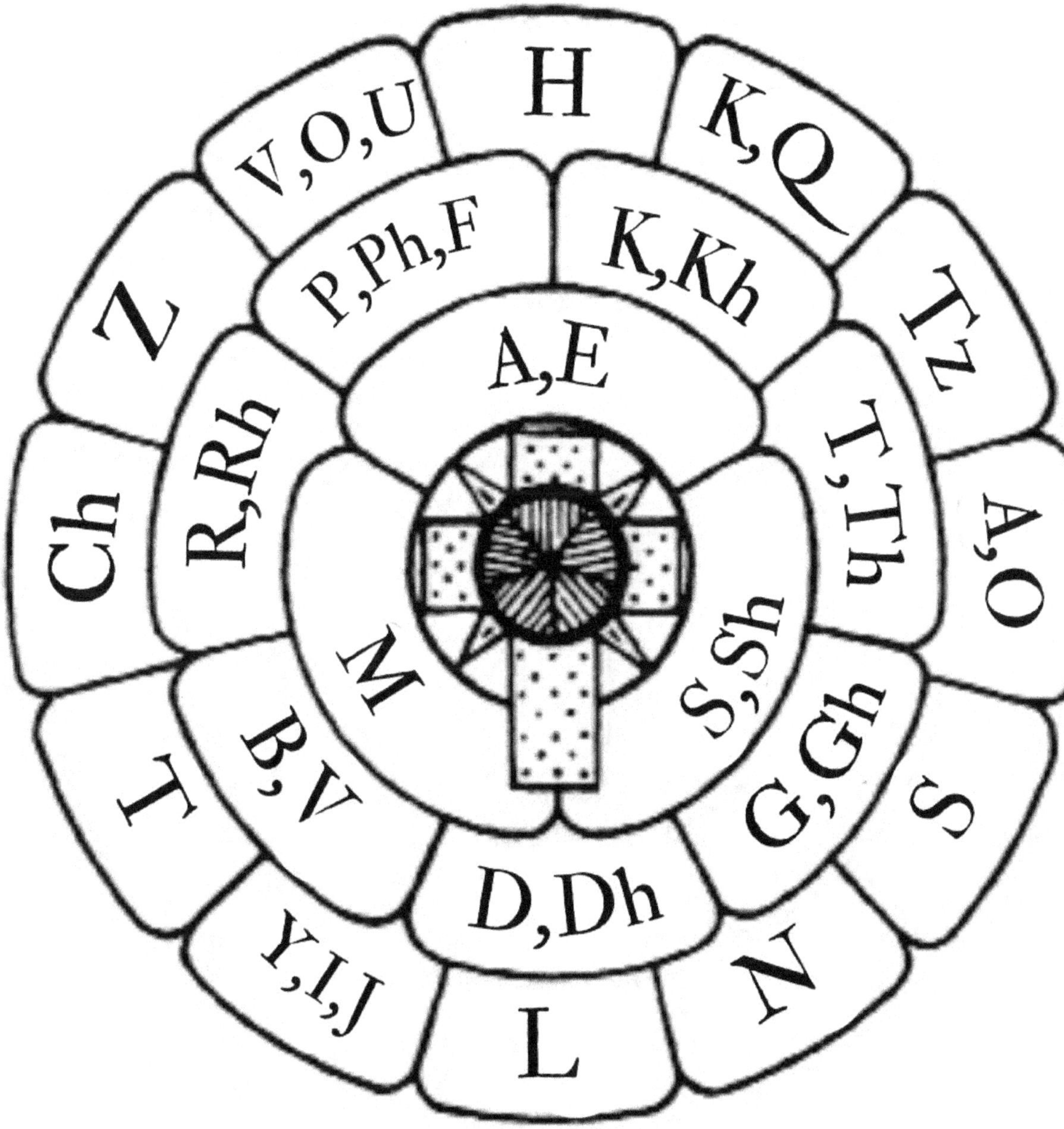

Rose Cross Template

This Rose Cross template features blank petals so you can fill it with the letters or other graphemes of any language you choose.

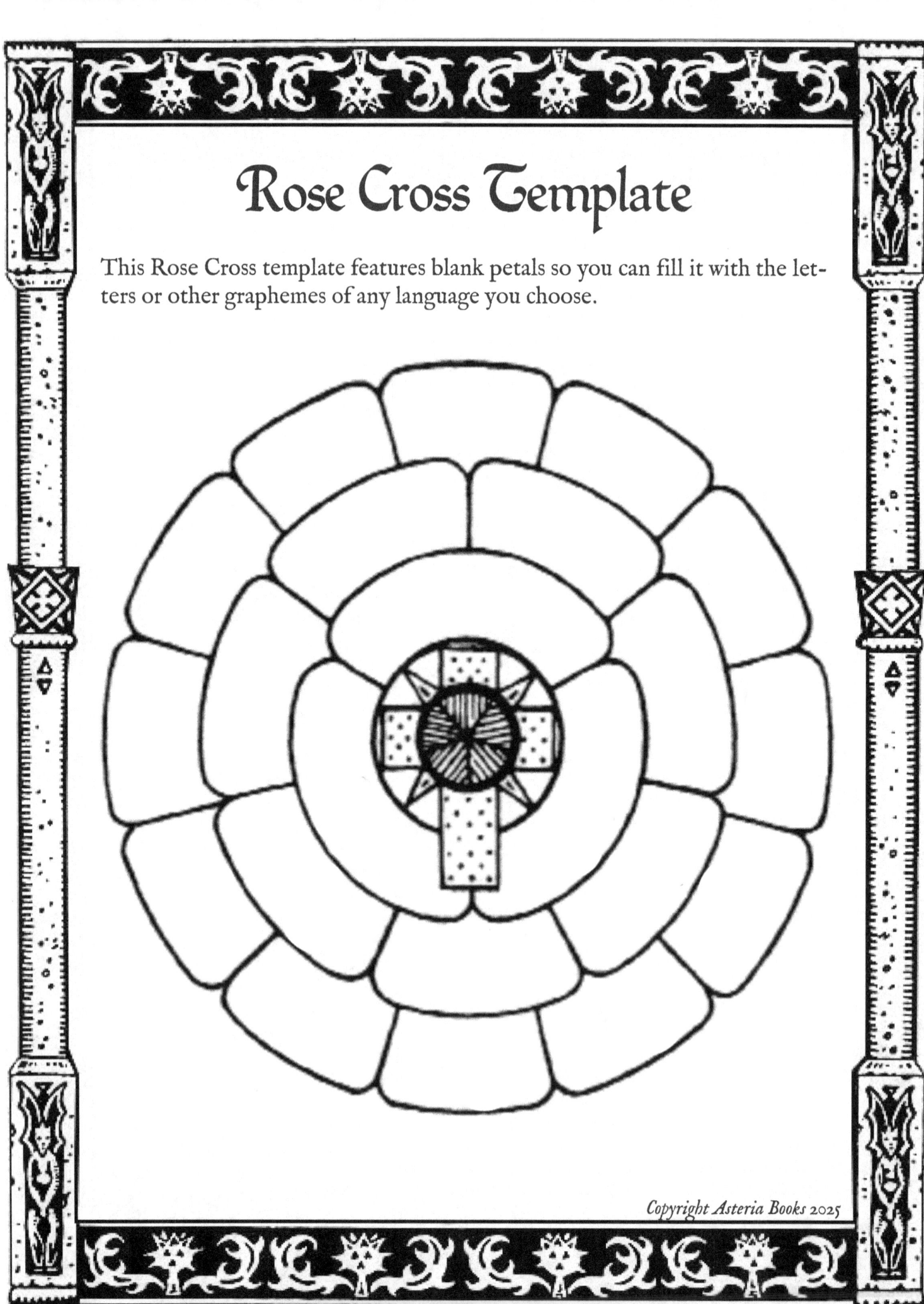

Sigil Craft: Kamea Method

Agrippa writes about the Kamea method in *Three Books of Occult Philosophy*.

In its simplest terms, you start with the magic number table related to the planet whose energy aligns to your magickal goal. Venus for love, romance, or sex. Jupiter for power, career, or wealth. Etc

You then decide on a name, word, or phrase to sigilize. Assign all the letters of the alphabet to numbers. Use the table provided on the next page to do it in English.

It is worth noting that, like the Rosy Cross method, the Kamea method usually utilizes Hebrew letters, which have deep symbolism and numerical associations within a practice called gematria.

Then plot their course from number to number across the square.

A couple of notes: It is traditional to use a small circle to indicate the starting point and a perpendicular line to indicate the end. You can make little bumps or zigzags to denote repeated numbers, and you can curve the lines for visibility.

Also, there's some numeric gymnastics that has to happen when you do this in anything other than Hebrew. In some cases, you will have to choose how best to modify your numbers to make them work. For example, the letter M is associated with the number 40. In some situations, it will make sense to drop the 0 and treat this as the number 4.

At first blush, it might seem overly complicated, but it really isn't. Plus remember: some of the sorcery is in the work!

Letters to Numbers

A	1	N	14
B	2	O	15
C	3	P	16
D	4	Q	17
E	5	R	18
F	6	S	19
G	7	T	20
H	8	U	21
I	9	V	22
J	10	W	23
K	11	X	24
L	12	Y	25
M	13	Z	26

Copyright Asteria Books 2025

Sun Kamea

6	32	3	34	35	1
7	11	27	28	8	30
19	14	16	15	23	24
18	20	22	21	17	13
25	29	10	9	26	12
36	5	33	4	2	31

Moon Kamea

37	78	29	70	21	62	13	54	5
6	38	79	30	71	22	63	14	46
47	7	39	80	31	72	23	55	15
16	48	8	40	81	32	64	24	56
57	17	49	9	41	73	33	65	25
26	58	18	50	1	42	74	34	66
67	27	59	10	51	2	43	75	35
36	68	19	60	11	52	3	44	76
77	28	69	20	61	12	53	4	45

Mercury Kamea

8	58	59	5	4	62	63	1
49	15	14	52	53	11	10	56
41	23	22	44	45	19	18	48
32	34	35	29	28	38	39	25
40	26	27	37	36	30	31	33
17	47	46	20	21	43	42	24
9	55	54	12	13	51	50	16
64	2	3	61	60	6	7	57

Mars Kamea

11	24	7	20	3
4	12	25	8	16
17	5	13	21	9
10	18	1	14	22
23	6	19	2	15

Copyright Asteria Books 2025

Venus Kamea

22	47	16	41	10	35	4
5	23	48	17	42	11	29
30	6	24	49	18	36	12
13	31	7	25	43	19	37
38	14	32	1	26	44	20
21	39	8	33	2	27	45
46	15	40	9	34	3	28

Jupiter Kamea

4	14	15	1
9	7	6	12
5	11	10	8
16	2	3	13

Copyright Asteria Books 2025

Saturn Kamea

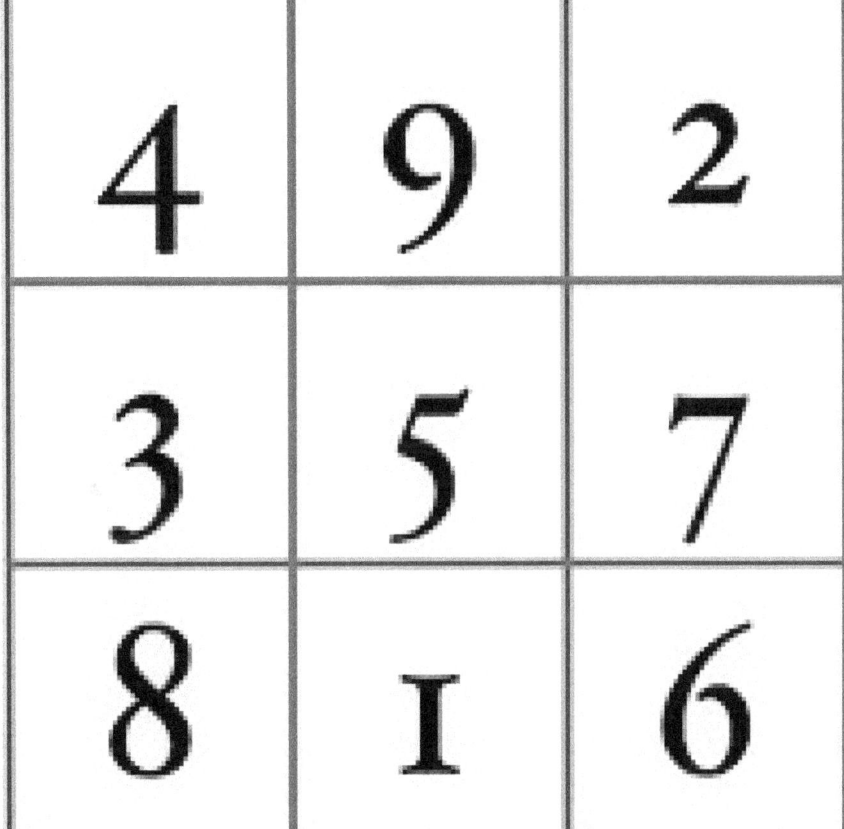

Sigil Craft: AO Spare Method

This method is named for one of the formative authors of Chaos Magick, Astin Osman Spare, and it is one of the methods that allows for more creativity. Spare was, after all, an artist.

To create a sigil with this method, you write your goal as a sentence or complete phrase. You'll want to put a good amount of thought into this -- just put great consideration into the phrasing of the intention for any spell work. As I am fond of saying, "Words mean stuff," -- so choose them carefully.

Write the phrase out on paper and then eliminate all the vowels and any duplicate letters. You are aiming for whittling that phrase down to a handful of letters that don't automatically read as the original phrase to a reader of your language.

With these letters, you are going to connect them so that they make a symbol or shape. It might not look like anything at all -- or it might look reminiscent of your desire in some way. That's up to you.

Usually, the goal with this method is forget or "let go of" the original intent so that the empowered sigil is free to work without constant interference from you "checking in on it."

Included here is an example of a sigil Spare created using this method.

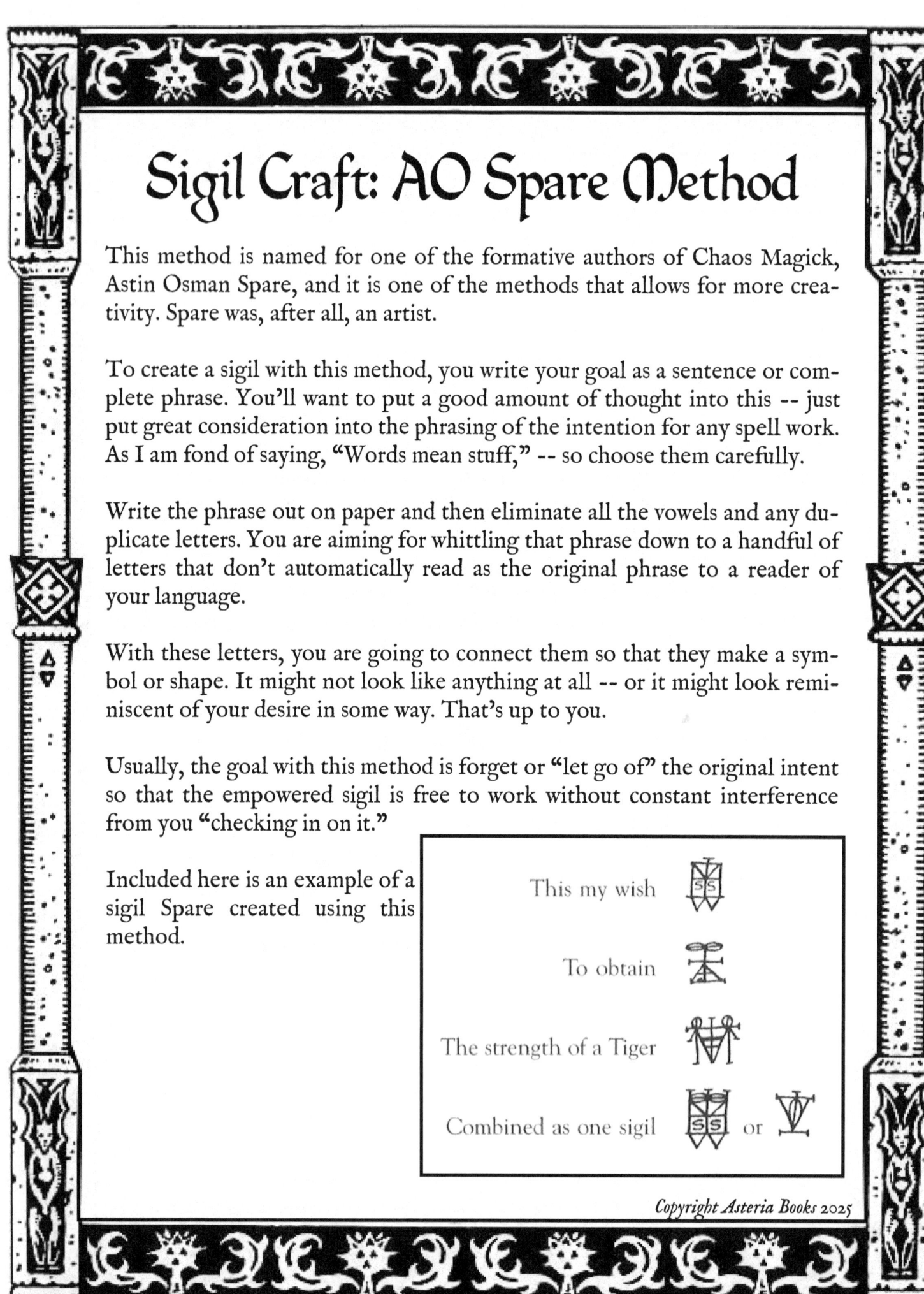

Copyright Asteria Books 2025

Sigil Craft: Spirit Method

It could be easily argued that the oldest method of getting a sigil is to enter into communication with a Spirit who then provides you with a symbol for use. Similar to this, and probably just as old, is entering into a trance state where the symbol is found in vision.

In cases like this, the symbol might be representative of the Spirit itself, who then does the task or tasks to help you achieve the desired outcome. Or it could be representative of the magickal goal or intention.

Examples of this type of sigil are the seals related to the 72 Spirits of the Lemegeton (the Goetia). With some of these Spirits, you will see 2 sigils offered for use. With all of them, the earliest grimoires did not include any sigils, as they were later additions that were received by one of the grimoire-keepers.

By the time Dr. Thomas Rudd copied out his grimoire -- which would become synonymous with the Goetia -- the sigils were known. But 100 years earlier, when Johann Weier was writing about almost exactly the same Spirits, he made no mention of them and didn't include the sigils in his own manuscripts.

Someone in the intervening time between these two occultists had received the sigils (undoubtedly through trance or scrying work) that are so well-known and well-used today. By the time Crowley and Mathers (another 250-ish years later) translated and published the Rudd manuscripts in the British Museum in about 1904, both the descriptions and sigils became highly codified in the working minds of magickal people. The descriptions had been somewhat fluid before that, and there was always an understanding that a Spirit could have more than one sigil.

A Spirit with a history of contact across the ages can give you a brand new sigil that nobody has ever seen before and it is perfectly valid for you. (It may not work for anyone else, but it is yours, and it is good!)

Copyright Asteria Books 2025

Sigil Craft: Symbolic Method

Laura Tempest Zakroff's sigil work is a great example of the symbolic method of sigil-crafting.

With this style of sigil crafting, you're creating a design that communicates your intention entirely in an idiosyncratic, pictographic manner -- meaning: the sigil you create is going to use symbols that have meanings to you (and maybe ONLY to you) in the combination that you have used them.

You can pull in numbers, letters, planetary symbols, alchemical symbols, runic devices, modern icons, childhood symbols -- pretty much any linear shape that holds meaning for you. And you'll put them together in a way that they become something larger -- something greater than the sum of their parts.

If you resonate with this method, I highly recommend developing a sort of "symbol lexicon" -- like a personal symbol dictionary. This is something that I recommend for my own students, in general, because it can be extraordinarily helpful in so many areas of your Craft. After all, what "snake" means in one culture is different than what it means in another place or time -- and ALL of that can be very different than your own personal relationship with Snake. Your first pet might have been a ball python named Miss Hiss who grew up alongside you and gave you sweet, noodly cuddles. Your personal experiences must, of necessity, inform how you incorporate snake symbolism into your sigil crafting -- and no author or symbolism expert can do that for you.

The sigil created will often have an artistic style that is reflective of yourself as a unique and creative soul. And it will typically "read" to an observer as a pictorial device conveying your overall intention.

Copyright Asteria Books 2025

Personal Symbol Lexicon

Use this page as a starting place for creating your own person lexicon of symbols. The page is pre-filled with a few common symbols, but the meanings are left blank for you to supply your own insights based on your personal understanding and interactions with these symbols.

Symbol	Meaning	Symbol	Meaning
♡		☆	
🍃		⚡	

Magickal Alphabets

Copyright Asteria Books 2025

Theban Alphabet

The earliest known source for the Theban alphabet is Cornelius Agrippa's *Three Books of Occult Philosophy* first published in Latin at Antwerp in 1531. The exact origins of the Witches' alphabet are shrouded in the mists of time, but it is often called "The Theban Alphabet" or "The Runes of Honorius" after its reputed inventor, Honorius of Thebes.

Copyright Asteria Publishing 2012

Celestial

The Celestial alphabet, which is also known as the Angelic alphabet, is derived from the Hebrew and Greek alphabets. It was created by Heinrich Cornelius Agrippa during the 16th Century and was used for communication with angels.

A	Aleph		L	Lamed	
B	Beth		M	Mem	
G	Gimel		N	Nun	
D	Daleth		S	Samech	
H	He		E	Ain	
V	Vau		P	Pe	
Z	Zain		Tz	Tzadi	
C	Cheth		K	Kaph	
Th	Theth		R	Resh	
I/J	Iod		Sch	Schin	
C	Caph		T	Tau	

Copyright Asteria Books 2022

Alphabet of the Magic

The Alphabet of the Magi was invented by Theophrastus Bombastus von Hohenheim (also known as Paracelsus) in the 16th century. He used it to engrave the names of angels on talismans which he claimed could treat illnesses and provide protection. It was probably influenced by the various other magical alphabets that were around at the time and also by the Hebrew script.

A	Aleph		L	Lamed	
B	Beth		M	Mem	
G	Gimel		N	Nun	
D	Daleth		S	Samech	
H	He		E	Ain	
V	Vau		P	Pe	
Z	Zain		Tz	Tzadi	
C	Cheth		K	Kaph	
Th	Theth		R	Resh	
I/J	Iod		Sch	Schin	
C	Caph		T	Tau	

Copyright Asteria Books 2022

Malachim

The Malachim alphabet is derived from the Hebrew and Greek alphabets. It was created by Heinrich Cornelius Agrippa during the 16th Century and is still used by Freemasons to a limited extent.

A	Aleph	⌘	L	Lamed	ʊ
B	Beth	ʊ	M	Mem	ⱨ
G	Gimel	ⱴ	N	Nun	ⱡ
D	Daleth	ⲧ	S	Samech	ⱥ
H	He	ⱨ	E	Ain	▢
V	Vau	⋏	P	Pe	⋈
Z	Zain	ⱴ	Tz	Tzadi	⋏
C	Cheth	▭	K	Kaph	ʊ
Th	Theth	⋏	R	Resh	ⱴ
I/J	Iod	⌒	Sch	Schin	⊹
C	Caph	▭	T	Tau	⋈

Copyright Asteria Books 2022

Masonic Cipher

The Masonic Cipher was an alphabet used largely used by Freemasons in the 18th century. A squared version is used for the uppercase and a rounded one for the lowercase. A few punction symbols are also used (comma, exclamation point, question mark, period, colon and semicolon), but these are the standard symbols.

Aa	⌐⌐	Nn	⌐⌐
Bb	⌴⌴	Oo	⌴⌴
Cc	⌊⌊	Pp	⌊⌊
Dd	⌐⌐	Qq	⌐⌐
Ee	▢▢	Rr	▢▢
Ff	⊏⊏	Ss	⊏⊏
Gg	⊓⊓	Tt	⊓⊓
Hh	⊓⊓	Uu	⊓⊓
Ii	⌐⌐	Vw	⌐⌐
Jj	∨∨	Ww	∨∨
Kk	»»	Xx	»»
Ll	««	Yy	««
Mm	∧∧	Zz	∧∧

Copyright Asteria Books 2022

Passing the River

Passing the River (called "Passage Du Fleuve" in French) is an occult alphabet derived from the Hebrew alphabet and first described in the Third Book of Occult Philosophy by Heinrich Cornelius Agrippa in 1553. The name of this alphabet perhaps refers to the time the Jews crossed the Euphrates during their return from Babylon to Jerusalem.

A	Aleph	✡	L	Lamed	⹋
B	Beth	⊐	M	Mem	⌑
G	Gimel	⌐	N	Nun	⼅
D	Daleth	⊢	S	Samech	⼅
H	He	⍡	E	Ain	⼁
V	Vau	⌒	P	Pe	⼂
Z	Zain	<	Tz	Tzadi	⼁
C	Cheth	⌐	K	Kaph	△
Th	Theth	⼂	R	Resh	⼓
I/J	Iod	⼕	Sch	Schin	⋁
C	Caph	⌐	T	Tau	⼕

Copyright Asteria Books 2022

Pictish Swirl

Recent archaeological evidence indicates that the Picts (or "Painted People" of eastern and northern Scotland) may very well have developed their own written system of language after encountering the Romans about 1700 years ago. This system isn't it. In fact, we are not likely to be able to decipher true Pictish writing without a "Rosetta Stone" to decode it. However, what is shared here is an alphabet that was popularized (and likely constructed by) author and Witch Raymond Buckland in his work on Scottish Witchcraft. (Looking closely, one can see the influences of Theban in this script.)

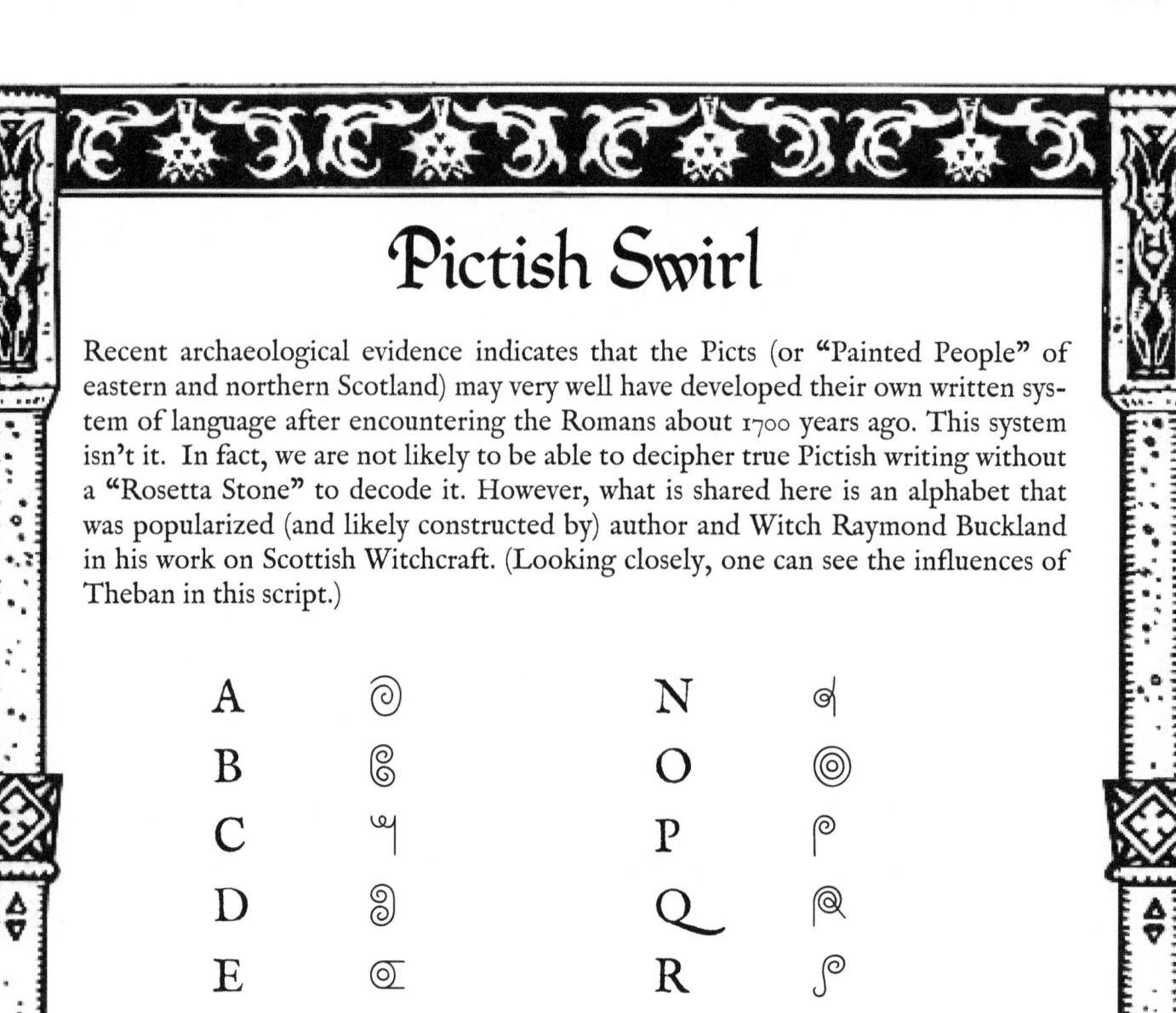

Copyright Asteria Books 2022

Theban

The Theban alphabet was first published in 1518 in Polygraphiae libri sex, a cryptographic work by Johannes Trithemius (1462-1516), a German abbot, lexicographer, chronicler, cryptographer and occultist. Trithemius attributed the alphabet to Honorius of Thebes, but it has also been attributed to Heinrich Cornelius Agrippa (1486-1535), a student of Trithemius. Theban is used as an alternative to the Latin alphabet and is popular among Witches, hence its nickname: the "Witch's Alphabet." It is used to write spells, inscriptions, and other texts. It serves to disguise the meaning of a text and to give it a mystical quality.

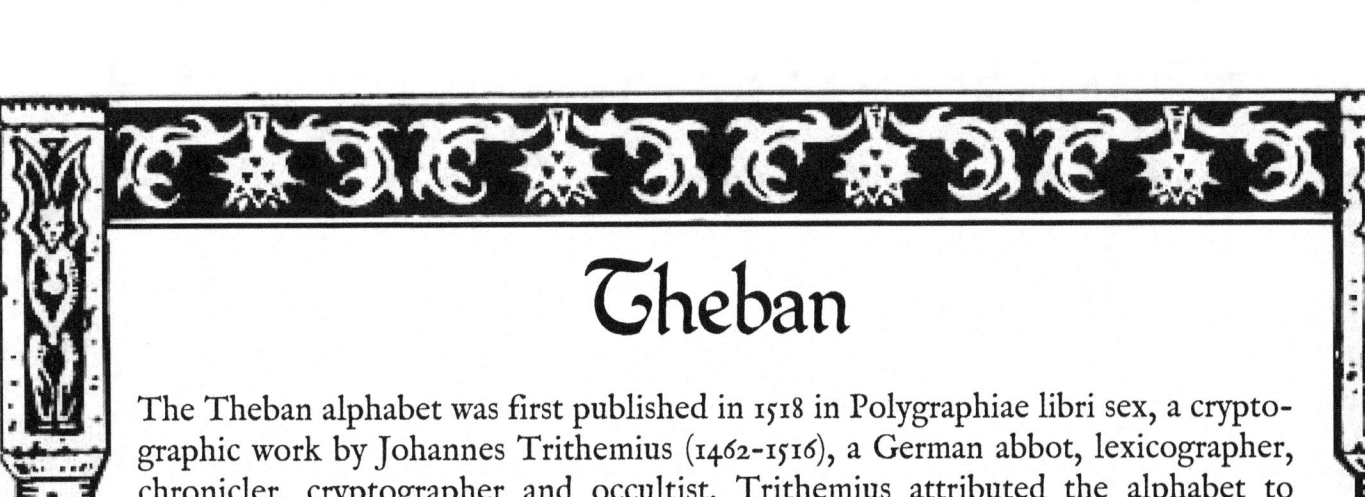

Copyright Asteria Books 2022

Crystal Magick

Birth Stones

The concept of birthstones, once a curiosity of ancient astrological and religious texts, has been refined and re-purposed for the modern practitioner. No longer are they merely symbolic—they are tangible talismans, infused with the energies of their corresponding months and the celestial influences that preside over them. Each stone is a key, unlocking a specific set of attributes and powers that can be harnessed for personal growth, protection, and focused spellwork.

> January -- Garnet, a stone of grounding and fortitude. Wield it to anchor new beginnings and to shed the skin of past failures.
> February -- Amethyst, with its tranquil violet hue, is an ally for the seeker of spiritual clarity and a ward against the anxieties of the mind.
> March' -- Aquamarine whispers secrets of the deep, enhancing communication and fostering emotional healing.
> April -- Diamond is a brilliant conduit for strength and clarity of intention.
> May -- Emerald offers prosperity and heart-centered wisdom.
> June -- Pearl, or moonstone, is a beacon for intuition and emotional balance.
> July -- Ruby burns with a fiery passion, igniting courage and confidence.
> August -- Peridot, a stone of the sun, purifies the aura and attracts good fortune.
> September -- Sapphire lends itself to truth and spiritual insight.
> October -- Opal, a prism of shifting colors, heightens creativity and adaptability.
> November -- Citrine is a joyous stone of abundance and manifestation.
> December -- Turquoise is a protective shield, connecting the practitioner to the wisdom of the earth and sky.

To work with your birthstone, simply carry it, wear it, or place it on your altar during ritual. Meditate with it to absorb its unique vibrations, or use it to charge your intention

Copyright Asteria Books 2025

Casting Stones

Casting stones, a form of divination known as lithomancy, is a deeply personal and ancient practice. Unlike the structured framework of the tarot, casting stones is an intuitive art, where the meaning of a reading is derived not only from the individual stones but from their relationships to one another and their placement on the casting surface. To begin, you'll need a set of stones, each chosen and consecrated with a specific purpose. You can collect your own from nature, or purchase a curated set.

One common approach is the 3-Stone Yes/No Set. For this, you would use three stones: one for "Yes," one for "No," and one as a marker. Hold the stones in your hand, focus on a clear, direct question, and gently toss them onto a cloth. The stone that lands closest to the marker stone is your answer.

For a more comprehensive reading, consider a Stone Tarot Set. Assign each of your stones to a specific major arcana card. (You can assign your own associations, or use the excellent version Scott Cunningham provides in his Encyclopedia of Crystal, Gem, and Metal Magic.) Cast all the stones at once. The "story" of the reading is found in how the stones land — which are close together, which are far apart, and what direction they are pointing. Alternatively, you can shake the bag holding the stones, reach in to grab a random selection, and cast those -- reading them as above.

Finally, for a simple and versatile method, a Four-Element Casting uses four stones representing Earth, Air, Fire, and Water. Hold the stones and ask for guidance. The stone that lands furthest from the others often reveals the most potent, or unseen, influence on your situation. The beauty of casting stones lies in its fluid, interpretive nature, allowing your intuition to be the ultimate guide.

Copyright Asteria Books 2025

Cleansing Your Crystals

Before a stone can become a tool for your magick, its energetic memory must be wiped clean. Cleansing is not about physical sanitation, but about clearing the residual energy imprinted by countless hands and environments before it came to you. This vital first step prepares the crystal to receive your intention, transforming it from a simple stone into a consecrated ally.

Several methods can be used, depending on the nature of the stone:

Sunlight: A powerful, purifying force. Place your crystals in direct sunlight for a few hours. Be mindful that vibrant stones like amethyst and rose quartz may fade with prolonged exposure.

Water: Running water (from a tap or a natural stream) is a simple and effective cleanser. Caution is key here. Avoid putting water-sensitive crystals like selenite, halite, or unpolished pyrite in water, as they can dissolve or rust.

Smoke: A gentle, universal method that is safe for all stones. Pass the crystal through the smoke of cleansing herbs like rosemary, frankincense, myrrh, or cedar. The smoke acts as a wash, carrying away unwanted energy.

Salt: A deeply absorbent and purifying agent. Place your crystals in a bowl of dry sea salt for a few hours. This is an excellent method for grounding and purification. Be mindful of soft or fragile stones, which may be scratched by salt, and again, be careful with water if using a salt water solution.

Copyright Asteria Books 2025

Charging Your Crystals

In ancient traditions, stones were revered for their inherent, immutable power. They were considered gifts from the earth, imbued with the raw energy of their formation. The modern practice of "charging" crystals is a relatively recent development, stemming from a desire to attune these natural energies to a specific intention or to amplify their already potent vibrations. Think not of this as filling an empty vessel, but rather as focusing and directing an existing torrent of energy.

There are many ways to work with this process. The celestial bodies offer potent forces. The full moon, with its reflective and intuitive energy, is a favorite for clearing and amplifying stones. Simply place your crystals in a safe spot outdoors or on a windowsill where they can bathe in the moonlight for the night. The sun, a source of invigorating and active energy, can also be used, but be mindful that some crystals (like amethyst or rose quartz) may fade with prolonged exposure.

The earth itself is a powerful charging station. Burying a stone in the soil for a day or a week allows it to reconnect with its source, renewing and grounding its energy. Sound is another effective tool. The vibrations from a singing bowl, tuning fork, or even a clear, focused chant can realign a stone's frequency. Finally, for a more personal touch, you can charge a crystal with your own energy by holding it in your hands and visualizing your intention flowing into it. Remember, the true magic is not in the "charge," but in the conscious connection you forge with the stone's timeless power.

Copyright Asteria Books 2025

Stone Altars

To a practitioner of stone magick, the altar is more than a workspace; it is a sacred focal point, a charged battery, and a direct line to the earth's ancient wisdom. A stone altar is built with intention, creating a sanctuary for your magickal tools and a dedicated space for your craft.

The construction of the altar can be as simple or as grand as you desire. An inexpensive, yet deeply effective, option is to arrange a few flat stones as your altar surface. A simple flagstone or large piece of slate or marble from a hardware store can serve as a potent, earthy foundation. For those with a more aspirational vision, consider a custom-cut slab of polished amethyst or a large geode split in half, creating a natural, glowing sanctuary. The core principle is to build with a material that resonates with the earth's energy.

Once the surface is chosen, populate it with your tools. Instead of a traditional chalice, a small, polished amethyst bowl can hold water for scrying. A wand crafted from selenite or clear quartz serves as a powerful instrument for directing energy. A mortar and pestle carved from solid agate can be used to grind herbs, while a pendulum of rose quartz can be used for divination. To amplify the entire space, place a large crystal cluster (like amethyst or clear quartz) at the center of the altar—this acts as the heart of your sacred space, constantly radiating and purifying energy. Your stone altar is a living extension of your will, a testament to the power of the earth itself.

For the most ambitious of practitioners, the concept of a stone altar can be expanded to a sacred outdoor space with standing stones. This is a powerful, permanent commitment to earth magick. Choose stones carefully from a natural source, and with permission, arrange them in a circle or alignment that speaks to you. Each stone, once set, becomes a pillar of energy, creating a vortex for ritual and meditation. This sacred space is where you can conduct grand ceremonies, connect with the land spirits, and anchor your magick directly into the earth itself. It is a timeless and profound act, creating a place of power that will resonate for generations.

Copyright Asteria Books 2025

Crystal Balls

The image of a seer gazing into a crystal ball is etched into our collective consciousness, but the practice of scrying is far older than popular fiction suggests. Known as crystallomancy, this form of divination has roots in ancient Celtic and Roman traditions. Scrying is not about actively "seeing" the future, but about achieving a trance-like state and allowing the mind to receive visions, symbols, or images from the subconscious or spirit world. The crystal ball acts as a focal point, a gateway to a deeper state of awareness.

While a perfectly clear quartz sphere is the classic choice, different crystals can be used to tune into specific types of visions.

Clear Quartz: The all-purpose scrying tool. It provides a clean slate, allowing for a wide range of visions from past, present, or future.

Obsidian: A dark and powerful mirror. This stone is ideal for deep shadow work, revealing hidden truths and confronting difficult aspects of the self.

Amethyst: A stone of high spiritual vibration. Amethyst scrying balls are excellent for receiving psychic messages and divine guidance.

Selenite: With its ethereal glow, selenite connects the practitioner to angelic realms and spirit guides, providing visions of pure light and healing energy.

Smoky Quartz: A grounding tool. Scrying with smoky quartz often yields practical, down-to-earth advice for navigating daily life and complex situations.

Each crystal is a unique lens through which to view the tapestry of fate. Choose the one that calls to you and trust the wisdom you find within its depths.

Copyright Asteria Books 2025

Crystal Bowls

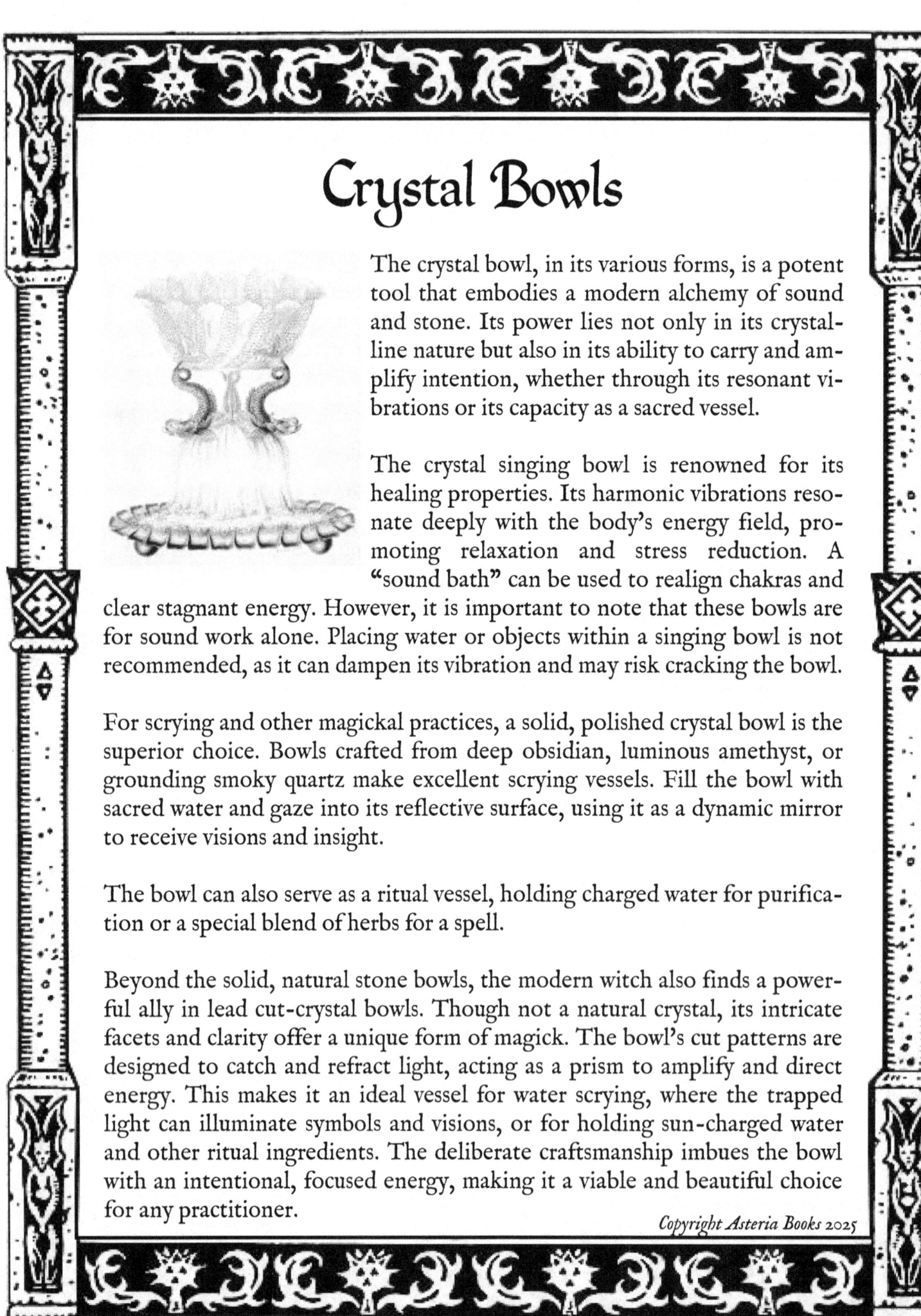

The crystal bowl, in its various forms, is a potent tool that embodies a modern alchemy of sound and stone. Its power lies not only in its crystalline nature but also in its ability to carry and amplify intention, whether through its resonant vibrations or its capacity as a sacred vessel.

The crystal singing bowl is renowned for its healing properties. Its harmonic vibrations resonate deeply with the body's energy field, promoting relaxation and stress reduction. A "sound bath" can be used to realign chakras and clear stagnant energy. However, it is important to note that these bowls are for sound work alone. Placing water or objects within a singing bowl is not recommended, as it can dampen its vibration and may risk cracking the bowl.

For scrying and other magickal practices, a solid, polished crystal bowl is the superior choice. Bowls crafted from deep obsidian, luminous amethyst, or grounding smoky quartz make excellent scrying vessels. Fill the bowl with sacred water and gaze into its reflective surface, using it as a dynamic mirror to receive visions and insight.

The bowl can also serve as a ritual vessel, holding charged water for purification or a special blend of herbs for a spell.

Beyond the solid, natural stone bowls, the modern witch also finds a powerful ally in lead cut-crystal bowls. Though not a natural crystal, its intricate facets and clarity offer a unique form of magick. The bowl's cut patterns are designed to catch and refract light, acting as a prism to amplify and direct energy. This makes it an ideal vessel for water scrying, where the trapped light can illuminate symbols and visions, or for holding sun-charged water and other ritual ingredients. The deliberate craftsmanship imbues the bowl with an intentional, focused energy, making it a viable and beautiful choice for any practitioner.

Copyright Asteria Books 2025

Crystal Wands

The magickal wand is a quintessential tool, an extension of the practitioner's will used to channel and direct energy. While traditionally made of wood, the modern practice has embraced the raw power of the mineral kingdom, giving rise to the crystal wand. This potent instrument, whether carved entirely from stone or adorned with it, becomes a living conductor for focused magick.

Wands carved from a single piece of crystal offer a pure, undiluted stream of energy. A wand of clear quartz is a versatile and powerful choice, acting as an amplifier for all forms of energy, perfect for channeling intention with clarity and precision. A selenite wand, with its ethereal light, serves as an unparalleled tool for cleansing and purification, both of a space and of the aura. These solid stone wands are like crystalline laser pointers, focusing the inherent energy of the stone into a directed beam of will.

A more eclectic and common approach is the embellishment of a wooden wand with crystals. In this form, the wand synergizes the grounding life energy of the wood with the specific properties of the crystals. Typically, a larger point of clear quartz or amethyst is affixed to the tip, acting as the primary focal point. Smaller stones, like rose quartz for matters of the heart or obsidian for protection, can be set along the shaft. This creates a multi-faceted tool, capable of directing a more complex blend of energies.

Ultimately, the choice of wand is a personal one. A solid crystal wand is a testament to the raw power of one stone, while an embellished wand is a composite of many. Both are formidable allies, waiting to be charged and wielded as an extension of your own magical self.

Copyright Asteria Books 2025

Getting to Know a Stone

A crystal or gemstone is more than just a beautiful object; it is a living entity of the earth, holding a unique energetic signature. To truly work with a stone, you must first build a relationship with it, a process of alignment where you attune to its specific frequency. This deep connection transforms a simple stone into a potent magical partner.

One of the most effective methods for this is continuous, close proximity. By carrying a stone in a pocket, a pouch, or worn as jewelry, you allow its energy to subtly merge with your own aura throughout the day. This creates a constant dialogue, allowing you to intuitively feel its influence on your thoughts, emotions, and environment. Similarly, placing a stone on your bedside table or slipping it into your pillowcase allows its energy to work with your subconscious mind during sleep, influencing your dreams and helping you integrate its properties on a deeper level.

For a more focused connection, meditation is a key practice. Hold the stone in your receptive hand, close your eyes, and allow yourself to feel its unique vibration. Visualize its color, texture, and inherent power flowing into you, and listen for any messages or feelings it may have to share. You can also align with a stone through a dedicated Stone Journal, where you record your experiences with each crystal. Note how you felt before and after working with it, and any insights or dreams that arose. This practice helps you track its specific effects and understand its "personality" over time.

Another powerful and intimate method is to use a water-safe crystal in a ritual bath. Place the cleansed stone in the bathwater and immerse yourself, allowing the water to act as a medium for the stone's energy to infuse your entire being. This is particularly effective with cleansing stones like clear quartz or heart-opening stones like rose quartz. (For crystals that are not water-safe, consider creating a gem elixir using the "indirect method," and adding this elixir to your bath.)

Lastly, you can align with a stone by giving it a place of honor. Dedicate a specific spot for it on your altar, allowing it to become a part of your sacred working space. This elevates its purpose and signals your respect and intention, deepening the bond between you and your crystalline ally.

Copyright Asteria Books 2025

Gemstone Jewelry

Throughout history, adornment has been more than a matter of aesthetics; it has been an act of magick. Gemstone jewelry, in particular, transforms a simple accessory into a personal talisman, a continuous channel for a stone's energy. Worn directly on the body, the gemstone can subtly influence the part of the body it touches and the energy centers associated with that area.

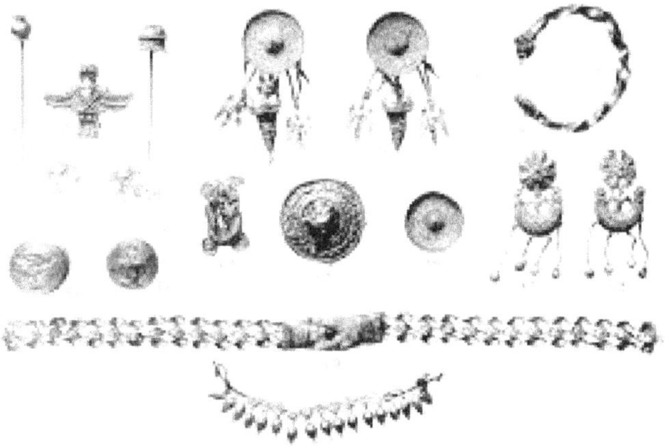

A necklace or pendant, for example, rests over the heart and throat. Wearing rose quartz here can foster self-love and compassion, while a lapis lazuli pendant can enhance communication and truth. The ancient Egyptians believed scarab necklaces of lapis lazuli offered protection and wisdom.

Rings, worn on the hands, can amplify intention and direct energy during spellwork or daily tasks. A simple carnelian ring might lend courage and vitality, while an amethyst ring can strengthen intuition.

Earrings, placed close to the mind, are perfect for enhancing psychic awareness. Moonstone earrings can heighten intuition and connect the wearer to lunar cycles, while labradorite can shield the aura and reveal hidden truths.

Bracelets and bangles, worn on the wrists, can either ground or energize the flow of energy through the body. A hematite bracelet can provide grounding and protection, while a citrine bracelet can attract abundance and joy.

By consciously choosing your gemstone jewelry, you are not merely accessorizing, but crafting a personal spell that is worn daily, an extension of your magical self into the world.

Copyright Asteria Books 2025

Stones in Magick

Since the dawn of human consciousness, stones have held a special place in ritual and folklore. The first tools, the first adornments, and the first objects of ceremony were all born of stone. The inherent power of the earth, its raw, slow-burning energy, was believed to be captured and concentrated within these mineral formations. This reverence is found in every corner of the globe, from the megalithic standing stones of Stonehenge to the jade amulets of ancient China.

In many ancient cultures, stones were not just inanimate objects but living beings with spirits. They were used to mark sacred places, to build altars, and to create protective boundaries. The Romans and Greeks, for example, used gemstones as talismans and amulets, believing they offered protection from evil spirits and brought good fortune.

The practice of lithomancy, or casting stones for divination, dates back to ancient times, with the patterns of their fall revealing answers to the mysteries of the universe.

While the healing properties of crystals are a popular modern focus, their historical use was far broader. Medieval grimoires often mention stones as key ingredients in potions and powders, their essence imbued into a brew to lend courage, attract love, or ward off illness. They were carved into protective sigils and worn as rings, pendants, and bracelets, each stone with its own lore. Garnet was a stone of warriors, lending strength in battle; sapphire was a stone of royalty, representing truth and divine favor.

The folklore of stones is a global tapestry, rich with stories of power, protection, and the deep, abiding connection between humanity and the earth itself.

Copyright Asteria Books 2025

Stones in Healing

Long before modern medicine, cultures around the world recognized the subtle yet profound energetic properties of minerals, believing they could influence the body's natural rhythms and restore balance. The ancient Egyptians, for instance, used stones like lapis lazuli and carnelian to aid in the healing of the body and mind, often grinding them into powders and applying them topically or wearing them as protective talismans. Similarly, traditional Chinese medicine incorporated various jades and other stones to balance the body's chi.

The folklore of these practices is rich with specific examples. Amethyst has long been associated with sobriety and mental clarity, worn to ward off intoxication and calm an overactive mind. Rose quartz became known as the "stone of the heart," believed to mend emotional wounds and attract loving energy. The fiery carnelian was used to invigorate the life force, or kundalini, and increase physical vitality. These traditions, passed down through generations, form the foundation of our modern understanding of crystal healing.

For the modern witch, integrating these practices into healing work is a simple yet powerful act. Here are some ways to use stones for healing:

- GRIDWORK: Arrange specific stones in a geometric pattern around the body to create a focused energy field. A simple grid of clear quartz points can amplify all healing energy, while a grid of rose quartz can be used to soothe emotional pain.
- MEDITATION: Hold a stone that resonates with your healing intention while meditating. Visualize the stone's energy flowing into you, mending and restoring.
- ELIXIRS (Indirect Method): As noted in another entry in this grimoire, create an elixir to internalize a stone's energy by placing a cleansed crystal in a small bowl inside a larger vessel of water. The elixir can then be used in baths, beverages, and other healing applications.
- TOPICAL PLACEMENT: Place a specific stone on a part of the body that needs healing, such as amethyst on the forehead to relieve headaches or rose quartz over the heart to soothe grief.

Copyright Asteria Books 2025

Crystal Grids

A crystal grid is a powerful ritual tool that combines the inherent energy of multiple crystals with the sacred geometry of a specific pattern. Unlike a single stone, a grid amplifies and focuses energy through the synergy of its components. The grid's power is derived from the geometric relationship between the stones, creating a vortex of energy that can be directed toward a specific intention.

To create a grid, you will need a central focus stone, which holds the primary intention of the grid. This is typically a large, powerful crystal point or sphere. Around the focus stone, you will arrange a series of surround stones, smaller crystals that support and amplify the central energy. The grid is activated by tracing a line of intent between each stone, often with a quartz point, to create a continuous flow of energy.

The pattern of the grid is a crucial element. The shape of the grid itself dictates the nature of the energy you are calling forth. While you can create your own pattern, some popular choices include:

The Flower of Life: A sacred geometric pattern for creation, harmony, and interconnectedness. It is often used for grids focused on universal healing or personal growth.

The Seed of Life: A foundational pattern for new beginnings and manifestation. It is ideal for grids focused on starting new projects or attracting new opportunities.

The Pentagram: A classic symbol of protection and balance, representing the four elements and the spirit. It is an excellent choice for grids designed to ward off negative energy or create a safe space.

The Spiral: A dynamic and ancient symbol of cosmic energy and evolution. It is used to draw energy in or out, depending on the direction of the spiral, and is perfect for spells of banishment or attraction.

Seed of Life

Hexagram

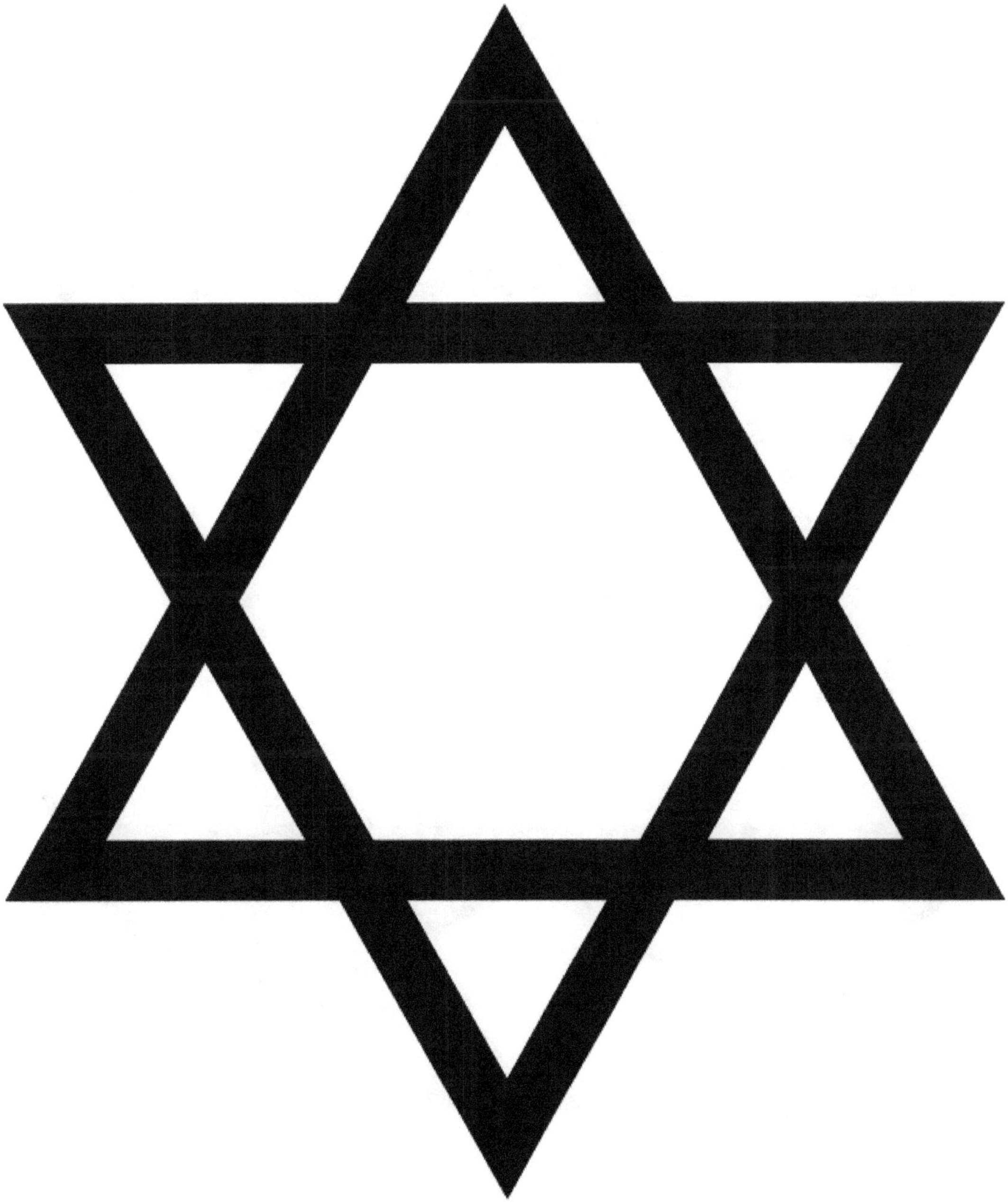

12-Pointed Star

9-Pointed Star

Gem Elixirs

In the world of crystal magick, gem elixirs (water infused with a stone's energy) are a potent tool for internalizing the properties of a specific crystal. They are consumed or used topically, allowing the stone's vibration to resonate directly with your body's energy field. However, it's crucial to approach this practice with caution and awareness. Never place stones directly into water intended for consumption. Many crystals, such as malachite, azurite, and cinnabar, contain toxic minerals that can leach into the water, posing serious health risks. Even seemingly safe stones can have microscopic fractures that harbor bacteria, or they may have been treated with chemicals or dyes that are not safe to ingest. And some stones, like selenite, will dissolve in water.

To create a safe and effective gem elixir, you can employ the "indirect method." This technique ensures that the water is infused with the crystal's energetic signature without any physical contact. To do this, you will need a large, clean glass container for your water and a smaller, clean glass bowl or cup. Place your chosen, cleansed crystal into the small glass bowl. Then, place the small bowl inside the larger container, ensuring the water surrounds it but does not touch the stone itself. Cover the large container to protect the water from dust or debris. Allow the water to sit for a period of time—a few hours or overnight under a full moon are common practices. The water will absorb the stone's energy through the glass without any risk of contamination. Once complete, remove the smaller bowl, and your gem elixir is ready to be used safely.

Your gem elixir can be added to skin- and haircare products, herbal preparations of all sorts, and it can be used for anointing the body, magickal tools, and candles.

Copyright Asteria Books 2025

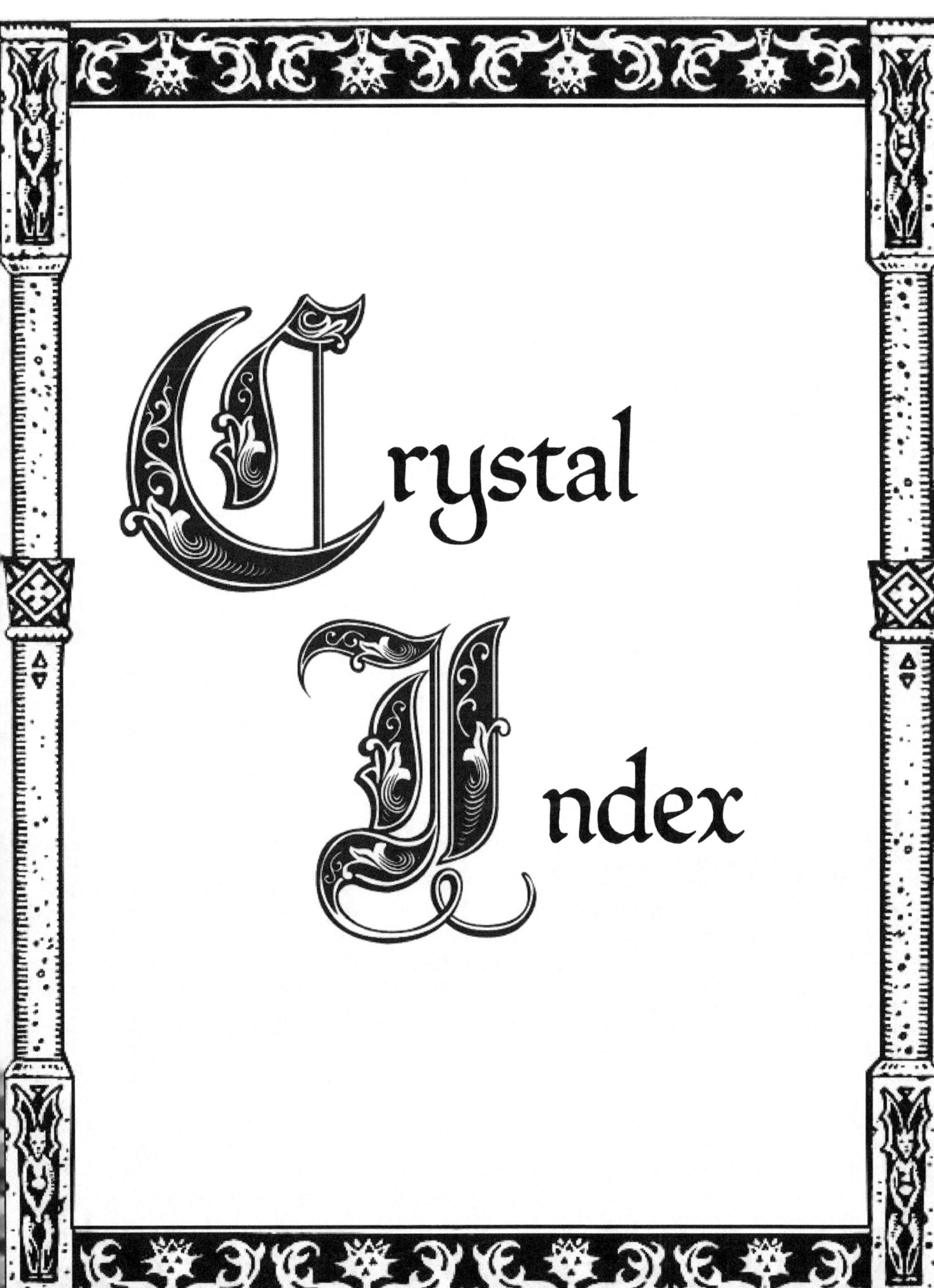

Crystal Index

Agate

Folk Names: Stone of the Earth, Banded Agate
Color(s): Clear, white, gray, brown, red, black, and others, often banded
Mohs scale: 6.5–7
Planetary association: Mercury
Element: Earth
Deities: Gaia, Cerridwen, Bona Dea
Powers: Grounding, courage, protection, healing

HEALING LORE: Agate has long been prized for its stabilizing and harmonizing properties. In ancient traditions, it was believed to soothe and calm the spirit, offering comfort during times of stress and emotional turmoil. The stone is often used to bring balance to the body's subtle energy fields, and its gentle vibrations are said to aid in physical healing by strengthening the body's internal systems. Different colors of agate were used for specific ailments; for example, fiery red agate was believed to invigorate the blood, while blue lace agate was used to soothe throat ailments and promote peaceful communication.

MAGIC AND RITUAL LORE: As a stone of the Earth element, agate is a powerful tool for grounding and connection to the natural world. It is a staple in protection spells, with its banded layers symbolizing the many layers of a magical shield. Agate is also used to promote courage and confidence, giving the practitioner the strength to face their fears. It is an excellent stone for scrying, as its gentle, swirling patterns can act as a natural mirror for intuitive insights. Agate amulets were worn to ward off negative energy and to attract good fortune, making it a universal ally for a wide range of magical practices.

Copyright Asteria Books 2016

Amber

Folk Names: Stone of the Sun, Electrum, Tears of the Sun, Gold of the North
Color(s): Yellow, orange, brown, red, sometimes green or blue
Mohs scale: 2.0–2.5
Planetary association: Sun
Element: Fire, Akasha (Spirit)
Deity: Freya, Ra
Powers: Healing, protection, purification, wisdom

HEALING LORE: Amber is not a mineral, but a fossilized tree resin, and its healing properties are as old as the sun that gave it life. Historically, amber has been used to draw out negative energy from the body, and its gentle, warm vibrations are believed to soothe and calm. It is often worn as a necklace or bracelet, especially by children, to alleviate pain and promote general well-being. It is said to be particularly effective for ailments of the throat, chest, and thyroid. The ancient Romans believed that wearing amber could prevent ailments of the ear and eye. Its connection to the Sun gives it a naturally uplifting energy, making it an ideal stone for emotional healing and combating seasonal depression.

MAGIC AND RITUAL LORE: As a stone of the Sun and the element of Fire, amber is a beacon of light, courage, and vitality. It is a powerful tool for purification and protection, used to cleanse both a ritual space and the aura of the practitioner. Its light, golden color and ancient origins make it an excellent stone for ancestral work and for connecting with ancient wisdom. Amber is also a powerful attractor, used in spells of manifestation and abundance. Because of its electric properties (the word "electrum" is the Latin word for amber), it is an excellent stone for charging other crystals or for directing a magical current. In folklore, it was believed to be the hardened tears of the sun, and as such, is a stone of divine grace and spiritual enlightenment. Amber is a quintessential witch stone, often being worn in combination with jet – and in some traditions, also with bone.

Copyright Asteria Books 2016

Amethyst

Folk Names: Stone of Sobriety, Bishop's Stone, Violet Quartz
Color(s): Purple (from pale lilac to deep violet)
Mohs scale: 7
Planetary association: Jupiter, Neptune
Element: Water
Deity: Bacchus, Diana
Powers: Intuition, protection, purification, sobriety

HEALING LORE: The healing properties of amethyst have been revered for centuries, particularly for the mind and spirit. It is a powerful stone for stress relief, believed to calm an overactive mind and soothe emotional turmoil. Ancient Greek and Roman texts speak of its ability to prevent intoxication, hence its name, which comes from the Greek amethystos meaning "not drunk." It is a superb ally for those dealing with anxiety or insomnia, as its serene energy promotes restful sleep and peaceful dreams. It is also believed to aid in the healing of physical ailments of the head, such as headaches and migraines, when placed on the third eye or temples.

MAGIC AND RITUAL LORE: Amethyst is one of the most significant stones in a witch's toolkit, a bridge between the physical and spiritual realms. As a stone of the element of Water, it is deeply connected to intuition and psychic abilities. It is an essential tool for divination, meditation, and scrying, as its high vibration helps to open the third eye and crown chakras. Amethyst is a powerful protective stone, used to ward off negative energy and psychic attack. It is also an excellent tool for cleansing and purifying other crystals. In ritual, it is placed on altars to bless a sacred space and to promote spiritual enlightenment. Its vibrant purple color is a symbol of transformation and divine connection, making it an invaluable stone for all manner of spiritual work.

Copyright Asteria Books 2016

Ammonites

Folk Names: Naga Stone, Serpent Stone
Color(s): Iridescent, brown, gray, black
Mohs scale: 3.5–4
Planetary association: Saturn
Element: Earth, Water, Akasha
Deity: Naga (serpent deities)
Powers: Past life recall, grounding, prosperity, protection

HEALING LORE: The Ammonite's powerful, spiraling energy is believed to be a key for deep healing and chakra alignment. Its spiral shape, a classic symbol of sacred geometry, helps to draw in and release energy, making it an excellent tool for overcoming blockages. It is often used in healing practices to relieve both physical and emotional trauma, providing a sense of grounding and stability. The stone's ancient energy is said to connect to the root chakra, anchoring the user to the earth's timeless wisdom and promoting a sense of inner peace and well-being.

MAGIC AND RITUAL LORE: Ammonite is a potent talisman for those working with past life exploration and ancestral wisdom. Its spiral symbolizes the journey back through time, making it a perfect tool for past life regression and for connecting with ancient energies. In ritual, it is used to attract prosperity and abundance, with its spiral representing a continuous flow of wealth and opportunity. The stone's connection to the serpent deities of folklore makes it a powerful protective amulet, warding off negative energy and guarding sacred spaces.

Copyright Asteria Books 2016

Apache Tear

Folk Names: Stone of Grief, Obsidian Tears
Color(s): Black, dark brown (translucent when held to light)
Mohs scale: 5–5.5
Planetary association: Pluto, Saturn
Element: Earth
Deity: Tezcatlipoca, Itzapapalotl, Sekhmet, Pele, Hecate, Persephone
Powers: Grief release, protection, grounding, truth

HEALING LORE: Apache's Tear is a deeply compassionate healing stone, primarily known for its ability to aid in the processing of grief and emotional pain. Folklore tells of a tribe of Apache warriors who, facing a losing battle, rode their horses off a cliff to avoid capture. The tears of their mourning loved ones were said to have solidified into these unique, translucent obsidian stones. The stone's gentle energy helps to cleanse and purify the aura, releasing deep-seated trauma and sorrow. It is a powerful ally for emotional support, offering a calm and steady presence during times of loss. Unlike other forms of obsidian, Apache's Tear is said to work without overwhelming the user, providing a gentle yet profound healing experience.

MAGIC AND RITUAL LORE: As a form of black obsidian, Apache's Tear is an incredibly protective stone, used to ward off negative energy and psychic attack. It is a stone of grounding, helping to anchor the practitioner to the earth and stabilize their energy field. In ritual, it is often placed on the altar or carried as a talisman to provide a shield of protection during shadow work or other difficult practices. Its connection to the underworld, ruled by deities like Hecate and Persephone, makes it a potent stone for communing with ancestors and for journeying into the depths of the subconscious mind. Apache's Tear is a stone of truth, revealing hidden patterns and helping the witch to see themselves and their situation with clarity and honesty.

Copyright Asteria Books 2016

Aquamarine

Scientific mineral name: Beryl
Folk Names: Stone of the Sea, Mariner's Stone
Color(s): Light blue, blue-green
Mohs scale: 7.5–8
Planetary association: Moon, Neptune
Element: Water
Deity: Poseidon, Aphrodite, Yemaya
Powers: Communication, clarity, courage, emotional healing

HEALING LORE: Aquamarine, with its serene blue color, is a stone of calm and emotional healing. It has long been used to soothe and purify the spirit, offering a sense of peace in times of stress and anxiety. It is particularly associated with ailments of the throat and lungs, believed to aid in communication and to clear blockages in the throat chakra. In ancient times, it was used by healers to promote a sense of well-being and to calm an overactive immune response. Its gentle, flowing energy is said to aid in the release of anger and emotional turmoil, bringing the heart and mind into a state of harmony.

MAGIC AND RITUAL LORE: As a "Stone of the Sea," aquamarine's magical properties are deeply tied to the element of Water. It is a powerful tool for witches who work with the sea, the moon, and the ebb and flow of emotions. It is a stone of courage, offering the strength to face one's fears and to speak one's truth with clarity and confidence. It is a classic stone for divination, particularly for scrying with water, as its clear blue color reflects the depths of the subconscious mind. Sailors and travelers once carried aquamarine as a protective amulet, believing it to be a charm against drowning and a guide for safe journeys. Its calming energy makes it an excellent stone for meditation, helping the practitioner to access a deeper, more intuitive state of consciousness.

Copyright Asteria Books 2016

Aventurine

Folk Names: Stone of Opportunity, Fairy Stone, Stone of the Gambler
Color(s): Green, blue, peach, red
Mohs scale: 7
Planetary association: Mercury, Venus
Element: Earth
Deity: Fortunata, Lakshmi
Powers: Luck, opportunity, prosperity, courage

HEALING LORE: Aventurine is a powerful and versatile healing stone, known for its ability to calm the heart and balance the emotions. It is a stone of comfort, believed to soothe anxiety and bring a sense of inner peace. Green aventurine, in particular, is associated with the heart chakra, and is used to heal emotional wounds and attract loving energy. It is a stone that encourages compassion and empathy, and its gentle vibrations are said to aid in the healing of the physical heart and circulatory system. In ancient times, it was used to clear blockages and promote a healthy flow of energy throughout the body.

MAGIC AND RITUAL LORE: As the "Stone of Opportunity," aventurine is a staple in spells of luck, prosperity, and manifestation. It is a powerful attractor, drawing new opportunities and good fortune to the practitioner. Its connection to the element of Earth makes it an excellent stone for grounding and stability, providing a solid foundation for new ventures. Aventurine is also a stone of courage, offering the strength to step outside of one's comfort zone and take risks. It is a popular tool for gamblers and those seeking to attract abundance. In ritual, it can be placed in a money bowl, a prosperity sachet, or carried as a talisman to attract good luck and help manifest your desires. Its beautiful, shimmering qualities are a reminder that magic is all around us, and that good fortune is waiting to be found.

Copyright Asteria Books 2016

Belemnites

Folk Names: Thunderbolts, Elf Arrows, Devil's Fingers
Color(s): Dark brown, gray, amber
Mohs scale: 5–5.5
Planetary association: Jupiter, Mars
Element: Water, Air
Deity: Thor, Jupiter
Powers: Protection, strength, lightning magick, courage

HEALING LORE: Belemnites are an energizing and protective stone, believed to promote physical strength and vitality. They are often used in healing practices to aid in the strength of bones and joints, drawing on their unique, hardened form. Their ancient energy is a powerful tool for releasing blockages and for stimulating a healthy flow of energy throughout the body. Their connection to the elements of Water and Air gives them a harmonizing energy, and they are said to be particularly useful for ailments of the throat and lungs.

MAGIC AND RITUAL LORE: The Belemnite's folklore as a "thunderbolt" from the sky makes it a powerful tool for storm magick and for working with the elements of Air and Fire. It is a powerful protective amulet, believed to offer protection from lightning, storms, and all forms of negative magick. In ritual, it is used to command energy with authority and to bring about change with a powerful, focused intent. It is an excellent stone for spells of courage and strength, with its ancient, pointed form symbolizing a clear and direct path to success.

Copyright Asteria Books 2016

Bloodstone

Folk Names: Heliotrope, Christ's Blood, Stone of the Martyr, Sunstone
Color(s): Dark green with red speckles
Mohs scale: 6.5–7
Planetary association: Mars
Element: Fire, Earth
Deity: Mars, Ares
Powers: Courage, vitality, healing, protection

HEALING LORE: As its name suggests, Bloodstone is a powerful healing stone associated with the blood and physical vitality. In ancient times, it was used to staunch bleeding, purify the blood, and aid in the healing of wounds. Its invigorating energy is believed to strengthen the body's life force and provide courage and endurance. It is an excellent stone for athletes and those recovering from illness, as its energy helps to rebuild and restore the physical body. Bloodstone is also used to calm the emotions and soothe anger, offering a sense of grounded strength and resilience.

MAGIC AND RITUAL LORE: Bloodstone is a warrior's stone, a talisman of courage and protection. It is a powerful tool for spells of strength, vitality, and overcoming adversity. In ritual, it is placed on the altar or carried as a protective amulet to ward off negative energy and psychic attack. Its connection to the element of Fire makes it a great stone for banishing and for commanding energy with authority. In ancient lore, it was said to be the stone of the martyr, and its red flecks were believed to be the blood of Christ. As such, it is also a stone of sacrifice and selfless action, used to bring about positive change.

Copyright Asteria Books 2016

Boji Stones

Other Names: Moqui Marbles, Shaman Stones, Kansas Pop Rocks, Mushroom Stones
Planet: Earth, Mars
Other Astrological: Aquarius, Scorpio, Leo, Taurus
Element: Earth
Deities: Gaia, Mother Earth
Magical Properties: grounding, balancing, healing, protection, spirit journeying, manifestation, cleansing

MYTHS: Boji stone myths center on their origin from a sacred mound in Kansas. The stones, seen as a gift from the Earth, are believed to be found in male and female pairs. This dual nature is said to be essential for balancing a person's energy, with the myth claiming the stones lose power if separated.

HEALING: Boji stones are said to help release emotional blockages, reduce anxiety, and promote a sense of inner peace. They are thought to help a person feel more centered and secure. Some practitioners believe they can help with physical pain, tissue regeneration, and cellular healing. It is believed that placing the stones on an affected area can draw out negative energy and promote the body's natural healing process. They are considered protective stones that can shield a person's aura from negative energy, psychic attacks, and electromagnetic smog.

MAGIC AND RITUAL: Boji stones are thought to have a self-cleansing property, meaning they do not need to be energetically cleared as often as other crystals. They are also used to cleanse and recharge other stones. They are sometimes referred to as "shaman stones" because they are believed to aid in spiritual journeys and help a person connect with animal guides or spiritual realms. It is believed that by holding the stones and focusing on an intention, a person can use their grounding energy to help manifest their desires.

Copyright Asteria Books 2025

Calcite

Folk Names: Honey Calcite, Optical Calcite, Iceland Spar
Color(s): White, yellow, orange, blue, green, pink, clear
Mohs scale: 3
Planetary association: Sun, Moon
Element: Fire, Air
Deity: Varies by color
Powers: Clarity, amplification, memory, purification

HEALING LORE: Calcite is a gentle yet powerful healing stone that is known for its ability to clear and purify. It is believed to cleanse the body of toxins and to aid in the absorption of vitamins and minerals. Different colors of calcite have specific healing properties; for example, green calcite is used for emotional healing and to soothe the heart, while blue calcite is used to calm the nerves and promote peaceful communication. Its clear, crystalline structure is said to help a person see a clear path forward, both physically and emotionally.

MAGIC AND RITUAL LORE: As a stone of amplification, calcite is a powerful tool for charging other crystals and for magnifying magical intent. It is an excellent stone for memory work and for improving mental clarity. Clear calcite, also known as Iceland Spar, is used for scrying and for seeing through illusions, as its double-refracting properties can help a person to see both sides of a situation. Calcite is also a stone of purification, used to cleanse a ritual space of stagnant or negative energy. Its gentle, yet powerful vibrations make it a versatile and essential tool for any magical practice.

Copyright Asteria Books 2016

Carnelian

Folk Names: Stone of the Sun, Sard
Color(s): Red, orange, reddish-brown
Mohs scale: 7
Planetary association: Sun, Mars
Element: Fire
Deity: Isis, Ra
Powers: Courage, vitality, creativity, motivation, passion

HEALING LORE: Carnelian is a stone of life force and vitality. Its fiery, warm energy is believed to stimulate the metabolism and invigorate the body's life force, or chi. In ancient times, it was used to aid in fertility and to promote a healthy flow of blood. It is an excellent stone for boosting confidence and motivation, and its fiery energy is said to help overcome inertia and procrastination. Carnelian is also a powerful stone for the sacral chakra, used to heal and balance a person's creativity and passions.

MAGIC AND RITUAL LORE: As a stone of the Sun and the element of Fire, Carnelian is a beacon of light, courage, and vitality. It is a powerful tool for spells of motivation, creativity, and passion. In ritual, it is placed on the altar or carried as a talisman to give the practitioner the courage to face their fears and to follow their heart's desires. It is a powerful attractor, used in spells of manifestation and abundance. Its connection to ancient Egyptian lore, where it was associated with the goddess Isis and the sun god Ra, makes it a potent stone for connecting with divine feminine and masculine energy.

Copyright Asteria Books 2016

Cat's Eye

Folk Names: Cymophane
Color(s): Honey, green, brown
Mohs scale: 8.5
Planetary association: Moon, Saturn
Element: Earth
Deity: Sekhmet, Bastet
Powers: Protection, insight, clarity, psychic ability

HEALING LORE: The healing properties of Cat's Eye are deeply connected to its ability to bring clarity and focus. Its unique, shimmering band of light is said to represent the power of the third eye, and its energy is used to strengthen a person's intuition and aid in seeing through illusions. It is believed to help in the healing of the physical eyes and to improve night vision. As a stone of protection, it is used to ward off negative energy and to calm the emotions, offering a sense of grounded stability.

MAGIC AND RITUAL LORE: Cat's Eye is a powerful protective stone, a talisman that is said to be able to ward off the evil eye and other forms of negative magick. It is a stone of insight and clarity, used in divination and scrying to reveal hidden truths and to see through deceit. Its connection to feline deities like Sekhmet and Bastet makes it a great stone for witches who work with cat spirits and for those who seek to embody the grace, cunning, and independence of the feline. In ritual, it is placed on the altar or carried as a protective amulet to create a shield of energy that is both powerful and subtle.

Copyright Asteria Books 2016

Celestite

Folk Names: Celestine, Angel Stone
Color(s): Light blue, white, clear
Mohs scale: 3–3.5
Planetary association: Neptune
Element: Air
Deity: Varies (often associated with angels and spirits)
Powers: Angelic communication, peacefulness, stress relief, spiritual development

HEALING LORE: Celestite, with its ethereal blue color, is a stone of peace and tranquility. Its gentle, soothing energy is said to calm the nerves and promote deep relaxation, making it an excellent stone for those dealing with stress, anxiety, or insomnia. It is believed to aid in the healing of the physical body, particularly in the case of stress-related ailments. Its connection to the throat chakra makes it a great stone for promoting peaceful and harmonious communication.

MAGIC AND RITUAL LORE: As the "Angel Stone," celestite is a powerful tool for communicating with angels and spirit guides. Its high vibration helps to open the crown chakra and to create a clear channel for spiritual communication. In ritual, it is placed on the altar or used in meditation to create a sacred space that is filled with light and spiritual energy. It is an excellent stone for scrying and for dream work, as its gentle energy can help to access a deeper, more intuitive state of consciousness. Celestite is also a stone of protection, used to create a shield of light that is both powerful and peaceful.

Copyright Asteria Books 2016

Chalcedony

Folk Names: Speaker's Stone
Color(s): Translucent, milky, blue, white, gray, pink
Mohs scale: 7
Planetary association: Moon
Element: Water, Air
Deity: Diana, the Triple Goddess
Powers: Emotional balance, harmony, communication, stability

HEALING LORE: Chalcedony is thought to soothe emotional turmoil, reducing anxiety, stress, and worry, and fostering a sense of inner peace and tranquility. It can help process and release past emotional trauma, promoting emotional healing and forgiveness. It is believed to replace negativity with positive energy, fostering kindness, generosity, and an optimistic outlook. It is said to help stabilize emotions, aiding those who easily get worried or experience mood swings. Especially Blue Chalcedony, it is linked to the Throat Chakra, improving verbal dexterity, listening skills, and enhancing clear communication. It is believed to aid in healing the lungs and clearing the respiratory system, potentially helping with conditions like allergies, bronchitis, and asthma. It's a popular choice for those struggling with insomnia. It is reputed to improve blood circulation, reduce inflammation, and help eliminate toxins, purifying the body and strengthening the immune system. It's associated with relieving kidney problems, including gallstones, and soothing throat infections.

MAGIC AND RITUAL LORE: Chalcedony is often called the "Speaker's Stone" and is associated with enhancing communication and self-expression. It's believed to help individuals articulate thoughts and feelings clearly and confidently. This includes improving public speaking abilities and fostering honest dialogue. Chalcedony is believed to connect individuals with their inner wisdom and intuition. It can facilitate meditation and spiritual exploration, encouraging a deeper understanding of one's spiritual path and opening channels to higher realms. Blue Chalcedony, specifically, is associated with spiritual growth and the development of intuition. As a stone of balance, it is said to dispel fear-based thinking, encourage generosity, and shield against negative energies and psychic attacks.

Copyright Asteria Books 2016

Chrysocolla

Folk Names: Stone of the Sage, Copper Gem
Color(s): Blue-green, blue, green
Mohs scale: 2.5–3.5
Planetary association: Venus, Neptune
Element: Water
Deity: The Great Mother, Gaia
Powers: Wisdom, communication, peace, expression

HEALING LORE: Chrysocolla is often used to soothe anxiety, reduce nervousness, and promote relaxation. It helps release emotional blockages, encourage forgiveness, and foster self-acceptance. Chrysocolla is believed to bring a sense of tranquility and balance to one's emotional state. It is thought to enhance communication skills, allowing for clearer and more authentic expression. Chrysocolla is often associated with the throat chakra and is believed to help with throat-related issues like sore throats, laryngitis, and voice clarity. It is also thought to aid respiratory function. Some believe it can assist with digestive problems. Chrysocolla may help regulate blood pressure and blood sugar levels. It is thought to support the immune system and promote overall physical vitality.

MAGIC AND RITUAL LORE: Chrysocolla is believed to enhance communication skills, allowing for more honest and compassionate self-expression. It can empower individuals, fostering self-confidence and a sense of personal strength. Chrysocolla is thought to enhance spiritual awareness, intuition, and psychic abilities. It can facilitate a deeper connection with one's inner self and the spiritual realm. Chrysocolla is often used in meditation to deepen spiritual practices and promote clarity of thought. Some believe it can offer protection against negative energies and emotional manipulation. It is also thought to have grounding properties, helping to create a sense of stability and security. Chrysocolla is associated with creativity and can inspire artistic expression. It is believed to help balance rocky relationships and promote understanding. Chrysocolla is connected to the heart chakra, fostering compassion, self-love, and deeper connections. It is believed to enhance intuition and connect individuals with their inner wisdom and the divine feminine energy.

Copyright Asteria Books 2016

Citrine

Folk Names: Stone of the Merchant, Success Stone, Light Citrine
Color(s): Yellow, orange, brownish-yellow
Mohs scale: 7
Planetary association: Sun
Element: Fire
Deity: Fortuna, Apollo
Powers: Abundance, prosperity, manifestation, joy

HEALING LORE: Citrine is a joyous, uplifting stone that is known for its ability to bring a sense of happiness and well-being. Its warm, sunny energy is believed to stimulate the metabolism and invigorate the body's life force, or chi. In ancient times, it was used to aid in digestion and to promote a healthy flow of blood. It is an excellent stone for boosting confidence and motivation, and its fiery energy is said to help overcome inertia and procrastination. Citrine is also a powerful stone for the solar plexus chakra, used to heal and balance a person's will and personal power.

MAGIC AND RITUAL LORE: As a stone of the Sun and the element of Fire, Citrine is a beacon of light, courage, and vitality. It is a powerful tool for spells of abundance, prosperity, and manifestation. In ritual, it is placed in a money bowl, a prosperity sachet, or carried as a talisman to attract good fortune and help manifest your desires. Its connection to the sun makes it a great stone for spells of banishment and for commanding energy with authority. In folklore, it was believed to be the stone of the merchant, and its warm, sunny energy was said to attract wealth and success. Citrine is a powerful cleanser of other stones and ritual objects, as it brings the light of the sun with itself. Because of this, it keeps itself cleansed and free of unwanted energies, as well.

Copyright Asteria Books 2016

Clear Quartz

Folk Names: Rock Crystal, Master Healer, Ice of the Gods
Color(s): Clear, translucent, white
Mohs scale: 7
Planetary association: Sun, Moon, All Planets
Element: All Elements, Akasha
Deity: Varies
Powers: Amplification, healing, cleansing, spiritual connection

HEALING LORE: Clear Quartz is known as the "Master Healer" for its ability to amplify and direct energy. Its pure, crystalline structure is believed to clear blockages and to promote a healthy flow of energy throughout the body. It is a versatile stone, used to aid in the healing of all physical and emotional ailments. Its clear energy is a great aid for calming an overactive mind and soothing anxiety. It is also an excellent tool for enhancing intuition and promoting a deeper, more spiritual awareness.

MAGIC AND RITUAL LORE: Clear Quartz is a quintessential witch's stone, a powerful tool for amplification and manifestation. Its pure energy is a great aid for charging other crystals and for magnifying magical intent. In ritual, it is placed on the altar or carried as a talisman to attract good fortune and help manifest your desires. Its connection to all elements and the cosmos makes it a great stone for all forms of magick and for commanding energy with authority. Among some Indigenous people in Australia and the Americas, clear quarts is especially associated with the Ancestors and Spirit communication.

Copyright Asteria Books 2016

Coal

Other Names: Anthracite Black Stone
Color(s): Black, dark gray
Mohs scale: 1–2
Planetary association: Saturn
Element: Earth
Deity: Hades, Persephone
Powers: Grounding, protection, shadow work, ancestor connection

HEALING LORE: While not a typical healing stone, coal has a unique and powerful energy. Its deep, dark color and ancient origins make it a great stone for grounding and for connecting with the earth. Activated charcoal is a well-established treatment for overdoses and poisonings, as it can bind to and help remove toxins from the body. Some proponents claim it can aid with digestive issues, reduce gas, and lower cholesterol, though scientific evidence supporting these claims is limited. Activated charcoal is used in some skincare products and dental products, with claims of detoxifying and whitening effects, but more research is needed.

MAGIC AND RITUAL LORE: As a stone of the underworld and the element of Earth, coal is a powerful tool for shadow work and for communing with ancestors. Coal is believed to help alleviate stress and anxiety by promoting a sense of stability. Anthracite is used in spiritual practices to shield against negative energies, making it useful during meditation and psychic work. It's thought to aid in self-discovery and personal development. Interestingly, some traditions associate coal with attracting wealth and abundance. Activated charcoal is known for its ability to absorb toxins and impurities. In magical practices, it's used to cleanse spaces, objects, and even the aura of negative energies. It's a popular ingredient in banishing rituals, helping to remove negativity and unwanted influences. Its ability to absorb and neutralize energy makes it a protective tool in spells and rituals. The dark, mysterious nature of charcoal is associated with the shadow self and can be used to facilitate inner reflection and self-discovery.

Copyright Asteria Books 2016

Coral

Folk Names: Gorgeia, Goral, Langgan, Red Gold
Color(s): Red, pink, white, blue, black
Mohs scale: 3–4
Planetary association: Mars, Neptune
Element: Water
Deity: Poseidon, Yemaya, Medusa
Powers: Protection, emotional balance, fertility, healing

HEALING LORE: Coral is a powerful healing stone associated with the blood and the physical vitality. Its fiery, warm energy is believed to stimulate the metabolism and invigorate the body's life force, or chi. In ancient times, it was used to aid in fertility and to promote a healthy flow of blood. It is an excellent stone for boosting confidence and motivation, and its fiery energy is said to help overcome inertia and procrastination. Coral is also a powerful stone for the sacral chakra, used to heal and balance a person's creativity and passions.

MAGIC AND RITUAL LORE: Coral is widely believed to offer protection from negative energies, evil spirits, and misfortune. It's used as an amulet to ward off accidents, illness, and curses. Coral, especially red coral, is associated with enhancing intuition, promoting spiritual connection, and aiding in meditation. It's believed to balance chakras, particularly the root and heart chakras. Coral is linked to attracting success, wealth, and happiness. It's also thought to bring good luck and enhance love and sensuality. Coral is known to calm emotions, relieve stress, and foster inner peace. It can help overcome fear, depression, and panic. In some cultures, coral is associated with fertility and is used to strengthen the maternal bond during pregnancy. It's also believed to promote harmony in relationships and encourage a love of life.

Copyright Asteria Books 2016

Crinoid Columns

Folk Names: Fairy Money, Star Stones, Indian Beads
Color(s): White, gray, brown
Mohs scale: 7
Planetary association: Venus, Moon
Element: Water, Earth
Deity: Faeries, Mermaids
Powers: Luck, prosperity, healing, protection

HEALING LORE: Crinoid columnals, with their delicate, ancient energy, are deeply comforting and soothing. They are believed to be excellent for emotional healing and for calming the spirit, particularly for those dealing with stress and anxiety. Their connection to the sea gives them a harmonizing energy, and they are said to aid in the healing of the heart and to promote a sense of inner peace. Their gentle, nurturing vibrations make them a great stone for children or for those who need a reminder of the simple joys of life.

MAGIC AND RITUAL LORE: As their folk names suggest, Crinoid columnals are a powerful tool for prosperity and faery magick. They are a classic offering to faeries, placed on altars or in gardens to invite their presence and protection. They are also a potent talisman for luck and good fortune, with their star shape symbolizing a connection to the cosmos and the stars. In ritual, they are used for protection, with their small, compact form symbolizing a tight and secure magical shield.

Copyright Asteria Books 2016

Diamond

Folk Names: Adamant, King of Gems, Stone of Innocence
Color(s): Clear, yellow, pink, blue, green, black
Mohs scale: 10
Planetary association: Sun
Element: Fire, Akasha (Spirit)
Deity: Indra, Zeus, Cupid, Ra
Powers: Purity, strength, courage, protection, love

HEALING LORE: The diamond, the hardest natural substance on Earth, is a powerful healer for the mind and spirit. Its pure, radiant energy is believed to clear the aura and dissolve blockages in the crown chakra, promoting mental clarity and spiritual enlightenment. It is an excellent stone for those dealing with mental or spiritual confusion, as its clear energy helps to bring a sense of purpose and direction. In ancient times, it was believed to aid in the healing of the brain and nervous system, and to amplify the healing properties of other stones.

MAGIC AND RITUAL LORE: The diamond is a stone of purity, strength, and protection. Its radiant energy is a powerful tool for spells of protection, as its perfect crystalline structure is believed to be able to deflect all forms of negative energy. Diamonds are believed to bring clarity of mind and purpose, enhancing focus and concentration. Diamonds are believed to amplify energy, both physical and spiritual, making them powerful tools for manifestation and healing. Diamonds are thought to offer protection from negative energies and bad dreams, and also to instill courage and self-esteem. They are associated with spiritual enlightenment, helping individuals connect with their higher selves and experience inner peace.

Copyright Asteria Books 2016

Echinoids

Folk Names: Sea Urchin fossils, Faery Loaves, Faerie Cakes, Thunderstones
Color(s): White, gray, brown
Mohs scale: Varies
Planetary association: Moon, Venus
Element: Water, Earth
Deity: Yemaya, Poseidon, Faeries
Powers: Emotional healing, grounding, protection, spiritual balance

HEALING LORE: Sea urchins, specifically their spines and pigments, are believed to possess various healing properties, including anti-inflammatory, antioxidant, and antimicrobial effects. They are also being explored for their potential in bone regeneration. Echinoids are believed to possess metaphysical healing properties, particularly related to grounding, emotional healing, and accessing ancient wisdom. They are thought to transmute negative energy, release past-life karmic patterns, and promote a sense of peace and stability.

MAGIC AND RITUAL LORE: Echinoids are a powerful tool for water magick and for connecting with the sea and its deities. They are a classic offering to sea gods and goddesses, placed on altars or in gardens to invite their presence and protection. And ss their folk name (Faery Loaves) suggest, they are also a powerful tool for faery magick and for connecting with the Fae. They are a classic offering to faeries, placed on altars or in gardens to invite their presence and protection. They are also a potent talisman for emotional balance and spiritual growth, with their ancient energy providing a clear and steady channel to the deep past. In ritual, they are used for protection, with their intricate form symbolizing a shield of energy that is both powerful and subtle.

Copyright Asteria Books 2016

Emerald

Folk Names: Stone of the Heart, Gem of Venus
Color(s): Green
Mohs scale: 7.5–8
Planetary association: Venus
Element: Earth
Deity: Venus, Aphrodite, Saraswati, Thoth
Powers: Love, prosperity, wisdom, emotional healing

HEALING LORE: The emerald, a stone of the heart, is a powerful healer for the emotions. Its gentle, soothing energy is believed to calm the nerves and promote deep relaxation, making it an excellent stone for those dealing with stress, anxiety, or insomnia. It is an excellent stone for boosting confidence and motivation, and its fiery energy is said to help overcome inertia and procrastination. The emerald is also a powerful stone for the heart chakra, used to heal and balance a person's creativity and passions.

MAGIC AND RITUAL LORE: As a stone of the Earth and the element of Venus, the emerald is a powerful tool for spells of love, prosperity, and manifestation. In ritual, it is placed on the altar or carried as a talisman to attract good fortune and help manifest your desires. Its connection to the heart makes it a great stone for spells of love and for commanding energy with authority. In folklore, it was believed to be the stone of the heart, and its gentle, soothing energy was said to calm the nerves and promote a sense of inner peace. It is also an excellent tool for scrying, as its deep green color can act as a natural mirror for intuitive insights.

Copyright Asteria Books 2016

Flint

Folk Names: Stone of Fire, Arrowhead Stone
Color(s): Dark gray, black, brown
Mohs scale: 7
Planetary association: Mars
Element: Fire
Deity: Mars, Vulcan
Powers: Protection, strength, banishing, creativity

HEALING LORE: Flint, a stone of the Earth and Fire, is a powerful healer for the mind and spirit. It's known for its grounding and protective properties, aiding in emotional balance and introspection. It can also be used to access ancient knowledge, potentially helping to integrate lessons from past lives. Physically, flint is associated with kidney health, bone strength, and calming the nervous system. Flint can help balance the physical and emotional bodies, promoting introspection and inner insight.

MAGIC AND RITUAL LORE: As a stone of Fire, flint is a powerful tool for spells of protection and banishing. Some believe flint facilitates access to past life knowledge and the integration of lessons learned. It can enhance connection with the spiritual world, including awakening, self-discovery, and communication with spirit guides. Some believe that meditating with flint can help access and learn from past life experiences. Flint can be used to sever karmic ties and break free from negative patterns or addictions. Flint is associated with ancient strength, stability, and resilience, making it a good choice for those needing to assert themselves or overcome challenges. Flint has been traditionally used to protect travelers.

Copyright Asteria Books 2016

Flourite

Folk Names: Stone of the Rainbow, Fluor Spar
Color(s): Clear, blue, purple, green, yellow, pink, black
Mohs scale: 4
Planetary association: Neptune
Element: Air
Deity: Hermes, Athena
Powers: Clarity, focus, intuition, protection, purification

HEALING LORE: Flourite, a stone of the Rainbow, is a powerful healer for the mind and spirit. Its clear, crystalline energy is believed to cleanse the aura and dissolve blockages in the crown chakra, promoting mental clarity and spiritual enlightenment. It is an excellent stone for those dealing with mental or spiritual confusion, as its clear energy helps to bring a sense of purpose and direction. In ancient times, it was believed to aid in the healing of the brain and nervous system, and to amplify the healing properties of other stones.

MAGIC AND RITUAL LORE: As a stone of the Air and the element of Neptune, flourite is a powerful tool for spells of clarity, focus, and intuition. In ritual, it is placed on the altar or carried as a talisman to give the practitioner the courage to face their fears and to follow their heart's desires. Its connection to the element of Air makes it a great stone for spells of manifestation and for commanding energy with authority.

Copyright Asteria Books 2016

Garnet

Folk Names: Almandine, Pyrope, Carbuncle Stone, Arizona Ruby
Color(s): Red, brown, orange, pink
Mohs scale: 6.5–7.5
Planetary association: Mars
Element: Fire
Deity: Sekhmet, Ra, Demeter, Persephone, Noah, Aphrodite, Druids
Powers: Passion, protection, strength, vitality, courage

HEALING LORE: Garnet is a powerful healing stone associated with the blood and physical vitality. Its fiery, warm energy is believed to stimulate the metabolism and invigorate the body's life force, or chi. In ancient times, it was used to staunch bleeding, purify the blood, and aid in the healing of wounds. Its invigorating energy is believed to strengthen the body's life force and provide courage and endurance. It is an excellent stone for athletes and those recovering from illness, as its energy helps to rebuild and restore the physical body.

MAGIC AND RITUAL LORE: Garnet is a powerful protective stone, said to shield the wearer from negative energies and psychic attacks. It's believed to create a protective barrier, fostering a sense of safety and security. Its connection to the root chakra helps to ground and stabilize, providing a sense of security. Garnet is thought to promote spiritual ascension and growth. It is associated with emotional balance and can help with feelings of depression. Garnet is believed to reignite passion and creativity, particularly when associated with the sacral chakra. It can help clear the mind, organize thoughts, and enhance creative thinking. Garnet is associated with attracting prosperity and abundance. It is believed to enhance courage and strengthen willpower. Garnet is associated with physical love and fidelity, especially in romantic relationships.

Copyright Asteria Books 2016

Goldstone

Folk Names: Stone of Ambition, Star Stone
Color(s): Gold, blue, red
Mohs scale: 6–6.5
Planetary association: Sun, Mars
Element: Fire
Deity: Varies
Powers: Ambition, courage, vitality, protection, prosperity

HEALING LORE: Goldstone, a stone of Ambition, is a powerful healer for the mind and spirit. Its fiery, warm energy is believed to stimulate the metabolism and invigorate the body's life force, or chi. In ancient times, it was used to aid in fertility and to promote a healthy flow of blood. It is an excellent stone for boosting confidence and motivation, and its fiery energy is said to help overcome inertia and procrastination. Goldstone is also a powerful stone for the sacral chakra, used to heal and balance a person's creativity and passions.

MAGIC AND RITUAL LORE: As a stone of the Sun and the element of Fire, Goldstone is a beacon of light, courage, and vitality. It is a powerful tool for spells of abundance, prosperity, and manifestation. In ritual, it is placed in a money bowl, a prosperity sachet, or carried as a talisman to attract good fortune and help manifest your desires. Its connection to the sun makes it a great stone for spells of banishment and for commanding energy with authority. In folklore, it was believed to be the stone of the merchant, and its warm, sunny energy was said to attract wealth and success.

Goshenite

Folk Names: White Beryl, Mother of Crystals
Color(s): Colorless, Transparent
Mohs scale: 7.5-8
Planetary association: Moon, Mercury
Element: Spirit, Air
Deity: Hecate, Athena, The Fates
Powers: Truth, Clarity, Mental Focus, Psychic Development, Honesty, Purity

HEALING LORE: Known as "The Eye Stone" in ancient lore, goshenite is often used to improve vision and eye health. Placing it on the third eye or crown chakra can help clear mental clutter, enhance memory, and sharpen intellectual abilities. It's an excellent stone for those who need to stay mentally sharp and focused. As a booster stone, it can amplify the healing properties of other crystals, making it a versatile tool for any healing layout. Its pure energy helps cleanse the aura and purify the energetic body.

MAGIC AND RITUAL LORE: Goshenite is a stone of unclouded truth and spiritual purity. As the colorless variety of beryl, it is a blank slate, a pure conduit for cosmic energy. It is perfect for scrying and meditative work, as it facilitates a clear connection to the spiritual world. Its clarity makes it an excellent stone for divination and accessing Akashic records. Use it in rituals to promote honest communication and to expose lies or deceit. Place it on your altar to amplify the power of other stones in a grid or spell. Carrying goshenite can help you speak your truth with confidence and integrity, and it can be used to create a powerful energetic shield against manipulation and psychic interference.

Copyright Asteria Books 2016

Gryphaea

Folk Names: Devil's Toenails, Stone of the Sea
Color(s): Gray, brown, black
Mohs scale: Varies
Planetary association: Saturn
Element: Water, Earth
Deity: Ancestors
Powers: Protection, grounding, ancestral wisdom, patience

HEALING LORE: Gryphaea, with their ancient, shell-like forms, are powerful healers for the mind and spirit. Their energy is said to be excellent for promoting patience and for calming the spirit, particularly for those dealing with stress and anxiety. Their connection to the sea gives them a harmonizing energy, and they are said to aid in the healing of the heart and to promote a sense of inner peace. Their gentle, nurturing vibrations make them a great stone for children or for those who need a reminder of the simple joys of life.

MAGIC AND RITUAL LORE: As their folk names suggest, Gryphaea are a powerful tool for protection and grounding. They are a classic amulet, carried to ward off negative energy and to create a shield of strength. In ritual, they are used to connect with ancestral wisdom and for spells of patience and stability. Their connection to the ancient seas and the deep past makes them a powerful tool for scrying and for connecting with the origins of all life.

Copyright Asteria Books 2016

Heliador

Folk Names: Golden Beryl, Sun Stone
Color(s): Clear yellow to yellowish-green.
Mohs scale: 7.5-8
Planetary association: Sun
Element: Fire, Air
Deity: Ra, Apollo, Sif
Powers: Willpower, Confidence, Intellect, Leadership, Protection, Joy

HEALING LORE: Physically, heliodor is a powerful ally for the solar plexus chakra. It's said to aid in strengthening the digestive system, liver, and spleen, helping the body process both food and emotional energy. Use it to combat fatigue and seasonal affective disorder, as its sunny energy is a powerful revitalizing force. Emotionally, it can help dissipate the fear of failure and encourage a sunny outlook on life, boosting the immune system and the body's innate healing abilities.

MAGIC AND RITUAL LORE: Heliodor, a radiant sun-warmed stone, is a crystal of pure, assertive willpower. It doesn't scream for attention; rather, it shines with a steady, commanding light. Named from the Greek words helios (sun) and doron (gift), this stone is a direct line to solar energy, imbuing the bearer with the golden courage of a lion. It is a beacon for those who feel lost in their own shadow, and a tool for those who seek to illuminate their true path and purpose. Use heliodor on your altar to call upon the energy of the sun during any spellwork. It is particularly effective in rituals of manifestation, success, and leadership. Place it on your desk to enhance mental clarity and focus when working on complex projects. For protection, carry a heliodor to create a shield of light around your aura, deflecting negativity and psychic attacks. Its energy is direct and unyielding, making it a powerful focal point for any magical working that requires a strong sense of self.

Copyright Asteria Books 2016

Hematite

Folk Names: Stone of the Mind, Black Diamond, Iron Ore, Bloodstone
Color(s): Silver-gray, black, reddish-brown
Mohs scale: 5.5–6.5
Planetary association: Mars
Element: Earth
Deity: Varies
Powers: Grounding, protection, stability, focus

HEALING LORE: Hematite is a cornerstone of healing for its powerful grounding effects. Its dense, metallic energy is said to dissolve negativity and provide a sense of stability and balance. Historically, it has been used to calm the mind and improve focus, making it a great ally for those struggling with scattered thoughts. The stone's connection to the blood has also led to its use in traditional healing to strengthen the circulatory system and promote vitality. Its ability to absorb and neutralize energy makes it a wonderful tool for detoxifying the body on both a physical and energetic level.

MAGIC AND RITUAL LORE: Known as a formidable protective stone, Hematite is an essential tool for creating a solid magical shield. Its mirrored surface is believed to reflect negative energy back to its source, making it a perfect warding stone for any ritual space or personal talisman. Witches often use Hematite for grounding before and after spellwork, ensuring they remain anchored to the Earth. Its metallic luster and connection to the planet Mars lend it a martial, strengthening energy, making it an excellent choice for spells of courage and overcoming adversity.

Copyright Asteria Books 2016

Herkimer Diamond

Folk Names: Herkimer Quartz, Stone of Attunement
Color(s): Clear
Mohs scale: 7.5
Planetary association: Mercury
Element: Air
Deity: Angerona, Hekate, Latona
Powers: Psychic ability, amplification, dream recall, spiritual connection

HEALING LORE: This unique form of quartz, found in Herkimer, New York, is renowned for its high vibrational energy. It's often called a "stone of attunement," as its pure, double-terminated crystalline structure is said to align the physical, mental, and spiritual bodies. Healers use Herkimer Diamond to clear blockages and to aid in the healing of the energetic body. Its luminous energy is also believed to improve dream recall and promote a deeper, more restorative sleep. It is a powerful tool for spiritual and emotional cleansing.

MAGIC AND RITUAL LORE: Though not a true diamond, the Herkimer Diamond's clarity and potency make it a prized possession for any magical practitioner. Its double-terminated nature allows it to both transmit and receive energy, making it a powerful amplifier for other crystals and for magical intent. It's an excellent stone for dreamwork, helping the user to consciously enter the dream state and to receive messages from the subconscious. Its clear, crystalline energy is perfect for scrying and divination, as it can be used to open the third eye and crown chakras, creating a clear channel for psychic information.

Copyright Asteria Books 2016

Jade

Folk Names: Stone of Heaven, Royal Jade
Color(s): Green, white, yellow, purple, black
Mohs scale: 6–7
Planetary association: Venus
Element: Earth, Water
Deity: Guanyin (Kwan Yin), Yu Huang (Jade Emporer), Chalchiuhtlicue
Powers: Wisdom, prosperity, harmony, protection, love

HEALING LORE: The ancient Chinese believed Jade to be a sacred stone of healing and longevity. Its soothing, gentle energy is a powerful balm for emotional wounds, promoting a sense of peace and harmony. Jade is also a stone of physical healing, particularly for the kidneys and heart. It's believed to aid in detoxification and to promote a healthy flow of energy throughout the body. The stone's folklore suggests it offers a sense of stability and serenity, making it a wonderful tool for those who feel overwhelmed or out of balance.

MAGIC AND RITUAL LORE: As a stone deeply connected to prosperity and wisdom, Jade is a powerful talisman for attracting abundance and good fortune. Its serene energy makes it an ideal stone for rituals of peace and harmony, as it can be used to calm and balance a sacred space. Its protective qualities are legendary; it was often carved into amulets to ward off evil spirits and negative energy. The stone's association with the divine feminine makes it a perfect tool for witches who work with goddesses of love, compassion, and wisdom.

Copyright Asteria Books 2016

Jasper

Folk Names: Supreme Nurturer, Rainbringer
Color(s): Red, green, yellow, brown, black, often patterned
Mohs scale: 7
Planetary association: Mars, Saturn
Element: Earth
Deity: Gaia, Bona Dea, Chirakan-Ixmucane, Callisto
Powers: Grounding, protection, stability, courage

HEALING LORE: Jasper is known as the "Supreme Nurturer," and its healing energy is deeply rooted in the Earth. It provides a sense of comfort and stability, particularly during times of great stress or emotional upheaval. Different colors of jasper are used for specific ailments; for example, red jasper is a stone of physical strength and vitality, while green jasper is a powerful healer for the heart. It is believed to aid in the healing of chronic illness, as its energy helps to ground and stabilize the physical body, promoting resilience and endurance.

MAGIC AND RITUAL LORE: This stone is a powerful tool for protection and grounding. Witches often use jasper to create a protective shield during ritual, as its strong, earthy energy can absorb and neutralize negative influences. Its connection to the element of Earth makes it an excellent stone for spells of stability and manifestation. In folklore, jasper was used by rain shamans to bring rain, and its energy is said to be able to connect the user to the deep wisdom of the planet.

Copyright Asteria Books 2016

Jet

Folk Names: Witches' Stone, Black Amber
Color(s): Black
Mohs scale: 2.5–4
Planetary association: Saturn
Element: Earth
Deity: Hecate, Kybele, Persephone
Powers: Protection, grounding, grief, banishing

HEALING LORE: Jet is a deeply comforting and protective healing stone. Its gentle, sorrow-absorbing energy is a powerful ally for those dealing with grief and loss. It is believed to aid in the healing of emotional wounds and to provide a sense of grounded stability during times of great upheaval. The stone's ancient, fossilized energy is said to help release deep-seated trauma and to calm an overactive mind. It is a wonderful stone for those who need a reminder that even in the darkest of times, there is still strength to be found.

MAGIC AND RITUAL LORE: Jet is a classic witch's stone, often worn in combination with amber -- and in some traditions, with bone as well. Jet is widely recognized as a powerful protection stone, guarding against negative influences, evil spirits, and even psychic attacks. It's believed to create a shield of positive energy around the wearer, offering a sense of security and safety, especially during challenging times or spiritual journeys. Jet is also associated with purification, both physically and energetically. It's thought to cleanse the aura, dispel negativity, and promote a sense of lightness and clarity. As a stone connected to the earth, jet is known for its grounding properties. It helps individuals feel more connected to the physical world, fostering a sense of stability and balance. Jet is believed to have a calming and soothing effect, helping to alleviate anxiety, nervousness, and temperamental outbursts. It's also thought to aid in processing negative emotions and promoting emotional healing. Some believe jet can enhance intuition and spiritual awareness, helping individuals connect with their inner wisdom and higher consciousness. Jet is also associated with luck, clarity during difficult times, and even pain relief (headaches and stomach problems). It is also believed to help break negative behavioral patterns and promote self-confidence.

Copyright Asteria Books 2016

Labradorite

Folk Names: Stone of Magick, Rainbow Moonstone
Color(s): Gray, black, with flashes of blue, green, gold, and purple
Mohs scale: 6–6.5
Planetary association: Moon, Uranus
Element: Water
Deity: Arianrhod
Powers: Intuition, magickal ability, spiritual awakening, protection

HEALING LORE: Labradorite is a powerful healing stone for the mind and spirit. Its shimmering, iridescent energy is a great aid for calming an overactive mind and soothing anxiety. It is a stone of transformation, believed to aid in the healing of emotional wounds and to provide a sense of courage during times of great change. Its connection to the third eye chakra makes it an excellent tool for enhancing intuition and promoting a deeper, more spiritual awareness.

MAGIC AND RITUAL LORE: This "Stone of Magick" is a staple in a witch's toolkit. Its mesmerizing flashes of color are a symbol of its true power, representing the veil between the worlds and the Witch Fire. Labradorite is used to enhance intuition and psychic abilities, making it an essential tool for divination and scrying. Its protective qualities are legendary; it is said to create a powerful shield of energy, protecting the practitioner from negative influences and psychic attack. The stone's ability to reveal hidden truths makes it a great ally for shadow work and for journeying into the depths of the subconscious mind.

Copyright Asteria Books 2016

Lapis Lazuli

Folk Names: Stone of the Stars, Royal Blue, Star Sapphire
Color(s): Deep blue with gold flecks
Mohs scale: 5–5.5
Planetary association: Jupiter, Neptune
Element: Water
Deity: Isis, Ishtar, Inanna
Powers: Truth, wisdom, communication, spiritual enlightenment

HEALING LORE: Lapis Lazuli is a powerful healing stone for the mind and spirit. Its deep, celestial energy is said to soothe and calm the spirit, and it has a long history of use for relieving stress and anxiety. It is believed to aid in the healing of the physical body, particularly for the throat, larynx, and vocal cords. The stone's connection to the third eye chakra makes it an excellent tool for enhancing intuition and promoting a deeper, more spiritual awareness. Lapis lazuli is traditionally believed to support the immune system and promote overall wellness. It's thought to alleviate pain, particularly headaches and migraines, and may assist with recovery from injury or physical trauma. Lapis Lazuli is associated with aiding conditions like insomnia, vertigo, and throat issues, and may benefit the respiratory and nervous systems. It's believed to support the thyroid gland's proper functioning.

MAGIC AND RITUAL LORE: Lapis Lazuli is a stone of truth and wisdom. Its deep blue color and shimmering gold flecks are a symbol of the night sky, making it a powerful tool for connecting with the cosmos and the divine. The stone is a great aid for spells of communication and for commanding energy with authority. In ancient times, it was used by priests and royalty to connect with the gods and to gain spiritual enlightenment. Its powerful, protective energy makes it a great warding stone for any ritual space.

Copyright Asteria Books 2016

Lava

Folk Names: Basalt, Fire Stone
Color(s): Black, dark gray
Mohs scale: 3–3.5
Planetary association: Mars, Pluto
Element: Fire, Earth
Deity: Pele
Powers: Grounding, courage, strength, emotional release

HEALING LORE: Lava stone is a primal healing tool, born of the Earth's fiery heart. Its raw, ancient energy is deeply grounding, offering a sense of stability and strength. It's often used to help release emotional trauma and to soothe an overactive mind. The stone's porous texture makes it a great carrier for essential oils, allowing it to provide a continuous, gentle therapeutic effect. Its fiery origins lend it an invigorating energy, promoting physical and mental vitality.

MAGIC AND RITUAL LORE: The stone's connection to the goddess Pele makes it a great ally for witches who work with the elements of fire and earth. Lava stones are strongly associated with grounding properties, connecting the individual to the earth's energy. This is believed to provide a sense of stability, security, and rootedness, particularly during times of change or upheaval. Due to their origin in the fiery depths of volcanoes, lava stones symbolize raw power and determination. They are believed to empower the wearer with strength and courage to face challenges and overcome obstacles. They are often used to represent shedding old patterns and embracing positive change and personal growth. They are believed to help release negative feelings like anger, resentment, and fear, promoting emotional balance and a sense of tranquility. Lava stones are considered protective, forming a shield against negative energies and influences. In some traditional Witchcraft practices, a basalt stone is embedded in a broom or gandreid used for Spirit flight.

Copyright Asteria Books 2016

Libyan Desert Glass

Folk Names: N/A
Color(s): Pale yellow, clear
Mohs scale: 6–6.5
Planetary association: Sun
Element: Fire, Air
Deity: Ra
Powers: Spiritual growth, psychic ability, manifestation, healing

HEALING LORE: Lybian Desert Glass is a powerful healing stone with a unique, high vibrational energy. It's believed to be a stone of spiritual awakening, helping to clear blockages and to promote a deeper, more spiritual awareness. Its clear, luminous energy is a great aid for calming an overactive mind and soothing anxiety. It is also a stone of physical healing, particularly for the stomach and digestive system. The stone's ancient origins and connection to the Sun gives it a naturally uplifting energy, making it an ideal stone for emotional healing and combating depression.

MAGIC AND RITUAL LORE: This rare tektite (star stone) is thought to amplify intentions and aid in manifesting desires, particularly in areas of prosperity and personal growth. It is believed to resonate with the solar plexus chakra, promoting resilience, confidence, and transformation. It's also said to activate the light body and connect with ancient wisdom. Some believe it creates a protective shield around the aura, warding off negative energies and energy vampires. While also linked to higher consciousness, Libyan Desert Glass is also associated with grounding, connecting the spiritual and physical realms, and bridging different worlds. It is believed to facilitate personal transformation, including overcoming fears, releasing what no longer serves, and stepping into one's true potential.

Copyright Asteria Books 2016

Lodestone

Other Names: Magnetite, Ston of Hercules, Leading Stone, Loadstone
Planet: Saturn, Mars
Other Astrological: Virgo, Capricorn, Aries
Element: Earth
Deities: Hercules/Herakles, Venus and Mars, Ancestors
Magical Properties: Attraction, Manifestation, Protection, Grounding, Empowerment, Communication

MYTHS: A Roman myth tells of an iron statue of the war god Mars and a lodestone statue of the love goddess Venus that were drawn to each other at a festival. The ancient Greek philosopher Thales, who was one of the first to study magnetism, believed that lodestone had a "psyche" or a "breath of life" because of its mysterious power to move other objects.

HEALING: L is placed on the body to draw out pain and inflammation. This belief is based on its magnetic properties, which are thought to rebalance the body's energy fields. Due to its high iron content, it is believed to be beneficial for blood-related issues, helping to improve circulation and vitality. The stone's grounding energy is said to help reduce stress and anxiety, promoting a sense of calm and stability. Lodestone is believed to help balance the body's magnetic fields and energy flows, leading to a feeling of overall harmony and well-being.

MAGIC AND RITUAL: Lodestone's primary magical property is its ability to attract and draw things to the user. This is often used in spells and rituals to attract money, love, success, and good fortune. Placing a lodestone in a cash box or a wallet is a common folk practice to attract wealth. Lodestone provides strong grounding and protection. It is used to create a psychic shield, ward off negative energy, and anchor a person's energy to the physical world, making it a good tool for those who feel uncentered or disconnected. Lodestone is used to "feed" or "charge" other stones, particularly iron-based ones like hematite. It is also believed to empower magical tools and talismans, infusing them with its powerful magnetic energy. Some traditions believe that lodestone can help open channels to communicate with the spirit world, especially in ancestor veneration rituals.

Copyright Asteria Books 2025

Malachite

Folk Names: Stone of Transformation, Peacock Ore
Color(s): Dark green, often with bands of lighter green
Mohs scale: 3.5–4
Planetary association: Venus, Pluto
Element: Earth
Deity: Hathor, Venus, Mistress of the Copper Mountain
Powers: Transformation, protection, emotional healing, prosperity

HEALING LORE: Malachite is a powerful healing stone for the emotions. Its rich, deep green energy is a great aid for calming the mind and soothing anxiety. It is a stone of transformation, believed to aid in the healing of emotional wounds and to provide a sense of courage during times of great change. Its connection to the heart chakra makes it an excellent tool for enhancing intuition and promoting a deeper, more spiritual awareness. Important Note: Malachite contains copper and can be toxic if ingested. Do not use in elixirs via the direct method.

MAGIC AND RITUAL LORE: Malachite is known as a stone of transformation, encouraging personal growth and positive change. It can help individuals embrace new beginnings and overcome fears. Malachite is believed to shield against negative energies and electromagnetic pollution. It's thought to absorb negativity and protect the wearer. Malachite has been historically used for protection against the evil eye and as a remedy for stomach ailments. It is also believed to stimulate creativity and imagination.

Copyright Asteria Books 2016

Marble

Color(s): White, gray, black, pink, green, yellow
Mohs scale: 3–5
Planetary association: Moon
Element: Earth
Deity: Hephaestos, Aphrodite, Galatea
Powers: Clarity, stability, grounding, protection

HEALING LORE: While not traditionally recognized for physical healing properties, marble is believed to have psychological benefits and can be used in holistic practices. It's been associated with detoxification, pain relief, and emotional balance. The calcium content in marble is believed to help the body flush out toxins. Marble is thought to help harmonize emotions, bringing calm and serenity, especially during stressful times. Marble stones are used in massage therapy to reduce inflammation, relieve pain, and encourage blood flow. Marble is suggested to ease pain related to arthritis, osteoporosis, and joint disorders.

MAGIC AND RITUAL LORE: Marble is a classic stone for altars and sacred spaces. Its smooth, cool surface provides a stable and grounded foundation for ritual work. Its connection to the element of Earth makes it a great stone for spells of protection and grounding, as it can be used to create a shield of energy that is both powerful and subtle. Marble is often linked to a calming and balancing energy, promoting inner peace and emotional stability. Marble is thought to enhance meditation practices, supporting deeper states of focus and aiding in the recall of dreams. Marble is believed to promote self-mastery and enhance one's common sense and ability to make sound decisions.

Copyright Asteria Books 2016

Megalodon Teeth

Folk Names: Giant Shark Tooth, Stone of the Deep
Color(s): Black, gray, brown, red
Mohs scale: 5–6
Planetary association: Saturn, Mars
Element: Water, Fire
Deity: Poseidon, ancient sea gods
Powers: Immense protection, immense power, authority, ancient wisdom

HEALING LORE: Megalodon Teeth are an immensely powerful healing stone, believed to promote physical strength and vitality. They are often used in healing practices to aid in the strength of bones and teeth, drawing on their unique, hardened form. Their ancient energy is a powerful tool for releasing blockages and for stimulating a healthy flow of energy throughout the body. Their connection to the elements of Water and Fire gives them a harmonizing energy, and they are said to be particularly useful for ailments of the throat and lungs.

MAGIC AND RITUAL LORE: Some cultures believe megalodon teeth act as powerful talismans, bringing good luck and warding off evil or negative energy. Shark teeth, including those from megalodons, are believed to offer protection from danger, both physical and spiritual. Some traditions associate shark teeth with cleansing and purifying energies, helping to release negative emotions and attachments. Megalodon teeth can be seen as a link to the primal instincts and the power of the ocean's depths. Fossilized shark teeth can be used to access past lives or connect with the wisdom of the Earth. They can be used in shamanic practices to connect with the energy of the shark and the spirit world.

Copyright Asteria Books 2016

Moldavite

Folk Names: Grail Stone, Bouteille Stone, Vltavin, Bokemian Peridot
Color(s): Olive green, dark green
Mohs scale: 5.5
Planetary association: Uranus
Element: Air
Deity: Lucifer, Tubelo, Michael, Cintamani, Venus of Willendorf, Hermes Trismegistus
Powers: Transformation, spiritual evolution, psychic ability, otherworldly communication

HEALING LORE: Moldavite is an incredibly powerful healing stone with a unique, high vibrational energy. It is believed to be a stone of spiritual awakening, helping to clear blockages and to promote a deeper, more spiritual awareness. Its clear, luminous energy is a great aid for calming an overactive mind and soothing anxiety. It is also a stone of physical healing, particularly for the stomach and digestive system. The stone's otherworldly origins and connection to the cosmos gives it a naturally uplifting energy, making it an ideal stone for emotional healing and combating depression.

MAGIC AND RITUAL LORE: Moldavite is a catalyst for rapid spiritual growth, helping to release old patterns and beliefs. It facilitates communication with the divine, guides, and extraterrestrial energies, aiding in spiritual awakening and understanding. Moldavite can enhance manifestation abilities, bring unexpected solutions, and promote mental clarity. Artifacts of moldavite have been found near the Venus of Willendorf, a Paleolithic sculpture, suggesting its use in rituals associated with the divine feminine. Moldavite can activate and balance all chakras, particularly the heart and third eye chakras. It helps release energetic blockages and emotional trauma, promoting overall healing and well-being.

Copyright Asteria Books 2016

Moonstone

Folk Names: Stone of the Moon, Adularia
Color(s): Clear, white, blue, gray, peach, rainbow
Mohs scale: 6–6.5
Planetary association: Moon
Element: Water
Deity: Diana, Selene, all lunar goddesses
Powers: Intuition, emotional balance, feminine energy, love

HEALING LORE: Moonstone is a deeply compassionate healing stone, primarily known for its ability to Moonstone is believed to help individuals understand their emotions and make more informed decisions by enhancing their intuition. Its gentle, soothing energy can help reduce feelings of stress, tension, and anxiety, promoting a sense of inner peace. Moonstone is thought to help individuals regulate their emotions, fostering emotional stability and reducing emotional turmoil. Moonstone is often used to support women's reproductive health, including regulating hormones, menstrual cycles, and easing PMS symptoms. It's also believed to be helpful for those trying to conceive. Moonstone can help increase energy levels and improve overall vitality. It's believed to aid in improving digestive health and reducing inflammation.

MAGIC AND RITUAL LORE: As the "Stone of the Moon," moonstone's magical properties are deeply tied to the element of Water and the divine feminine. It is a powerful tool for witches who work with the moon, the tides, and the ebb and flow of emotions. Its calming energy makes it an excellent stone for meditation, helping the practitioner to access a deeper, more intuitive state of consciousness. Placing moonstone under the pillow is said to encourage restful sleep and pleasant dreams, which can be helpful for those experiencing insomnia or nightmares. Moonstone is believed to enhance love, understanding, and emotional connection between partners. It is thought to support individuals embarking on new chapters in their lives, providing a sense of optimism and hope.

Copyright Asteria Books 2016

Morganite

Folk Names: Pink Beryl, Rose Beryl, Pink Emerald
Color(s): Pink, peach, salmon
Mohs scale: 7.5-8
Planetary association: Venus, Moon
Element: Water
Deity: Aphrodite, Ishtar, Quan Yin
Powers: Divine Love, Emotional Healing, Compassion, Harmony, Patience, Serenity

HEALING LORE: Morganite is the ultimate crystal for the heart and circulatory system. It is said to ease stress and anxiety, particularly in matters of the heart, and can be used to alleviate the symptoms of panic attacks. Place it on your chest during meditation to gently clear and activate the heart chakra, allowing for emotional release and healing. This stone promotes a sense of peace and can be beneficial for those struggling with grief or deep-seated emotional trauma, providing a soft landing for a heavy heart.

MAGIC AND RITUAL LORE: In ritual, morganite is a powerful stone for attracting and deepening loving relationships, both platonic and romantic. It's perfect for spells of self-love and radical acceptance. Place it on your altar with a lit pink candle to attract a soulmate or to heal discord in an existing partnership. Use it in a crystal grid for creating a harmonious home environment. Morganite's energy is not forceful; it works through gentle attraction and a deep, abiding sense of peace. Carry it to cultivate compassion and patience in daily interactions. It opens the heart chakra to receive and give love in its purest form, unburdened by ego or expectation. Morganite helps us see the beauty in every emotional experience, transforming pain into wisdom and frustration into patience. Its soft, nurturing energy is like a warm, loving embrace for the wounded inner child, reminding us that we are always worthy of love, especially our own.

Copyright Asteria Books 2016

Mother-of-Pearl

Other Names: Nacre
Color(s): White, iridescent, pink, blue, gray
Mohs scale: 2.5–4.5
Planetary association: Moon
Element: Water
Deity: Varies
Powers: Emotional healing, prosperity, protection, spiritual balance

HEALING LORE: Mother of pearl is known for its gentle, soothing energy, which can help calm emotions, reduce stress, and promote a sense of inner peace. It is believed to help individuals process and balance their emotions, fostering a more positive outlook. It is believed to promote skin regeneration, improve skin tone, and help with issues like acne, pigmentation, and age spots. Some believe it can aid digestion and soothe inflammation in the digestive system. Mother of pearl is sometimes associated with alleviating joint and muscle pain. It is believed to strengthen the immune system and potentially aid in recovery from illnesses.

MAGIC AND RITUAL LORE: Mother-of-Pearl is a powerful stone of emotional balance and harmony. It is a staple in spells of peace, tranquility, and emotional healing. In ritual, it is placed on the altar or carried as a talisman to create a sacred space that is filled with light and spiritual energy. Its connection to the Moon and the Triple Goddess makes it a great stone for witches who work with the divine feminine and for those who seek to embody the grace, compassion, and wisdom of the goddess. Mother-of-Pearl is also a stone of communication, used to help a person speak their truth with clarity and confidence.

Copyright Asteria Books 2016

Obsidian

Folk Names: Volcanic Glass, Stone of Truth, Apache's Tears
Color(s): Black, black with flecks of white (snowflake), black with rainbow sheen (rainbow)
Mohs scale: 5–5.5
Planetary association: Pluto, Saturn
Element: Earth, Fire
Deity: Varies
Powers: Protection, grounding, truth, shadow work

HEALING LORE: Obsidian, a volcanic glass, is believed to possess various healing properties, particularly in emotional and spiritual realms. It's known for its grounding, protective, and purifying effects, aiding in emotional release, mental clarity, and physical well-being. Obsidian is a powerful protective stone, shielding against negative energies and psychic attacks. It helps ground individuals to the present moment and promotes a sense of stability. Obsidian is thought to help release emotional blockages, past traumas, and limiting beliefs. It encourages self-reflection and helps individuals understand their true selves. Obsidian is used in lithotherapy to relieve pain, particularly muscle pain associated with conditions like arthritis. Some believe it aids in detoxification and supports the digestive system. It is thought to improve blood circulation and aid in tissue regeneration.

MAGIC AND RITUAL LORE: Obsidian is a powerful shield against negative energies, psychic attacks, and emotional harm. It connects one to the Earth, promoting stability and a sense of security. It enhances mental clarity, aids in decision-making, and encourages introspection. Obsidian supports self-discovery, expands consciousness, and opens new horizons. It can be used in meditation to ground, clear negative energy, and stabilize the mind. Some believe obsidian can be placed under the pillow to guide journeys through the spiritual realms. Obsidian is used to clear negative energy from spaces and the body. Golden Sheen Obsidian also attracts wealth and prosperity, aligns personal power with the Divine, and helps manifest one's true calling

Copyright Asteria Books 2016

Onyx

Folk Names: Stone of Longevity, Black Onyx
Color(s): Black, black with white bands
Mohs scale: 7
Planetary association: Saturn
Element: Earth
Deity: Varies
Powers: Protection, grounding, self-control, strength

HEALING LORE: Onyx is believed to strengthen bones, teeth, and nails. It is associated with increased physical stamina and endurance, making it a talisman for athletes. Onyx is said to support the nervous system and may aid in recovery from illness or fatigue. Some believe it can help with childbirth, foot and lower body ailments, and even glaucoma, though this should be used a spiritual healing supplement to more traditional approaches. It is believed to ground and stabilize one's energy, promoting a sense of security and connection to the earth. Onyx is thought to help balance emotions, soothe the mind, and promote inner peace, particularly during stressful times. Onyx is believed to help heal past traumas and emotional wounds.

MAGIC AND RITUAL LORE: Onyx is known for its grounding properties, helping to connect the wearer to the earth's energy and create a sense of stability. It's considered a protective stone, believed to absorb negative energy and psychic attacks, guarding against harm and misfortune. Onyx is thought to help release negative emotions, promote emotional stability, and ease grief and traumatic memories. Onyx is believed to sharpen mental focus, improve concentration, and enhance memory. It is associated with physical and mental strength, promoting self-control, willpower, and perseverance. Some believe onyx can stimulate intuitive powers and aid in spiritual growth. Black onyx is sometimes called the "stone of longevity." It's also believed to attract prosperity and abundance. Onyx can boost self-confidence and help overcome fears. Onyx is often used by politicians, leaders, and those in influential positions for its ability to enhance mental clarity and strategic thinking. Black onyx is considered a protective stone for travelers, warding off accidents and misfortune.

Copyright Asteria Books 2016

Opal

Folk Names: Eye Stone, Rainbow Jewel
Color(s): All colors of the rainbow, with a unique play of light
Mohs scale: 5.5–6.5
Planetary association: Neptune
Element: Water
Deity: Zeus, Cupid, Venus, Persephone
Powers: Intuition, creativity, transformation, emotional healing

HEALING LORE: Opals are believed to help release emotional blockages and promote emotional healing.
They are thought to encourage self-love, self-esteem, and acceptance. Some sources suggest opals can soothe grief and comfort those who are grieving. Different colors of opal are associated with specific emotional benefits. Blue Opals may help with throat and thyroid issues, improving communication. Yellow Opals promote creativity, spontaneity, and a sense of fun. Green or Pink Opals may reduce jealousy and grudges. Owyhee Opal helps release negativity and promotes kindness, love, and compassion. Some believe opals can strengthen the immune system and improve memory. Certain types, like black opals, are thought to soothe skin irritations and regulate body hydration. Opals may also be used to treat eye conditions and improve vision. Olive Opal is believed to reduce fever and infections. Purple Opal is thought to aid respiratory illnesses, lung damage, and asthma.

MAGIC AND RITUAL LORE: ften associated with creativity, passion, and amplifying emotions, precious opal is thought to help individuals express their true selves. Known for its vibrant energy, fire opal is believed to stimulate creativity and bring forth ecstatic vibrations for spiritual enlightenment. A powerful stone for protection and manifestation, black opal is said to shield the aura from negative influences and enhance psychic abilities. Opals are known to help regulate emotions, promote inner peace, and release emotional blockages. Many believe opals enhance intuition, spiritual insight, and connection to higher consciousness. Opals are thought to stimulate creativity, artistic pursuits, and the free flow of ideas. Certain opals, like black opal, are believed to shield from negative energies and psychic attacks.

Copyright Asteria Books 2016

Pearl

Folk Names: variations of Margaret mean Pearl
Color(s): White, cream, pink, black
Mohs scale: 2.5–4.5
Planetary association: Moon
Element: Water
Deity: Aphrodite, Venus
Powers: Emotional balance, harmony, purity, love, prosperity

HEALING LORE: Pearl is a deeply calming and soothing stone, known for its ability to bring a sense of peace and emotional balance. It is believed to calm the nerves and to aid in the healing of stress-related ailments. Its connection to the throat chakra makes it a great stone for promoting peaceful and harmonious communication, and its gentle, flowing energy is said to help release anger and emotional turmoil. It is also a stone of wisdom, believed to help a person to see a clear path forward and to make decisions that are in their highest good. Because of their soothing properties, pearls are often used in healing applications related to the skin, digestion, UTI's, bipolar disorder, and inflammatory conditions like arthritis.

MAGIC AND RITUAL LORE: Pearls are strongly linked to the moon and water, symbolizing divine feminine energy, nurturing, and fertility. Their radiant, unblemished surfaces are often seen as symbols of purity, innocence, and inner beauty. Some believe pearls can deflect negative energy and offer psychic protection. Pearls are associated with love, wisdom, and inner beauty, often exchanged as gifts to express deep affection. They are thought to calm and soothe, promoting serenity and emotional balance. Pearls are believed to enhance intuition and connection with one's inner wisdom. They are often associated with loyalty and faithfulness, making them popular for wedding jewelry.

Copyright Asteria Books 2016

Peridot

Folk Names: Olivine, Chrysolite, Evening Emerald
Color(s): Olive green, yellow-green
Mohs scale: 6.5–7
Planetary association: Sun, Venus
Element: Earth, Fire
Deity: Pele, Pax, Lakshmi, Apollo
Powers: Protection, prosperity, healing, spiritual cleansing

HEALING LORE: Peridot is believed to have a calming effect on the mind, helping to alleviate stress, anxiety, and even depression. It is thought to help balance emotions, dispel negative feelings like anger and resentment, and encourage feelings of joy and contentment. Peridot can boost self-esteem and encourage individuals to embrace their authentic selves. It is believed to help release past emotional wounds, guilt, or regret, facilitating emotional healing and personal growth. Peridot is associated with mental clarity and focus, making it useful for mindfulness practices and meditation. Peridot is thought to aid in physical detoxification, particularly of the liver, and help with issues related to the kidneys, bladder, gall bladder, and stomach. It is believed to have regenerative properties, aiding in cell and tissue repair. Peridot is associated with strengthening the body and enhancing biological functioning, potentially improving the immune system. It may help with stomach pain, improve metabolism, and ease digestive issues. Some believe it can help with skin problems like acne, blemishes, and inflammation. Peridot is thought to balance blood pressure and improve circulation, potentially benefiting heart health.

MAGIC AND RITUAL LORE: It helps individuals forgive themselves and others, fostering emotional healing and reconciliation. Peridot is thought to awaken intuition and connect individuals with higher realms of consciousness. It aligns the heart and solar plexus chakras, promoting love, compassion, self-esteem, and willpower. Some believe peridot can attract good luck, wealth, and success. Peridot is considered a protective stone, warding off negativity and harmful influences. It is believed to enhance memory, comprehension, and concentration, making it beneficial for students. Peridot is associated with love, compassion, and forgiveness, which can contribute to stronger relationships.

Copyright Asteria Books 2016

Petrified Wood

Folk Names: Fossil Wood, Tree Quartz, Wood Agate, Woodstone
Color(s): Brown, gray, red, green, black
Mohs scale: 7
Planetary association: Saturn
Element: Earth, Akasha
Deity: Dryads, Tree spirits
Powers: Ancestral work, grounding, transformation, past life recall

HEALING LORE: Petrified Wood embodies the grounding and stabilizing power of the Earth. Its ancient, fossilized energy is a powerful tool for promoting physical and mental stability. It is often used to soothe anxiety and to calm an overactive mind, offering a sense of deep-rooted strength. It is believed to aid in the healing of bone and joint ailments, drawing on the natural strength of the original tree. It is a stone of patience and inner growth, reminding the user that slow and steady progress leads to profound transformation.

MAGIC AND RITUAL LORE: As a stone that bridges the realms of wood and stone, Petrified Wood is an unparalleled tool for ancestral work and for connecting with ancient tree spirits. It is a powerful talisman for spells of deep transformation, helping the practitioner to shed old habits and embrace new beginnings. In ritual, it is placed on the altar to connect with the wisdom of the earth and the memory of the past. It is an excellent stone for past-life recall.

Copyright Asteria Books 2016

Pyrite

Folk Names: Fool's Gold, Healer's Gold, Firestone
Planet: Mars, Sun
Other Astrological: Leo
Element: Fire, Earth
Deities: Hephaestus, Vulcan, Pluto, Lakshmi, Apollo, Mars
Magical Properties: Prosperity, Protection, Grounding

HEALING LORE: In modern metaphysical practices, it is believed to help block or shield against electromagnetic pollution from computers and other devices. Pyrite is believed to be beneficial for the respiratory system, helping with conditions like bronchitis and asthma. It is thought to increase oxygen supply to the blood and strengthen the lungs. It is said to support the circulatory system, helping to improve blood flow and oxygenation throughout the body. Some practitioners believe pyrite can boost the immune system and help the body fight off infections. Pyrite is considered an energizing stone that can combat fatigue and burnout. It is thought to increase stamina and overall physical vitality. It is sometimes used to aid with digestion and reduce bloating or digestive discomfort.

MAGIC AND RITUAL LORE: Pyrite is famously known as a stone of prosperity and abundance. It is believed to attract money, success, and good fortune, often placed in homes or offices to draw in financial opportunities. The stone's grounding yet fiery energy is said to help a person manifest their ideas into physical reality. It encourages taking action and provides the willpower needed to achieve goals. Pyrite is considered a powerful protective stone that creates a defensive shield against negative energy, emotional vampires, and psychic attacks. It is often used to ward off jealousy and envy from others.

Copyright Asteria Books 2025

Rose Quartz

Folk Names: Stone of Love, Pink Quartz, Bohemian Ruby
Color(s): Pink, rosy pink
Mohs scale: 7
Planetary association: Venus
Element: Water
Deity: Aphrodite, Venus
Powers: Love, emotional healing, compassion, self-love

HEALING LORE: Rose Quartz is a gentle, compassionate healing stone, primarily known for its ability to heal the heart. Its soft, gentle energy is a powerful balm for emotional wounds, promoting a sense of peace and harmony. It is a stone of emotional healing, believed to aid in the healing of grief and emotional pain. Its connection to the heart chakra makes it an excellent tool for enhancing intuition and promoting a deeper, more spiritual awareness.

MAGIC AND RITUAL LORE: Rose Quartz is a powerful stone of love and emotional healing. It is a staple in spells of love, compassion, and self-love. In ritual, it is placed on the altar or carried as a talisman to attract good fortune and help manifest your desires. Its connection to the heart makes it a great stone for spells of love and for commanding energy with authority. In folklore, Eros/Cupid was said to sometimes gift this stone to humans in order to foster love, and Isis is credited with using this stone to preserve her youth and beauty. Rose quartz is also an excellent tool for scrying, especially when the querent comes with questions of the heart.

Copyright Asteria Books 2016

Ruby

Folk Names: King of Gems
Color(s): Red, dark pink, purple-red
Mohs scale: 9
Planetary association: Sun, Mars
Element: Fire
Deity: Isis, Aphrodite, Ares, Sekhmet, Krishna
Powers: Passion, protection, strength, vitality, courage

HEALING LORE: Ruby is believed to strengthen the heart, improve circulation, and regulate blood pressure. The stone's red color is linked to increased energy, making it helpful for combating fatigue and lethargy. Ruby is thought to aid with menstrual pain, fertility issues, and reproductive health, according to some sources. It's believed to assist in detoxifying the body, including the blood and lymph system. Ruby is also thought to support digestion, metabolism, and the adrenal glands. It is associated with increasing passion, enthusiasm, and a zest for life. Rubies are believed to boost self-confidence, courage, and inner strength. Ruby is used to treat fever and infections, according to some traditions. It is also associated with improving eye health. Ruby can help with mental clarity, focus, and balancing the brain hemispheres.

MAGIC AND RITUAL LORE: Rubies are believed to protect against psychic attacks, negative energy, and evil spirits. They are thought to shield the home from fire and intruders and can be worn discreetly for personal protection. The stone is associated with courage, bravery, and strength, helping to overcome fear and doubt. It is believed to inspire confidence and the ability to stand up for oneself and others. Rubies are strongly linked to love, passion, and romance. They are thought to enhance relationships, promote harmony and understanding, and rekindle love and passion in existing relationships. They are believed to invigorate the body and mind, increasing motivation and passion for life. Some believe rubies help ground spiritual energies, connecting one's physical self with their spiritual self. They are thought to activate the base chakra and stimulate the crown chakra, promoting spiritual wisdom. In ancient times, rubies were believed to make warriors invincible and protect them from wounds. Rubies are associated with wealth, prosperity, and good fortune in some cultures.

Copyright Asteria Books 2016

Salt

Color(s): White, pink, clear, grey
Mohs scale: 2.5
Planetary association: Moon
Element: Earth, Water
Deity: Huixtocihuatl, Salacia, Ma'l Oyattsik'i, Amphitrite, Hatta
Powers: Purification, protection, grounding, cleansing

HEALING LORE: Salt has been a valued healing tool for centuries, used for both its physical and spiritual properties. Its natural antiseptic qualities, stemming from its ability to draw out moisture from bacteria, made it a go-to remedy for disinfecting wounds in ancient times. Today, salt's healing uses are wide-ranging. Soaking in a warm salt bath, especially with Epsom salt, can help relieve sore muscles, reduce inflammation, and calm the nerves thanks to its magnesium content. Gargling with a saltwater solution is a proven way to soothe a sore throat and fight mouth infections. For skin conditions like eczema and psoriasis, baths with mineral-rich Dead Sea salts can reduce inflammation and moisturize. Additionally, halotherapy, or salt therapy, involves inhaling fine salt particles to help clear airways and improve lung function for conditions like asthma and allergies.

MAGIC AND RITUAL LORE: Salt's magical and ritual uses are ancient and diverse, rooted in its properties of purification and preservation. Salt is a primary tool for cleansing spaces, objects, and people. Its crystalline energy is believed to absorb negative energy, making it ideal for clearing away spiritual clutter. A common practice is burying magical tools like crystals in salt to remove unwanted energies. Salt is a powerful protective barrier. In many traditions, a line of salt is drawn across thresholds, windowsills, and doorways to prevent malevolent spirits or negative influences from entering. Creating a salt circle during a ritual is a way to create a sacred, protected space. Symbolically connected to the earth, salt can be used to ground energy and bring stability to a ritual or meditation. It helps to anchor intentions into the physical world. Just as it preserves food, salt is a symbol of permanence. It is used in rituals to strengthen a vow or a magical working, representing a lasting, unbreakable bond. Black salt, a specific blend often made with charcoal, is a potent tool for banishing, protection, and breaking hexes. It is used to get rid of negativity or unwanted guests. Salt is also added to purification baths to wash away negative energy from the body and mind.

Copyright Asteria Books 2016

Sapphire

Color(s): Blue, pink, yellow, green, violet, orange, white/clear, black
Mohs scale: 9
Planetary association: Saturn, Jupiter, Venus
Element: Water, Air
Deity: Apollo, Jupiter, Saturn, Athena, Shani
Powers: Wisdom, spiritual enlightenment, intuition, protection

HEALING LORE: The stone's serene and calming energy is thought to alleviate stress, anxiety, and feelings of depression. It is believed to bring a sense of peace and tranquility, helping to restore emotional balance. Historically, sapphire was used to treat ailments of the eyes and was believed to improve eyesight. It is also thought to help alleviate headaches and migraines. In some traditional practices, sapphire is used to cool and soothe inflamed areas of the body. Due to its association with the throat chakra, sapphire is believed to be beneficial for throat and thyroid issues.

MAGIC AND RITUAL LORE: Sapphire is often called the "wisdom stone." It's believed to calm the mind, remove unwanted thoughts, and enhance mental focus. This makes it a valuable aid for students, scholars, and anyone seeking to gain deeper insight or make clear decisions. Historically, sapphire was seen as a powerful amulet against negative energies, psychic attacks, and ill-wishing. It was worn to protect the wearer from envy, fraud, and even physical harm. In some traditions, it was thought to lose its luster if worn by an impure person, thus acting as a detector of deceit. The stone's celestial blue color connects it to the heavens and the divine. It is believed to stimulate the third eye and crown chakras, enhancing psychic abilities, intuition, and communication with higher realms. Sapphire has long been a symbol of loyalty, truth, and honesty. It is often used in rituals to strengthen vows, ensure fidelity in relationships, and encourage integrity in oneself and others. Sapphire has been used to adorn the rings of royalty and clergy for centuries, symbolizing their divine right to rule and their connection to heaven.

Copyright Asteria Books 2016

Selenite

Folk Names: Stone of the Moon, Gypsum
Color(s): White, clear, iridescent
Mohs scale: 2
Planetary association: Moon
Element: Water
Deity: Selene, Diana, all lunar goddesses
Powers: Cleansing, purification, spiritual connection, angelic communication

HEALING LORE: Selenite's gentle, calming energy is thought to soothe the nervous system, alleviate stress and anxiety, and promote emotional healing. It can help release old emotional wounds and bring a sense of peace and tranquility. The crystal's soothing energy is believed to clear mental clutter, bringing a sense of calm and clarity. It can help in making decisions, improving concentration, and fostering a clear perspective on life's challenges. Selenite's gentle, calming energy is thought to soothe the nervous system, alleviate stress and anxiety, and promote emotional healing. It can help release old emotional wounds and bring a sense of peace and tranquility.

MAGIC AND RITUAL LORE: Selenite is celebrated as a stone of pure white light. It's known for its ability to clear negative or stagnant energy from people, spaces, and other crystals. Unlike most crystals, selenite is self-cleansing and can be used to recharge other stones simply by placing them on a selenite plate or near a selenite wand. Place selenite wands or towers in the corners of a room or by doorways to create a protective grid that purifies the space and shields it from negative energy. A common practice is to "sweep" a selenite wand from the top of your head to your feet, a few inches away from your body, to cleanse and clear your aura of any unwanted energies. Placing a piece of selenite under your pillow or on your bedside table is believed to promote restful sleep and ward off nightmares by creating a serene and protective environment.

Copyright Asteria Books 2016

Seraphinite

Folk Names: Stone of the Angels, Green Chlorite, Angel Wing Stone
Color(s): Dark green with silvery, feathered chatoyancy
Mohs scale: 2-4
Planetary association: Neptune
Element: Earth
Deity: Angels, Sophia, Persephone
Powers: Angelic communication, emotional healing, spiritual growth, cleansing

HEALING LORE: Seraphinite is known for its ability to bring harmony and peace, helping to alleviate stress, anxiety, and depression. The stone gently cleanses the heart chakra, encouraging self-love and a balanced emotional state. It assists in releasing old emotional wounds and attachments that no longer serve a person's spiritual growth. The crystal has a restorative effect on the body, promoting cellular regeneration. It's thought to aid in the detoxification of the kidneys and liver, stimulate metabolism, and strengthen the heart and lungs. Seraphinite is believed to activate the spinal cord, releasing muscle tension, especially in the neck and shoulders. It infuses the body with light energy, promoting a sense of wholeness and well-being.

MAGIC AND RITUAL LORE: The most prominent magical property of seraphinite is its ability to facilitate communication with angels and spirit guides. It is believed to act as a bridge between the physical world and the angelic realms, making it easier to receive divine guidance, wisdom, and protection. Seraphinite is a stone of spiritual growth. It's believed to help a person recognize their spiritual path and purpose. It promotes self-healing on a deep, cellular level, working to dissolve negative emotional patterns and align the individual with their highest good. The stone is said to be a potent tool for cleansing the aura, clearing away any stagnant or negative energies. Its protective qualities are believed to guard against psychic attacks and negative influences.

Copyright Asteria Books 2016

Shark Teeth

Folk Names: Stone of the Sea, Serpent's Tongue
Color(s): Gray, black, brown, blue
Mohs scale: 5–6
Planetary association: Saturn, Mars
Element: Water, Fire
Deity: Poseidon, Shark deities
Powers: Protection, strength, courage, banishing

HEALING LORE: Fossilized Shark Teeth are an energizing and protective stone, believed to promote physical strength and vitality. They are often used in healing practices to aid in the strength of bones and teeth, drawing on their unique, hardened form. Ancient cultures revered shark teeth as symbols of protection, courage, and resilience, often associating them with warding off negative energy and providing a sense of security. Some believe shark teeth can help alleviate pain and promote physical healing, though this is less widely cited than the emotional benefits.

MAGIC AND RITUAL LORE: Shark teeth are believed to act as talismans, protecting the wearer from negative energies, harmful influences, and even physical danger. They are thought to deflect envy, anger, and fear, creating a shield of energy around the wearer. This protective quality is why they were often carried by sailors and travelers for safe journeys. Shark teeth are seen as symbols of strength, resilience, and the power of survival. They embody the primal spirit of the shark, reminding the wearer to be fierce, adaptable, and confident in the face of challenges. Shark teeth symbolize adaptability and change, encouraging flexibility and resilience in navigating life's transitions. They can be used to release old patterns and embrace new beginnings, facilitating personal transformation. This connection to change makes them useful for those undergoing major life shifts or ancestral work.

Copyright Asteria Books 2016

Smoky Quartz

Folk Names: Smoky topaz, Morion, Cairngorm, Whiskey Quartz
Color(s): Smoky brown, black, clear
Mohs scale: 7
Planetary association: Saturn, Pluto
Element: Earth
Deity: Hecate, Persephone, Crom Dubh
Powers: Grounding, protection, emotional healing, shadow work

HEALING LORE: Smoky quartz promotes a sense of practicality and organization. It can help clear a chaotic mind, allowing for more rational thought and the ability to solve problems with a clear head. The stone is thought to be detoxifying on all levels, assisting with the elimination of toxins from the body and supporting the digestive system. Smoky quartz is often used to help relieve chronic pain, muscle cramps, headaches, and tension in the back and shoulders. Many believe that smoky quartz can help protect against electromagnetic smog from computers, phones, and other electronics. It is also associated with benefiting the reproductive system, muscles, and nerve tissue.

MAGIC AND RITUAL LORE: As a stone of the Root Chakra, smoky quartz is one of the most effective tools for grounding spiritual energy. It helps to anchor you to the Earth, providing a sense of stability and security. This is particularly useful for those who feel scattered, overwhelmed, or uncentered. Smoky quartz is famous for its ability to absorb and transmute negative energy. It acts as a powerful shield, protecting the aura from psychic attacks, emotional stress, and negative influences. It is often used to clear a space of bad vibes and to convert negative emotions into positive ones. Beyond just absorbing negativity, smoky quartz is also used to create a protective barrier against unwanted entities and influences. It is a stone for warding off ill-wishing and for providing a sense of safety during spiritual work. Smoky quartz is a good stone for manifestation because it helps to ground your intentions into physical reality. By clearing away mental and emotional blockages, it allows you to focus your energy on what you want to create and bring it into being. In some traditions, particularly with the darker "morion" variety, smoky quartz has been used for scrying and divination. Its transparent yet smoky nature is believed to aid in seeing beyond the physical world.

Copyright Asteria Books 2016

Sodalite

Folk Names: Princess Blue, Poor Man's Lapis, Bluestone, Hackmanite
Color(s): Blue, violet, white/grey
Mohs scale: 5.5–6
Planetary association: Neptune, Jupiter
Element: Water
Deity: Athena, the Muses, Thoth
Powers: Intuition, wisdom, communication, spiritual enlightenment

HEALING LORE: Sodalite is strongly associated with the throat chakra. It is believed to help you speak your truth and to express your thoughts and feelings clearly and without fear. It can also help you become a better listener. Sodalite is often used to address thyroid issues and to balance the metabolism. It is believed to have a positive effect on the endocrine system. The stone's calming energy makes it a good choice for those who suffer from insomnia or sleep disturbances. Placing a piece under your pillow is believed to promote a peaceful, restful sleep. Sodalite is thought to help regulate blood pressure and to aid in fluid balance within the body. Because of its connection to the throat chakra, it is believed to be beneficial for a sore throat, hoarseness, and other issues affecting the vocal cords.

MAGIC AND RITUAL LORE: Sodalite is believed to open the third eye and connect you to your intuition. It is a powerful stone for spiritual growth, helping to deepen meditation and bring a greater understanding of your spiritual path. It can also help in connecting with your spirit guides. Known as the "poet's stone," sodalite is strongly associated with the throat chakra. It encourages you to speak your truth and express yourself with clarity and confidence. It helps you articulate your feelings and ideas without fear of judgment. Sodalite's energy helps to balance the head and the heart. It clears mental clutter and brings a sense of logic and objectivity to emotional situations. This makes it an excellent stone for those who need to make rational decisions without being swayed by overwhelming emotions. y helping to clear mental blockages and promoting clear thought, sodalite is said to inspire creativity and new ideas. It is a good stone for writers, artists, and anyone seeking to unleash their creative potential.

Copyright Asteria Books 2016

Staurolite

Folk Names: Fairy Cross, Fairy Stone
Color(s): Brown, reddish-brown, black
Mohs scale: 7–7.5
Planetary association: Earth
Element: Earth
Deity: Faeries, Earth Spirits
Powers: Protection, grounding, faery magick, healing

HEALING LORE: Historically, staurolite was used to help with fevers and is believed to aid in improving blood circulation and strengthening the body. The stone is thought to help with pain, particularly in the muscles and spine. It is believed to support cellular health, and some practices use it to help with a variety of physical ailments by balancing the body's energies. The stone is believed to help alleviate stress and promote a sense of inner peace. It has also been used in some traditions to assist with overcoming addictive behaviors.

MAGIC AND RITUAL LORE: Due to its natural cross formation, staurolite has long been revered as a protective talisman. It's believed to ward off evil spirits, ill-wishing, and negative energy. It's also considered a powerful good luck charm, with legends suggesting it can bring blessings and fortune to the wearer. Staurolite is said to act as a bridge between the physical and spiritual worlds. This makes it an excellent stone for communication with spirit guides, fairies, and other elemental beings. Placing staurolite under your pillow is believed to aid in lucid dreaming and provide protection from nightmares. Its ability to connect with higher realms can also help in developing psychic abilities and intuition.

Copyright Asteria Books 2016

Sugilite

Folk Names: Stone of the Violet Ray, Love Stone, Luvulite/Lavulite
Color(s): Purple, violet, pink
Mohs scale: 6–6.5
Planetary association: Jupiter, Neptune
Element: Water
Deity: Varies
Powers: Spiritual growth, emotional healing, protection, wisdom

HEALING LORE: Sugilite is a powerful emotional healing stone that helps alleviate stress, anxiety, and despair. It infuses the spirit with love, clearing the heart chakra to encourage self-acceptance and forgiveness. The stone helps to release emotional baggage and past traumas, transforming negative thoughts into positive ones. It's particularly beneficial for those struggling with feelings of alienation, isolation, or mental health issues like PTSD. Thanks to its high manganese content, sugilite is often used for pain relief, especially for headaches, muscle tension, and joint discomfort. It is believed to have a calming effect on the central nervous system, which can help with nerve-related pain and anxiety. Some believe that sugilite helps in the detoxification of the body and boosts the immune system.

MAGIC AND RITUAL LORE: Sugilite is often referred to as a "shield stone" because it is believed to create a protective barrier around the wearer's aura. This shield guards against negative energies, psychic attacks, and environmental stress. It helps sensitive individuals avoid absorbing the emotions and negativity of others, allowing them to maintain their own sense of peace and authenticity. As "The Stone of the Violet Ray," sugilite is a powerful tool for spiritual connection. It is thought to open the crown and third-eye chakras, making it easier to receive divine guidance, connect with spirit guides and angels, and enhance psychic abilities and intuition. It is a favored stone for meditation and channeling.

Copyright Asteria Books 2016

Sulfur

Folk Names: Brimstone, Sulphur
Color(s): Yellow
Mohs scale: 1.5–2.5
Planetary association: Sun, Mars
Element: Fire
Deity: Hephaestus, Vulcan, Mefitis, Hekate
Powers: Banishing, purification, protection, healing

HEALING LORE: Sulfur is a well-known and FDA-approved ingredient in many over-the-counter products for skin ailments. It has antibacterial effects that help fight the bacteria that cause acne, and its ability to promote the shedding of dead skin cells makes it effective for treating conditions like psoriasis, eczema, and seborrheic dermatitis. Many people find relief from joint and muscle pain by soaking in sulfur-rich hot springs, a practice known as balneotherapy. Sulfur is a component of cartilage and is believed to help reduce inflammation and pain associated with arthritis and other musculoskeletal disorders. Sulfur is a key component of several important amino acids and enzymes in the body that play a role in detoxification. It is thought to help the body eliminate toxins and harmful substances. In some historical and modern practices, sulfur springs are used for their purported benefits for respiratory conditions like bronchitis and asthma.

MAGIC AND RITUAL LORE: In metaphysical practices, sulfur is believed to have a strong cleansing energy that can purify the aura and remove stagnant or negative energy. Its fiery energy is believed to burn away stagnant or harmful influences. It's often used in spiritual baths, floor washes, or as an ingredient in incenses to banish negativity. Historically, sulfur was a key ingredient in spells and rituals for protection against evil spirits, psychic attacks, and hexes. It is said to create a strong barrier that negative entities cannot cross. In some traditions, it is sprinkled around a home to ward off ill-wishing or to break a curse. In alchemy, sulfur is one of the three foundational principles, along with mercury and salt. It represents the soul or the masculine principle, associated with the Sun and the element of Fire.

Copyright Asteria Books 2016

Sunstone

Folk Names: Aventurine Feldspar, Heliolite
Color(s): Orange, red, brown, with a shimmering effect
Mohs scale: 6–6.5
Planetary association: Sun
Element: Fire
Deity: Ra, Apollo, Helios, Surya, Sol
Powers: Joy, vitality, leadership, abundance, protection

HEALING LORE: Sunstone is a wonderful anti-depressant. It is believed to bring a sense of joy, optimism, and enthusiasm. Sunstone's warmth is believed to soothe anxiety and fear, bringing a sense of security and safety. Sunstone is an excellent stone for boosting vitality and life force energy. It is believed to increase metabolism, support the body's self-healing mechanisms, and help with chronic fatigue. The stone's gentle warmth is thought to help soothe pain and inflammation, particularly in cases of chronic pain and rheumatism. Due to its connection to the sun, sunstone is a great stone for combating the feelings of low energy and sadness that come with a lack of sunlight. It is also believed to help in recovery from sickness.

MAGIC AND RITUAL LORE: Sunstone is a stone of leadership and personal power. It's believed to help you step into your full potential, inspiring you to take action and pursue your dreams with confidence. It enhances your charisma and helps you attract others to your cause. The stone is considered a powerful talisman for good luck and abundance. It's believed to attract opportunities and blessings, and to help you manifest your desires into reality. Sunstone is an excellent protective stone that radiates light and positivity. It's believed to create a protective shield around the aura, warding off negative energies, psychic attacks, and ill-wishing. The stone's solar energy is said to have a cleansing effect on the chakras and the aura, helping to remove stagnant energy and promote a healthy flow of life force throughout the body.

Copyright Asteria Books 2016

Tektites

Folk Names: Star Stone, Inkstone of the Thundergod, Cosmic Glass; some well-known examples include Moldavite, Libyan Desert Glass, Australites, Indochinites, and Darwin Glass
Color(s): Black, dark green, dark brown
Mohs scale: 5.5–6
Planetary association: Uranus
Element: Fire, Air
Deity: Varies
Powers: Spiritual growth, psychic ability, manifestation, healing

HEALING LORE: Tektites are natural glasses formed by the impact of meteorites, and their healing properties are thought to be a blend of both earthly and extraterrestrial energies. While different types of tektites (like Moldavite and Libyan Desert Glass) have their own unique qualities, they share some common healing properties. Tektites are believed to stimulate the flow of energy throughout the body. This can help to remove blockages and promote overall vitality. Some people use tektites to help alleviate headaches, fatigue, and muscular tension. The stone is thought to have a restorative effect on the body, promoting cellular regeneration and helping with recovery from physical injuries.

MAGIC AND RITUAL LORE: Tektites are believed to be powerful catalysts for spiritual growth and transformation. As a stone of extraterrestrial origin, tektites are said to open the third eye and crown chakras, enhancing psychic abilities, intuition, and clairvoyance. As stones of cosmic energy, tektites are also powerful protective talismans. They are believed to create a protective barrier against negative energy and psychic attacks. They have a unique ability to ground you to the Earth while you explore higher states of consciousness, preventing you from feeling "spaced out." Tektites are said to amplify your intentions and help you manifest your desires more quickly.

Copyright Asteria Books 2016

Tiger's Eye

Folk Names: Tiger Iron
Color(s): Gold, brown, red, blue, with a chatoyant effect
Mohs scale: 7
Planetary association: Sun, Mars
Element: Fire, Earth
Deity: Ra, Sekhmet, Freyja, Durga, Bacchus,
Powers: Protection, courage, prosperity, grounding

HEALING LORE: Tiger's eye is valued for its ability to balance and ground energy, while also igniting a sense of confidence and personal power. Tiger's eye is often used to boost vitality and physical strength. It is believed to help fortify the blood, balance the endocrine system, and speed up a slow metabolism. The stone is thought to help relieve aches and pains in the neck, back, and shoulders, and may support recovery from spinal injuries. Tiger's eye has a historical reputation for benefiting the eyes and throat, and is believed to improve night vision. It is also associated with supporting the reproductive system.

MAGIC AND RITUAL LORE: Tiger's eye's magical properties are deeply tied to its appearance, which resembles a watchful, all-seeing eye. It is considered a strong protective stone that wards off negative energy, curses, and ill-wishing. Historically, it was worn as a talisman to protect against the "evil eye" and to provide courage and safety on the battlefield. Tiger's eye is a great stone for grounding and personal empowerment. It connects the energy of the sun (solar power, vitality) with the energy of the Earth (grounding, stability), helping to balance and center the wearer. It encourages you to tap into your inner strength, willpower, and confidence. The "all-seeing eye" aspect of the stone helps to sharpen inner vision and intuition. By clearing away mental fog and emotional clutter, tiger's eye is a potent stone for manifestation. The stone is said to balance the extremes of yin and yang energies within a person, promoting harmony and a sense of inner peace. It helps to integrate the spiritual and physical realms, bridging the gap between your aspirations and your actions.

Copyright Asteria Books 2016

Topaz

Color(s): Clear, yellow, gold, blue, pink, red
Mohs scale: 8
Planetary association: Sun
Element: Fire, Air
Deity: Apollo, Ra, Jupiter, Mefitis
Powers: Healing, protection, prosperity, creativity

HEALING LORE: Topaz is thought to have a positive effect on the digestive system and is sometimes used to aid with issues of metabolism and nutrient absorption. The stone is believed to support the immune system and promote overall physical health and vitality. In some traditional practices, topaz is used to help alleviate pain, particularly from conditions like arthritis and headaches. Historically, topaz was believed to improve eyesight and soothe strained eyes.

MAGIC AND RITUAL LORE: Topaz has a long-standing reputation as a protective talisman. In the Middle Ages, it was believed to ward off magic spells and curses. Ancient Egyptians and Greeks wore it as an amulet to protect against injury and ill-wishing. Due to its association with Jupiter, the planet of abundance and prosperity, golden and imperial topaz are potent stones for manifestation. Topaz is a stone for spiritual and intellectual pursuits. It is believed to connect the wearer to higher wisdom and divine guidance. The stone has a reputation for promoting truth and honesty. It is said to help you see the truth in others and to encourage integrity in your own actions. In some traditions, it was believed to change color if it was near poison, acting as a detector of falsehood.

Copyright Asteria Books 2016

Tourmaline

Folk Names: Rainbow Gem, Rubellite, Indicolite, Schorl, Ceylonese Magnet
Color(s): Black, pink, green, blue, yellow, watermelon
Mohs scale: 7–7.5
Planetary association: Varies
Element: Earth, Water
Deity: Black: Manat, Aradia; Green: Green Tara; Pink: Aphrodite, Quan Yin
Powers: Protection, grounding, healing, spiritual growth

HEALING LORE: All forms of tourmaline are considered protective stones. They are believed to create a shield of positive energy around the wearer, guarding against negative energies, psychic attacks, and environmental pollutants. Due to its wide spectrum of colors, tourmaline is considered a stone that can be used to balance and cleanse all the chakras. By matching the stone's color to the corresponding chakra, it helps to remove blockages and promote a healthy flow of energy throughout the body. Tourmaline is said to support the immune system and promote overall physical health. It is believed to have a revitalizing effect on the body and can help in detoxification.

MAGIC AND RITUAL LORE: The magical properties of tourmaline are deeply connected to its unique electrical properties and its ability to absorb and transmute energy. While different colors of tourmaline have specific attributes, a few core magical properties are shared across all varieties. They're believed to create a strong shield of positive energy around the wearer, warding off negative energies, psychic attacks, and ill-wishing. This protective quality extends to guarding against environmental pollutants and electromagnetic smog. Tourmaline is a highly effective grounding stone, particularly the black variety, which is known as schorl. It anchors you to the Earth, providing a sense of stability and security. This is useful for anyone who feels scattered, uncentered, or overwhelmed by spiritual or emotional energy. Tourmaline's most famous magical property is its ability to transmute negative energy into positive energy. It doesn't just absorb negativity; it actively transforms it. Because tourmaline comes in a wide spectrum of colors, it is considered a universal chakra cleanser. By using different colors of tourmaline, you can balance and align all seven of the main chakras, promoting a healthy and harmonious flow of energy throughout the body.

Copyright Asteria Books 2016

Trilobites

Folk Names: Stone of Time
Color(s): Gray, brown, black
Mohs scale: 7
Planetary association: Saturn
Element: Earth, Akasha
Deity: Cronos
Powers: Past life exploration, protection, grounding, wisdom

HEALING LORE: Trilobites, with their ancient, segmented forms, are powerful healers for the mind and spirit. Their energy is said to be excellent for promoting resilience and for healing old, karmic wounds. It is a stone of stability and grounding, offering a sense of calm and perspective during times of great change. It is believed to aid in the healing of physical ailments of the spine and bones, drawing on the strength of its ancient fossilized structure.

MAGIC AND RITUAL LORE: Trilobites are a "time-travel" stone, a unique tool for past-life regressions and for connecting with ancient wisdom. Its intricate, multi-segmented form is a symbol of protection, believed to ward off negative energy and to create a shield of strength. In ritual, it is placed on the altar or used in meditation to access the deep, ancient past and to receive guidance from the ancestors. Its connection to the primordial oceans and ancient life makes it a powerful tool for scrying and for connecting with the origins of all life.

Copyright Asteria Books 2016

Turquoise

Folk Names: Turkish Stone, Ferozah, Callais, Chalchihuitl
Color(s): Blue, blue-green, green
Mohs scale: 5–6
Planetary association: Venus, Neptune
Element: Water, Air
Deity: Hathor, Xiuhtecuhtli, Estsanatlehi
Powers: Protection, healing, communication, spiritual balance

HEALING LORE: Turquoise has a historical reputation for benefiting the respiratory system. It's believed to help with issues of the throat, lungs, and allergies. The stone is thought to strengthen the immune system and support the body's natural detoxification processes, reducing inflammation and promoting overall health. Turquoise is often used to help alleviate pain, particularly in the neck, head, and eyes. It is also believed to be beneficial for rheumatism, gout, and stomach issues.

MAGIC AND RITUAL LORE: Turquoise has been revered as a powerful magical stone for millennia, with its properties deeply tied to its sacred history and its unique color that bridges the realms of earth and sky. As one of its most ancient and well-known properties, turquoise is a powerful protective talisman. It's believed to ward off negative energy, evil spirits, and psychic attacks. Many cultures, from ancient Egypt to Native American tribes, used turquoise as a personal amulet to bring safety and good fortune. In some traditions, it was believed to change color to warn the wearer of impending danger or illness. Referred to as ferozah in ancient Persian, meaning "victorious," turquoise is a stone of good luck and success. It is believed to attract prosperity, abundance, and positive opportunities into your life. Turquoise is a stone that is said to unite the energies of heaven and earth. It helps to bridge the gap between the physical and spiritual realms, making it a valuable tool for meditation, spiritual insight, and connecting with divine wisdom.

Copyright Asteria Books 2016

Zircon

(Note: This entry is about the natural stone Zircon, not the lab-created Cubic Zirconia.)

Folk Names: Jacinth, Jargoon, Starlite, Matura Diamond
Color(s): Blue, green, red, brown, clear
Mohs scale: 7.5
Planetary association: Sun, Jupiter
Element: Fire, Water
Powers: Healing, protection, spiritual enlightenment, wisdom

HEALING LORE: Zircon is believed to stimulate clear thinking and concentration. It can help to quiet a chaotic mind, allowing for better decision-making and problem-solving. The stone's calming energy is thought to soothe emotional turmoil, reducing anxiety, stress, and feelings of inadequacy. In some traditions, zircon is used to help people cope with loss and grief, as it promotes a sense of hope and renewal. Zircon is thought to have a positive effect on the body's internal systems. It's believed to help with detoxification of the liver, improve digestion, and support a healthy immune system. The stone is sometimes used to help alleviate pain, particularly from menstrual cramps and muscle spasms. Zircon's calming energy is said to help with insomnia and restless sleep, promoting a sense of peace and tranquility that can lead to deeper, more restful sleep. Zircon is associated with strengthening the reproductive system and can be used to help with hormonal imbalances.

MAGIC AND RITUAL LORE: Zircon is sometimes used to aid in astral travel and to promote vivid, prophetic dreams. It is believed to provide a sense of spiritual protection during these journeys, ensuring a safe return. Zircon is a powerful protective talisman, believed to create a strong shield against negative energies and psychic attacks while purifying the aura of negative attachments. It is a potent tool for spiritual development, helping to open the third eye and crown chakras to connect with your higher self and receive divine guidance.

Known as a stone of truth, zircon encourages integrity and helps you discern honesty in others, making it ideal for clear decision-making. Its fiery energy also makes it an excellent ally for manifestation, amplifying your intentions with passion and vitality to bring your desires into reality.

Copyright Asteria Books 2016

Metal Index

Brass

Other Names: Yellow Copper, Orichalcum, Pinchbeck, Prince's Metal, Muntz Metal
Planet: Mars, Sun
Other Astrological: Leo, Aries
Element: Fire, Air
Deities: Hephaestus, Vulcan, Ogun
Magical Properties: Protection, Banishing,

MYTHS: In ancient myth, the legendary city of Atlantis was said to be adorned with "orichalcum," a metal described as a shining, reddish-gold material. Scholars believe this metal was likely a type of brass or a similar copper alloy, giving brass a link to this famous lost civilization. In Spirit lore, Solomon's spirit vessels are believed to be made of brass.

HEALING: In ancient traditions, brass was believed to possess healing properties. It was used in Ayurvedic medicine and other folk remedies, with the belief that wearing or touching the metal could help reduce joint inflammation and alleviate rheumatism. This belief likely stemmed from the anti-inflammatory properties attributed to copper. Brass is believed to stimulate the mind and improve mental clarity.

MAGIC AND RITUAL: The resonant sound of brass was a powerful tool for protection. The ringing of brass bells in temples and rituals was a common practice to purify a space, drive away negative spirits, and call in positive energy. Brass amulets and talismans were also worn to ward off evil and provide a shield against harm. In many folk traditions, brass was associated with masculine, "yang" energy. It was used to create tools and ceremonial objects that symbolized strength, courage, and action. Modern practitioners believe brass is a powerful metal for attracting wealth, prosperity, and success.

Copyright Asteria Books 2025

Bronze

Other Names: Copper Alloy, Red Brass, Tumbaga
Planet: Mars, Sun
Other Astrological: Aries, Leo, Taurus
Element: Fire, Earth
Deities: Hephaestus, Vulcan, Mars, Ares, Vishwakarma, Athena
Magical Properties: Manifestation, Grounding, Protection

MYTHS: In Greek mythology, Talos was a giant bronze automaton, or a living statue. Forged by the divine smith Hephaestus, Talos was given to King Minos to protect the island of Crete. The armor and weapons of heroes like Achilles were also described as being made of bronze, symbolizing their strength and heroic status.

HEALING: Historically, bronze has been worn to alleviate the symptoms of arthritis and rheumatism. This is a belief largely attributed to the copper content, which is thought to be absorbed in small amounts through the skin. As a conductor of energy, bronze is believed to help stimulate the flow of energy within the body's meridians. This is said to lead to greater vitality, reduced fatigue, and a sense of overall well-being. The tin component of bronze is believed to be essential for the production of hemoglobin and for maintaining adrenal health, which in turn can boost the immune system and increase energy.

MAGIC AND RITUAL: Bronze is believed to be a powerful tool for manifesting goals, especially those requiring strength and determination. Its grounding Earth energy and fiery, action-oriented properties work together to help bring a concept into reality. Like brass, bronze is a protective metal. Its use in ancient armor and weaponry gives it an association with shielding the user from physical and psychic harm. As a metal known for its durability and resistance to corrosion, bronze is said to instill these same qualities in its user, fostering resilience and the ability to endure through difficult times.

Copyright Asteria Books 2025

Copper

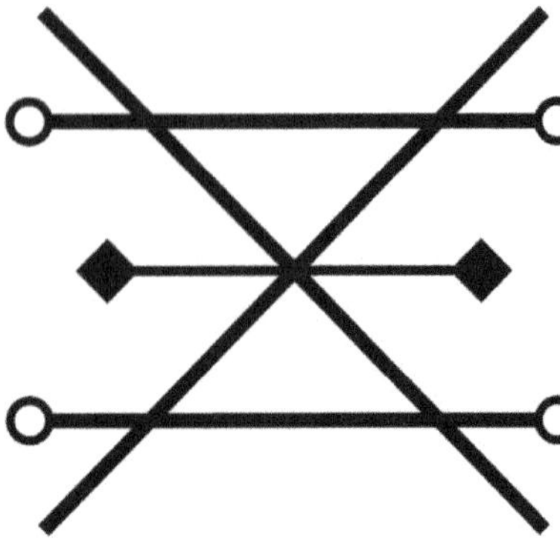

Other Names: Cuprum, Aes, Red Metal, Cop
Planet: Venus
Other Astrological: Taurus, Libra
Element: Water
Deities: Venus, Aphrodite, Hathor, Ishtar
Magical Properties: Grounding, Energizing, Love, Luck, Prosperity

MYTHS: The name "copper" originates from the Latin cuprum, meaning "metal of Cyprus," an island sacred to the goddess Aphrodite. This connection cemented copper's mythological association with love, beauty, and the divine feminine. In alchemy and astrology, the planet Venus, the Roman equivalent of Aphrodite, became copper's planetary ruler. Ancient traditions also viewed copper as a "living metal" with its own spirit, due to its ability to oxidize and change color, a process seen as a manifestation of its life force and interaction with the environment.

HEALING: Copper's healing properties, in both folk traditions and modern belief, are centered on its purifying and conductive nature. It is thought to cleanse negative energy from a person's aura and environment, while also balancing chakras. Historically, cultures like the Egyptians used copper for its antimicrobial properties to purify water and sterilize wounds, a belief now supported by science. Metaphysically, wearing copper is believed to support the immune system, stimulate blood circulation to combat fatigue, and promote overall vitality. As a protective shield, copper jewelry is worn to ward off illness and negative energy.

MAGIC AND RITUAL: Copper is renowned for its ability to conduct and amplify energy. It is often used in magical tools, wands, and healing practices to channel and direct energy. It is believed to enhance the properties of other crystals and stones it is paired with. Copper has strong grounding properties, connecting a person's energy to the Earth. It is used to balance the body's energy fields and prevent a person from feeling uncentered or disconnected. As a metal associated with the goddess Venus, copper is a symbol of love, luck, and prosperity.

Copyright Asteria Books 2025

Gold

Other Names: Aurum, Sun's Tears, King of Metals, Sol
Planet: Sun
Other Astrological: Leo, Aries
Element: Fire
Deities: Ra, Aphrodite, Inti, Apollo, Freyja, Lakshmi, Isis
Magical Properties: Abundance, Prosperity, Protection, Purification, Inner Wisdom

MYTHS: Gold's mythology is centered on its divine origins and solar radiance. In ancient Egypt, it was considered the "flesh of the gods," particularly the sun god Ra. Similarly, the Incas referred to it as the "sweat of the sun" and adorned temples with it to honor their sun god Inti. The Norse goddess Freya famously weeps tears of pure gold, a poetic symbol of its preciousness. Alchemists, meanwhile, viewed gold as the pinnacle of matter, a perfectly pure and incorruptible metal, and its creation was the ultimate goal of their craft. The tale of King Midas, whose touch turned everything to gold, serves as a timeless myth about its deceptive power.

HEALING: Gold is believed to possess physical healing properties rooted in its purported ability to balance the body's energy. It's thought that wearing gold jewelry can help with inflammation and alleviate symptoms of conditions like arthritis. Furthermore, its solar energy is said to support the body's natural life force, increasing overall vitality and combating fatigue. In ancient traditions, gold was even used to aid in blood circulation and maintain body temperature, with its warmth believed to be beneficial for overall physical health. Gold is used in modern healthcare for specific treatments like rheumatoid arthritis, cancer therapy, and dentistry, while in skincare, it's a popular ingredient in anti-aging and anti-inflammatory products.

MAGIC AND RITUAL: Gold is revered for its ability to amplify energy, making it a powerful conductor that enhances the properties of other crystals. As a symbol of the sun, it is believed to attract wealth, prosperity, and good fortune, drawing opportunities into one's life. Its radiant, pure energy is said to create a strong protective shield against negative energy and psychic attacks, purifying the aura and the surrounding environment. This divine connection also helps to unlock inner wisdom, intuition, and a greater sense of spiritual purpose.

Copyright Asteria Books 2025

Iron

Other Names: Ferrum, Pig Iron, Cast Iron, Wrought Iron
Planet: Mars
Other Astrological: Aries, Scorpio
Element: Fire, Earth
Deities: Mars, Ares, Hephaestus, Vulcan, Ogun, Brigid, Goibniu, Svarog
Magical Properties: Protection, Stability, Courage, Banishment

MYTHS: The discovery and forging of iron were seen as a divine act. The metal's creation was often attributed to a god of the forge, such as Hephaestus in Greek mythology or Ogun in Yoruba traditions. The blacksmith was often considered more than a craftsman; they were a shaman, a magician, and a crucial intermediary between the human and spiritual worlds.

HEALING: Iron is believed to be a powerful grounding agent, which helps combat physical fatigue and restore energy. Its connection to the blood and Earth element is thought to stimulate blood circulation and aid in the oxygenation of the body. In some traditions, it is used to support the body's natural defenses and provide a sense of physical strength and resilience. It's believed that wearing or holding iron can help a person feel more centered and vital, especially when feeling drained or lacking energy.

MAGIC AND RITUAL: Iron is a powerful metal in folklore, revered for its protective and grounding properties. Its dense, martial energy is believed to create a shield against evil spirits, curses, and negative forces, with horseshoes being a classic example. Iron's connection to the Earth makes it a strong grounding agent, providing stability and inner strength to those who feel disconnected. The metal is also thought to instill courage and willpower, helping people overcome challenges. In European folklore, iron was considered anathema to supernatural beings like fairies, used to banish them from sacred spaces.

Copyright Asteria Books 2025

Lead

Other Names: Plumbum, White Lead, Red Lead, Minium
Planet: Saturn
Other Astrological: Capricorn, Aquarius
Element: Earth
Deities: Saturn, Cronus, Hades, Pluto, Anubis
Magical Properties: Grounding, Banishment, Binding, Curses

WARNING: Lead is a highly toxic substance. It is a potent neurotoxin that can cause severe health problems if ingested, inhaled, or absorbed through the skin. In modern magic and ritual, it is strongly advised to avoid using actual lead. The properties discussed below are historical and symbolic, not a recommendation for use.

MYTHS: Lead's mythology is centered on its heaviness and its association with the planet Saturn. Alchemists considered it the base "first matter" and the metal of Saturn, whose transformation into gold was the ultimate goal of their craft. Its dense nature also linked it to the underworld and deities like Hades.

MAGIC AND RITUAL: Lead's heavy nature makes it a powerful symbol of the Earth element. It was used in rituals to provide a sense of grounding, stability, and endurance. It was believed to anchor a person's energy to the physical world, helping them feel secure and rooted. Its weight was metaphorically used to "weigh down" and bind unwanted spirits, curses, or negative influences. Talismans made of lead were believed to protect the wearer by banishing evil. Its weight and density made it a primary material for ancient curse tablets, which were inscribed with curses and then rolled or folded into small packets of lead to symbolically "weigh down" and imprison the spirit of the target.

Copyright Asteria Books 2025

Mercury

Other Names: Hydragyrum, Quicksilver, Silver-Water
Planet: Mercury
Other Astrological: Gemini, Virgo
Element: Water, Air
Deities: Hermes, Mercury, Thoth, Loki
Magical Properties: Communication, Safe Travel, Transformation, Luck, Protection, Communication, Divination

WARNING: Mercury is a highly toxic substance. It is a potent neurotoxin that can be absorbed through the skin, inhaled, or ingested. In modern magic and ritual, it is strongly advised to never handle or use actual mercury. Any historical or traditional healing practice involving mercury should never be attempted. Modern medicine has proven that mercury can cause severe and irreversible damage to the nervous system, kidneys, and other organs.

MYTHS: Quicksilver's myths are deeply tied to its unique liquid state. Alchemically, it was a foundational element representing duality and transformation, believed to be a living substance capable of transmuting base metals into gold. Its swift, elusive nature associated it with the gods Hermes and Mercury, casting it as a psychopomp—a guide for souls to the underworld—and a bridge between realms. In folklore, quicksilver was a protective and lucky substance, believed to deflect curses and attract wealth due to its reflective and scattering properties.

MAGIC AND RITUAL: Mercury is enhances a person's ability to communicate, to travel swiftly (both physically and spiritually), and to succeed in commerce and business. It is a substance that can exist between states, embodying the alchemical principle of change. It was considered a bridge between the physical and spiritual worlds. Mercury was thought to be a lucky substance that could attract good fortune. It was also used in some folk magic for protection, as its elusive nature was believed to make it difficult for curses or negative energies to attach to a person. Its reflective, fluid surface was sometimes used in scrying or divination rituals, as it was thought to reveal hidden truths or glimpses of the future.

Copyright Asteria Books 2025

Pewter

Other Names: Britannia metal, Queen's metal, Pot metal
Planet: Jupiter
Other Astrological: Sagittarius, Pisces
Element: Air
Deities: Jupiter, Zeus, Vishnu
Magical Properties: Wisdom, Spiritual Growth, Protection

MYTHS: Pewter's mythology is rooted in its role as the metal of the common person. Unlike the precious metals of royalty, it symbolized practicality, stability, and enduring prosperity for the hearth and home. In folklore, pewter also took on a protective role. It was believed that the metal could absorb and deflect curses or negative spells. This protective myth likely originated from its use in churches and religious objects, where it was thought to possess a sacred quality capable of guarding against evil.

HEALING: As a metal associated with Jupiter, pewter is believed to enhance mental clarity and promote sound judgment. In modern spiritual practices, pewter is often used in jewelry to symbolize forgiveness, peace, and grace. It's believed to help a person let go of emotional burdens and find a path toward inner peace. CAUTION: While modern pewter is lead-free, antique pewter is not. Do not eat or drink from antique pewter plates or cups, and do not wear antique pewter talismans directly against the skin.

MAGIC AND RITUAL: As a metal of Jupiter, pewter is believed to enhance wisdom and mental clarity. It's thought to help the user gain perspective, make sound judgments, and access inner knowledge. Pewter is considered a stone of good fortune and abundance. It's often used in rituals or carried as a talisman to attract prosperity, financial stability, and success in business ventures. In folklore, pewter was used for protection. It was believed to create a protective shield against negative energy and to ground a person's energy, helping them feel more centered and secure. Pewter is thought to facilitate spiritual growth and expansion. It is believed to help in meditation and to open the mind to higher learning, allowing for a deeper connection to the spiritual world.

Copyright Asteria Books 2025

Silver

Other Names: Argentum, Sterling
Planet: Moon
Other Astrological: Cancer
Element: Water
Deities: Selene, Luna, Isis, Hekate, Mama Quilla, Kuan Yin, Arianrhod, Tlazolteotl, Phoebe, Anahita, Nuit
Magical Properties: Protection, Reflection, Divination, Psychism, Purification, Divine Feminine

MYTHS: The ancient Egyptians believed that the bones of their deities were made of silver, making it more valuable and sacred than gold in some periods. The Incas revered silver as the "tears of the moon," a divine gift from their moon goddess, Mama Quilla. One of the most famous myths about silver is its power to kill werewolves and other supernatural creatures, which stems from its purity and light.

HEALING: Silver is seen as a metal of purification. It is believed to cleanse the body and aura of negative energy, promoting a feeling of spiritual purity and well-being. Silver is a common ingredient in bandages, wound dressings, and topical creams for burns. It prevents infection and promotes healing, especially in chronic wounds and severe burns. Silver diamine fluoride is a dental solution used to treat and prevent tooth decay, while silver is also a key component in some traditional dental fillings.

MAGIC AND RITUAL: Silver's magical properties are tied to its lunar connection and reflective nature. It's believed to be a powerful protective metal that acts as a mirror, reflecting negative energy and psychic attacks back to their source. As the metal of the Moon, silver is thought to enhance intuition, dreams, and psychic abilities. Its purifying nature is used to cleanse spaces, objects, and a person's aura of unwanted energy. Furthermore, silver is associated with love and emotional healing, helping to bring a sense of calm and balance to one's life.

Copyright Asteria Books 2025

Steel

Common Types: Carbon, Damascas, Stainless, Corten, Wootz
Planet: Mars
Other Astrological: Aries, Scorpio
Element: Fire, Earth
Deities: Most Forge Gods, most War-Gods
Magical Properties: Protection, Discipline, Grounding, Manifestation

MYTHS: In many cultures, the creation of a steel sword was not merely a physical act but a magical one. A blacksmith who could forge steel was seen as a master of a divine art. Legendary weapons like King Arthur's Excalibur are often described as being made of a steel so pure and strong that it was unbreakable. These myths elevated steel blades from mere weapons to symbols of sovereignty, destiny, and divine authority.

HEALING: Steel's grounding effect helps to combat fatigue and restore a person's physical energy. It is used to promote mental strength and focus. Its heavy, Earth-based energy is said to ground a person's emotions, helping to alleviate anxiety and stress.

MAGIC AND RITUAL: Based on both historical folklore and modern metaphysical beliefs, steel possesses magical properties that are a more refined and disciplined version of iron's raw power. Steel is renowned for its protective abilities. While iron is believed to repel negative energies and supernatural entities, steel's protection is more focused and unyielding. It is thought to create a strong, disciplined barrier against psychic attacks, curses, and ill will, acting as a mental and spiritual shield. It is a metal of mental fortitude, helping a person to stay focused on their goals and providing the energy to overcome obstacles with a determined spirit. Steel is a strong grounding agent. It is believed to help solidify intentions, bringing a person's thoughts and desires into tangible reality with a forceful, purposeful energy.

Copyright Asteria Books 2025

Tin

Other Names: Stannum, Plmbum candidum, White lead, Zinn, Kassiteros
Planet: Jupiter
Other Astrological: Sagittarius, Pisces
Element: Air, Water
Deities: Jupiter, Zeus, Tinia
Magical Properties: Prosperity, Luck, Wisdom, Communication, Protection

MYTHS: Myths arose that tin vessels, when used in rituals, could amplify intentions and hold the sacred energy of a blessing. This myth positioned tin as a vessel of divine favor, capable of containing and transmitting positive energy. Tin played a crucial role in the creation of bronze, an alloy that gave its name to an entire era of human history. Tin is the wise, older metal that, when combined with the fiery energy of copper, creates something stronger than either one alone.

HEALING: Tin is believed to be essential for maintaining a healthy adrenal system by reducing fatigue, boosting energy levels, and promoting a sense of overall well-being. Due to its association with vitality and energy, tin is also thought to support the immune system and aid in the body's natural healing processes. Tin is sometimes used for emotional healing. Its connection to Jupiter's forgiving and compassionate nature is believed to help a person let go of emotional burdens, resentment, and past grievances, allowing them to feel a sense of freedom and emotional expansion.

MAGIC AND RITUAL: Tin attracts prosperity, financial success, and lucky opportunities. Tin talismans and amulets are often used in rituals to increase one's wealth and bring positive outcomes in business ventures. Tin is thought to enhance mental clarity, wisdom, and intellectual pursuits. It is believed to aid in philosophical thinking and communication. Due to its benevolent and expansive energy, tin is also believed to provide a form of protection by creating an aura of good luck and positive vibrations that naturally repel ill will.

Copyright Asteria Books 2025

Animal Magick

Copyright Asteria Books 2025

Totemic Animals

Totemism is a spiritual practice that is a feature of many indigenous religions around the world. Although the term "totem" itself comes from the Algonquin language (one of several North American Indigenous cultures), many Indigenous peoples in North America, Australia, Africa, India, Oceania, and South America share a similar practice.

Totemism is a belief system centered around the existence of a mystical kinship or relationship between a human group (like a family clan) and a natural or supernatural being, such as an animal, tree, plant, or mythical creature. The totem is a symbolic emblem for that group's identity, and is often seen as an ancestral spirit for the entire group.

Members of a totemic group often place taboos on harming or killing their totem. They usually believe that the well-being of the totem animal is tied to the well-being of the human group.

There is some controversy in modern spiritual practice regarding totemism, which is considered by some to be a closed cultural practice. Totemism in general is actually common across the globe and cannot be considered closed, as a concept. However, specific rituals, tools, and the symbolic associations of animals or plants are closed.

In order to engage with totemic animals in a non-appropriative way, a person (or group) should research how their own culture viewed and interacted with a given animal, call upon family stories and myths involving that animal, and allow the Spirit of the animal to indicate the taboos, rituals, and or tools it will give the group.

Copyright Asteria Books 2025

Animal Spirit Allies

The shamanic practices of every culture include veneration and guidance by Spirit Allies in the guise of animals. I hesitate to call these beings "Spirit Animals" as that can have a specific meaning within certain Native American religious traditions, which I do not wish to conflate or appropriate. However, the concept of animals acting as guides and guardians in the Unseen Realms is not specific to any one culture, continent, or time period.

Spirit Allies are beings who appear in visionary workings, such as Witch Flight, spirit journeying, and lucid dreaming. These Allies can appear in many forms, and it is not at all uncommon for a Witch to be familiar with one or more Animal Spirits.

Animal Spirits, like other Allies, might act as teachers, healers, guides, and guardians to us. This relationship is often very personal, with the animal appearing to us in dreams as well as coming to us in both symbolic and literal forms during our waking consciousness. For example, we may dream of a rabbit, see one scampering across the dewy grass the following dawn, and then be given a bunny figurine by a friend the following day. Rabbit is trying to get our attention!

As with totemic animals, many individuals will honor taboos around the killing or consuming of an animal with whom they have a close allyship. Notable exceptions to this would be in cases where a practitioner undertakes a sacred hunt in order to integrate with the animal's spirit in a different way. Many will keep an ethically-sourced specimen of the animal's bone, hide, feathers, etc as a touch-point for connecting with the animal's energy.

Shapeshifting

Shapeshifting is another practice that spans the globe and seems to have been a part of the shamanic practices and mythic beliefs of nearly every culture. In Ancient Mesopotamia, the God Enki is known to be a shapeshifter, the forms he takes are not detailed in the literature. In ancient Greece, Zeus was also a notable shapeshifter, and the sorceress Circe was able to force Odysseus's crew to change into pigs. In Vedic myth, we see the shapeshifting abilities of Vishnu, the Rakshassa, the Naga, and others. European, East Asian, North and South American, African, and Caribbean lore are all filled with tales of shapeshifters — from the berserkers to selkies to kitsune to skin-walkers and loup-garou.

While shapeshifting may be reserved for specific individuals, according to a given culture, it is a widespread spiritual phenomenon that points to a certain universal truth in its existence.

Most contemporary Witches approach shapeshifting from within the landscape of guided meditations, Spirit Flight, or lucid dreaming. Here, we are talking about spiritual shapeshifting, rather than literal physical transformations. Spiritual shapeshifting can be useful for gaining insight and perspective, connecting deeply with an Animal Ally, or drawing on the power of that animal to help fuel a magickal working.

Masking is also a common and powerful technique that can be employed in ritual or meditative settings in order to shift one's shape.

Otherkin

The term Otherkin refers to those who identify as non-human on a deep, spiritual, or psychological level. This is not a choice, but an intrinsic knowing. The identity may manifest as a sense of being 'alien' to human society, a strong connection to a specific non-human species, or a feeling of carrying the soul or essence of a creature from myth or nature.

The Otherkin path is a journey of self-discovery and integration. It involves listening to the whispers of one's inner self and recognizing the "kin-type." This can be a fae creature, an elemental, a dragon, a wolf, a celestial being, or any other natural or supernatural being. The practice is not about transforming the physical body, but about aligning one's spiritual and emotional self with this deeper identity. Rituals often involve meditation, shadow work, and deep immersion in nature.

Otherkin don't seek to escape humanity, but to enrich it. They may find solace in shared community, practice unique forms of magick tied to their kin-type, and feel a deep sense of responsibility towards the natural world or a particular element. It is a path of both solitude and connection, where one walks in two worlds at once: the human and the Other.

Vulture Culture

To work with the remnants of creatures is to walk with the wild heart of the Earth, honoring the intricate dance of life and death. This spiritual path involves the mindful collection and use of animal parts—bones, fur, feathers, claws, and shed skins—not as trophies, but as sacred relics. This practice is fundamentally rooted in respect and is strictly non-harming; these are items found naturally, shed, or ethically sourced from an animal that has already passed. They are echoes of a life lived, carrying the spiritual essence and wisdom of the creature they belonged to.

Each part holds a unique kind of energy. Bones are potent tools for connection to the ancestors, grounding, and divination. They hold the fundamental structure and strength of a life, and can be used on altars to represent the cycle of regeneration and resilience. Feathers, gifted by the air itself, are used for cleansing, fanning smoke during smudging rituals, or to invoke the element of Air and the freedom of flight. They represent communication, swiftness, and spiritual ascension. Fur and shed skins carry a connection to instinct, protection, and the deep, primal wisdom of the land. These can be used in charms for personal protection or to establish a connection with an animal spirit guide.

This practice is an act of guardianship. By using these parts with gratitude, we honor the animal's sacrifice and ensure its spirit is remembered. It's a way of weaving the wild back into our lives, carrying a piece of the untamed world in our hands and on our altars.

Copyright Asteria Books 2025

Animal Index

Alligator

Alligator mississippiensis

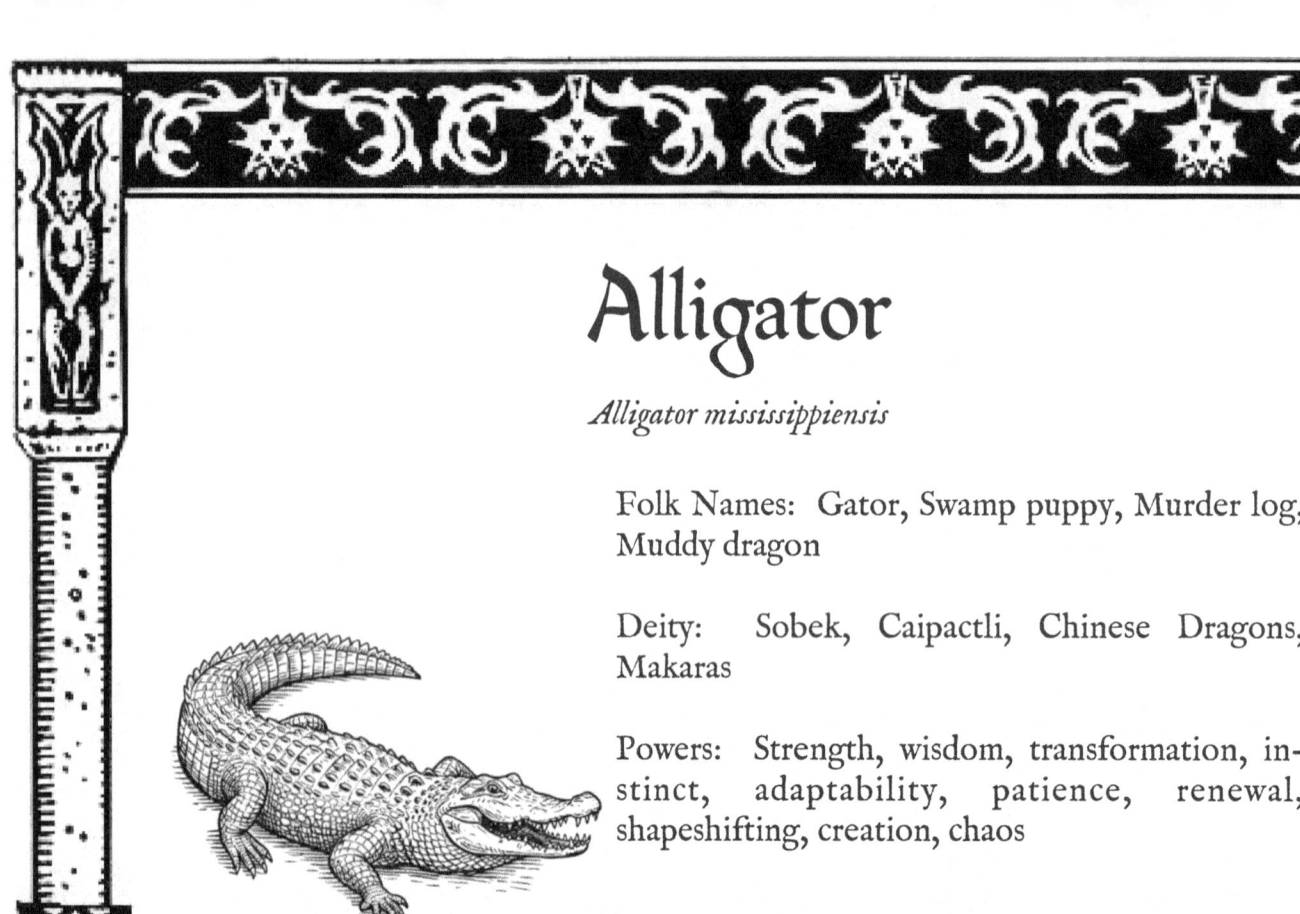

Folk Names: Gator, Swamp puppy, Murder log, Muddy dragon

Deity: Sobek, Caipactli, Chinese Dragons, Makaras

Powers: Strength, wisdom, transformation, instinct, adaptability, patience, renewal, shapeshifting, creation, chaos

MYTH, MAGIC, AND RITUAL: In ancient Egypt, the Nile crocodile was deified as Sobek, a god of fertility and military prowess, whose image was revered for protection and strength. Devotees would offer sacrifices to him to ensure a safe journey on the Nile and bountiful harvests. Similarly, some Mesoamerican creation myths feature a giant cosmic caiman, whose body formed the very earth and heavens. This creature symbolized the raw, creative energy of the natural world, a primal force from which all life emerged.

In North American folklore, particularly among southeastern Indigenous tribes, the alligator is a revered totem of strength, patience, and adaptability. It is seen as a guardian of the waters and a master of both worlds—land and sea—granting insight into hidden truths.

In modern magical practices, especially in traditions like Hoodoo and Conjure, the alligator's potent magic is accessed directly. The alligator foot, for example, is a well-known charm believed to attract luck and financial success. Other parts, such as the tooth or claw, are carried for protection, invoking the alligator's fierce and unyielding power to ward off harm and overcome obstacles. Through these rituals, practitioners connect with the ancient, untamed spirit of the alligator, channeling its primal energy for both defense and prosperity.

Copyright Asteria Books 2015

Bear

Ursidae

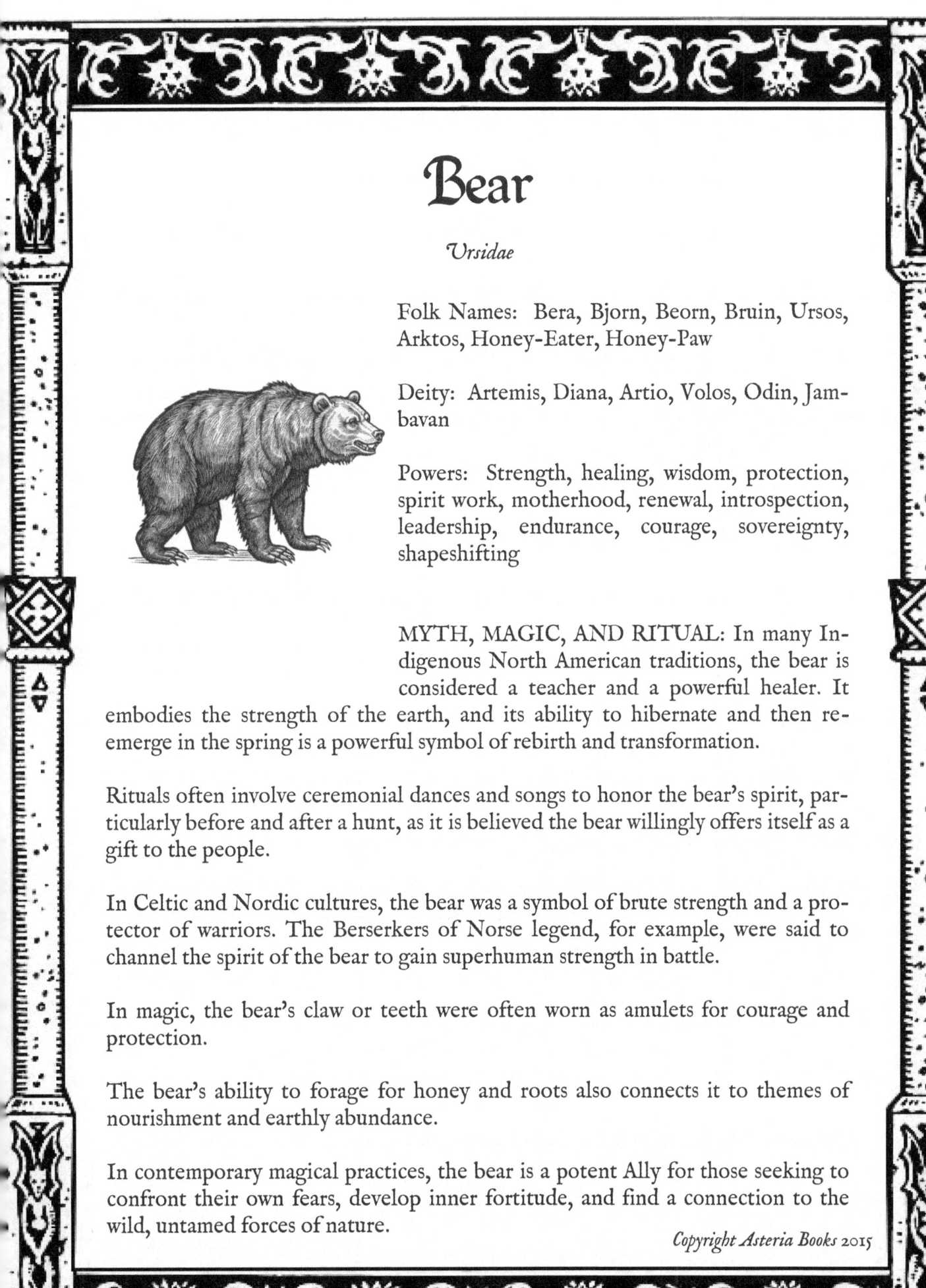

Folk Names: Bera, Bjorn, Beorn, Bruin, Ursos, Arktos, Honey-Eater, Honey-Paw

Deity: Artemis, Diana, Artio, Volos, Odin, Jambavan

Powers: Strength, healing, wisdom, protection, spirit work, motherhood, renewal, introspection, leadership, endurance, courage, sovereignty, shapeshifting

MYTH, MAGIC, AND RITUAL: In many Indigenous North American traditions, the bear is considered a teacher and a powerful healer. It embodies the strength of the earth, and its ability to hibernate and then re-emerge in the spring is a powerful symbol of rebirth and transformation.

Rituals often involve ceremonial dances and songs to honor the bear's spirit, particularly before and after a hunt, as it is believed the bear willingly offers itself as a gift to the people.

In Celtic and Nordic cultures, the bear was a symbol of brute strength and a protector of warriors. The Berserkers of Norse legend, for example, were said to channel the spirit of the bear to gain superhuman strength in battle.

In magic, the bear's claw or teeth were often worn as amulets for courage and protection.

The bear's ability to forage for honey and roots also connects it to themes of nourishment and earthly abundance.

In contemporary magical practices, the bear is a potent Ally for those seeking to confront their own fears, develop inner fortitude, and find a connection to the wild, untamed forces of nature.

Copyright Asteria Books 2015

Bee

Anthophila

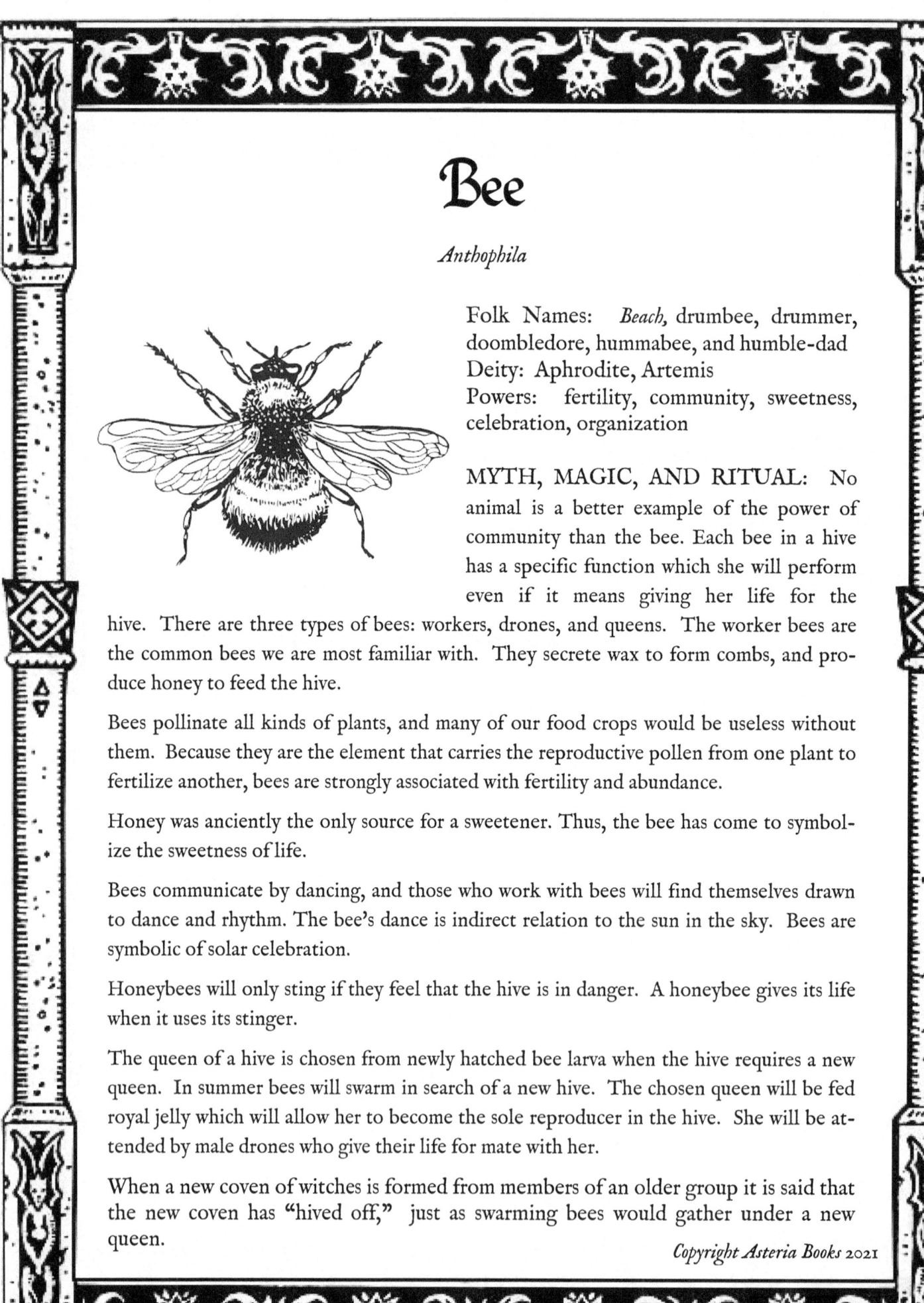

Folk Names: *Beach,* drumbee, drummer, doombledore, hummabee, and humble-dad
Deity: Aphrodite, Artemis
Powers: fertility, community, sweetness, celebration, organization

MYTH, MAGIC, AND RITUAL: No animal is a better example of the power of community than the bee. Each bee in a hive has a specific function which she will perform even if it means giving her life for the hive. There are three types of bees: workers, drones, and queens. The worker bees are the common bees we are most familiar with. They secrete wax to form combs, and produce honey to feed the hive.

Bees pollinate all kinds of plants, and many of our food crops would be useless without them. Because they are the element that carries the reproductive pollen from one plant to fertilize another, bees are strongly associated with fertility and abundance.

Honey was anciently the only source for a sweetener. Thus, the bee has come to symbolize the sweetness of life.

Bees communicate by dancing, and those who work with bees will find themselves drawn to dance and rhythm. The bee's dance is indirect relation to the sun in the sky. Bees are symbolic of solar celebration.

Honeybees will only sting if they feel that the hive is in danger. A honeybee gives its life when it uses its stinger.

The queen of a hive is chosen from newly hatched bee larva when the hive requires a new queen. In summer bees will swarm in search of a new hive. The chosen queen will be fed royal jelly which will allow her to become the sole reproducer in the hive. She will be attended by male drones who give their life for mate with her.

When a new coven of witches is formed from members of an older group it is said that the new coven has "hived off," just as swarming bees would gather under a new queen.

Copyright Asteria Books 2021

Blackbird

Turdus merula

Folk Names: Dru dubh
Deity: Rhiannon, Tubal Cain (and smith Gods)
Powers: territoriality, omens, enchantment, gateways

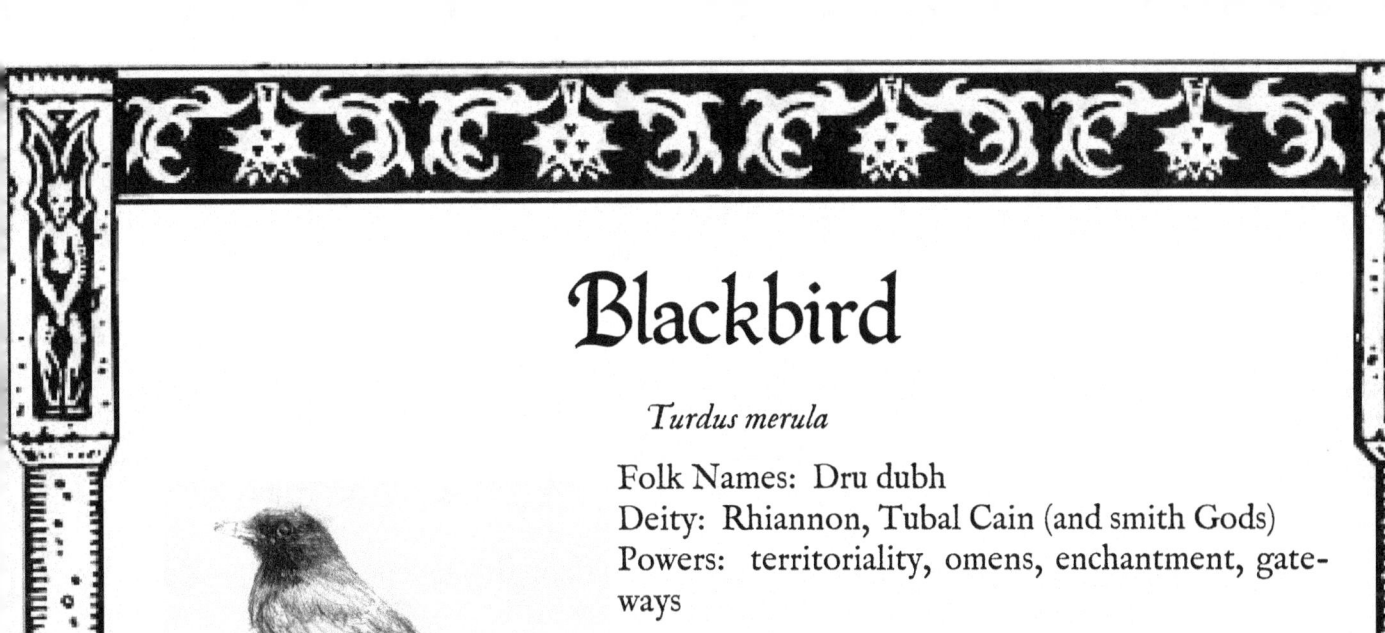

MYTH, MAGIC, AND RITUAL: The Blackbird notoriously sings at twilight and dawn -- the liminal times -- making it a guardian of the gateways and between-places. This makes it an ideal totem of January, the time when one year ends and another begins.

Rhiannon's birds were said to be blackbirds, as they are enchanted birds of the otherworld. They were said to "wake the dead and lull the living to sleep", another nod to their liminal singing, and a hint that the blackbird is capable of the shamanic work of dreamwalking and spirit communication.

The blackbird, or ousel, is the first animal Culhwch asks regarding the whereabouts of Mabon, as it was the oldest animal that Culhwch knew of. Again, the blackbird stands as the gateway to the animals that remain in the quest: stag, owl, eagle, and salmon.

The blackbird in Culhwch's tale, here named the Blackbird of Cilgwri, answers that he is so old that he found a smith's anvil when he first came to Cilgwri, but that time was so long ago that the anvil has long since worn away from his pecking at it. The blackbird is especially sacred to blacksmiths. In Irish ghobadhu means both blackbird and blacksmith. The blackbird has the unique habit of bashing snail shells and nuts on stones, much as a smith would use an anvil. For these reasons, and his coal-black feathers, the blackbird is sacred to smith gods, such as Tubal Cain.

Blackbirds are territorial, and seeing two together is considered a sign of good luck. It is also good luck to have a blackbird build its nest on your roof, or anywhere near your home.

In North America the red-winged blackbird is perhaps the most iconic of blackbirds. One Native American legend states that the blackbird tried to warn the people of a village that a man had set the marsh on fire. The man angrily threw stones at the bird, wounding its wings and staining them blood red. Thus, the blackbird is a bringer of omens, and of self-sacrifice.

Copyright Asteria Books 2021

Cat

Felis catus

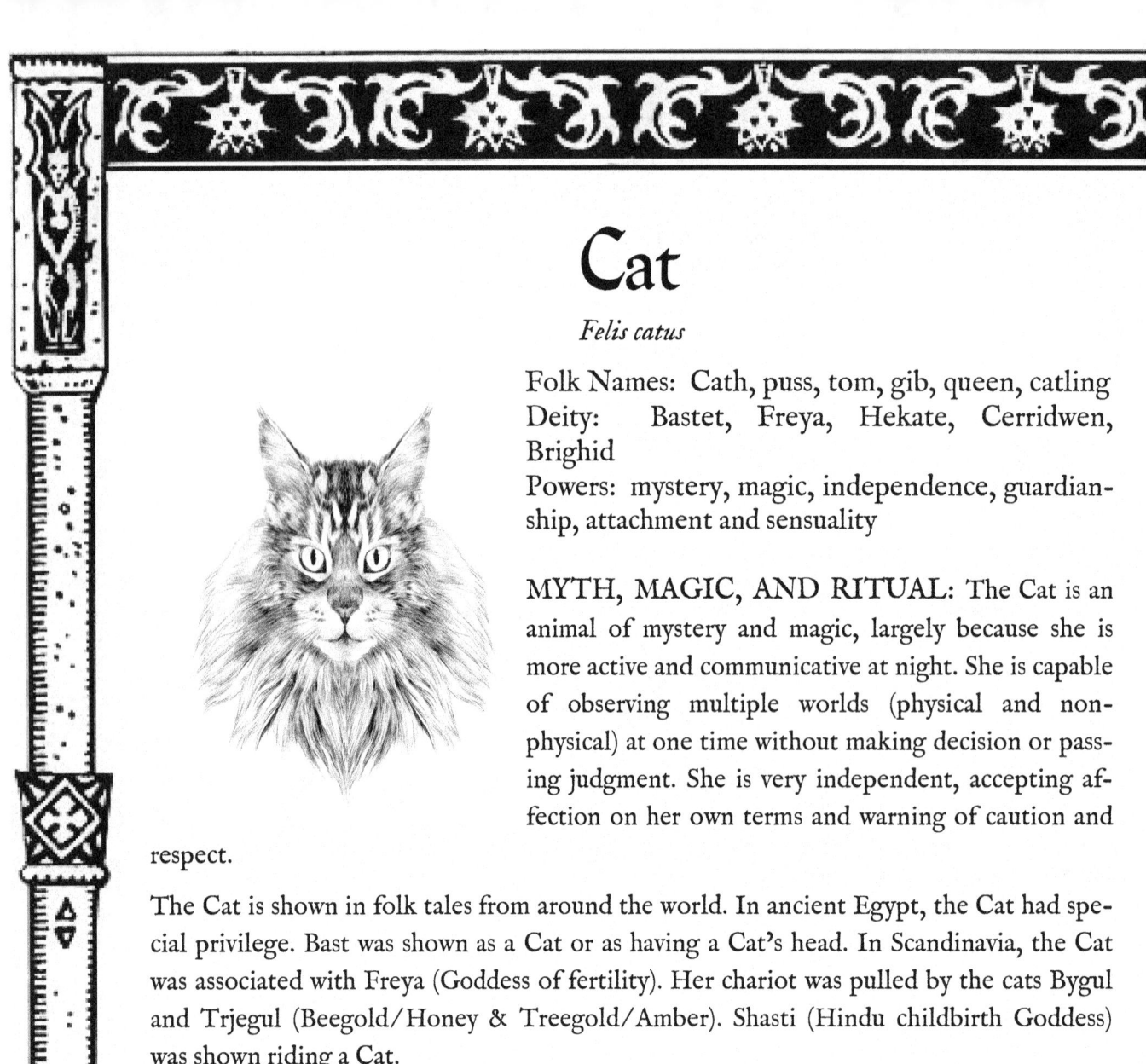

Folk Names: Cath, puss, tom, gib, queen, catling
Deity: Bastet, Freya, Hekate, Cerridwen, Brighid
Powers: mystery, magic, independence, guardianship, attachment and sensuality

MYTH, MAGIC, AND RITUAL: The Cat is an animal of mystery and magic, largely because she is more active and communicative at night. She is capable of observing multiple worlds (physical and non-physical) at one time without making decision or passing judgment. She is very independent, accepting affection on her own terms and warning of caution and respect.

The Cat is shown in folk tales from around the world. In ancient Egypt, the Cat had special privilege. Bast was shown as a Cat or as having a Cat's head. In Scandinavia, the Cat was associated with Freya (Goddess of fertility). Her chariot was pulled by the cats Bygul and Trjegul (Beegold/Honey & Treegold/Amber). Shasti (Hindu childbirth Goddess) was shown riding a Cat.

In Celtic world, warriors carried the skin of a wild Cat. The Cat's qualities of curiosity, 9 lives, independence, cleverness, unpredictability and healing would have been helpful to a warrior.

Because Cat can see and work in spirit world (which lead to the Church torturing and killing thousands of cats in Britain and France) it was believed that witches could take form of Cats. This lead to the belief that a witch's pet Cat was her familiar (spirit in the form of a Cat).

The Cat is associated with the Goddess and the feminine. Brighid had a cat as a companion. Cerridwen (as the great sow Henwen) gives birth to a wolf-cub, eagle, bee and kitten. The kitten grows into the Palug Cat - one of the 3 Plagues of Anglesey. Cerridwen is also attended by white cats who do her bidding.

The Cat is a fierce guardian (guardian of Otherworldly treasure) in the immrama of Maelduin. And the Celts have many sightings of Cath Sith (Faery Cats), which are Big Cats.

Copyright Asteria Books 2021

Cattle

Bos taurus

Celtic Name: Tarbh/Bò
Gender: Feminine
Planet: Moon
Element: Water
Deity: Io, Hathor, Brighid, Dionysos, Mithras
Powers: fertility, prosperity, protection, nourishment

MYTH, MAGIC, AND RITUAL: The bull is associated with health, potency, beneficence, fertility, abundance, prosperity, and power. The number of cattle owned were an indicator of wealth, a fact that is carried over in the term "Bull market" = rising stock market. The bull also appeared frequently on Celtic coins. Oxen (castrated bulls) were early power supply.

Bronze horns and bronze rattle (in the shape of bull's testes) spoke to the sacredness of the bull. Its horns are used as ceremonial drinking cups even today. An early Irish ritual ("bull sleep") told of the new king when the old one died. "Gateway ceremonies" involved ritual sacrifice of bulls.

The cow represents nourishment, motherhood and the Goddess. Certain herbs are associated with cows, such as cranberry (cowberry), cowslip, and milk-wort (field gentian). In Celtic lands, cows have long been considered sacred. In Britain there were sacred herds of white cattle. Ireland was gifted with cattle when three cows emerged from the sea - one red, one white, and one black. Brighid was reared on the milk of an Otherworld cow and is considered the patroness of cattle. Three of the four sacred festivals were related to cows (Samhain, Beltaine and Imbolc) Many Eastern traditions also hold the cow as sacred.

The cow is also a source of nourishment on many levels - milk, leather, meat, horn. The fact that is contributes to much to daily life is part of what makes it so sacred and special.

In folklore, the Milky Way is also called the Cow Path, and there are Fairy Cows called the "Crodh Shith." Many offerings are made of milk, and the breath and milk of the cow are considered healing.

Copyright Asteria Books 2020

Chicken

Gallus gallus domesticus

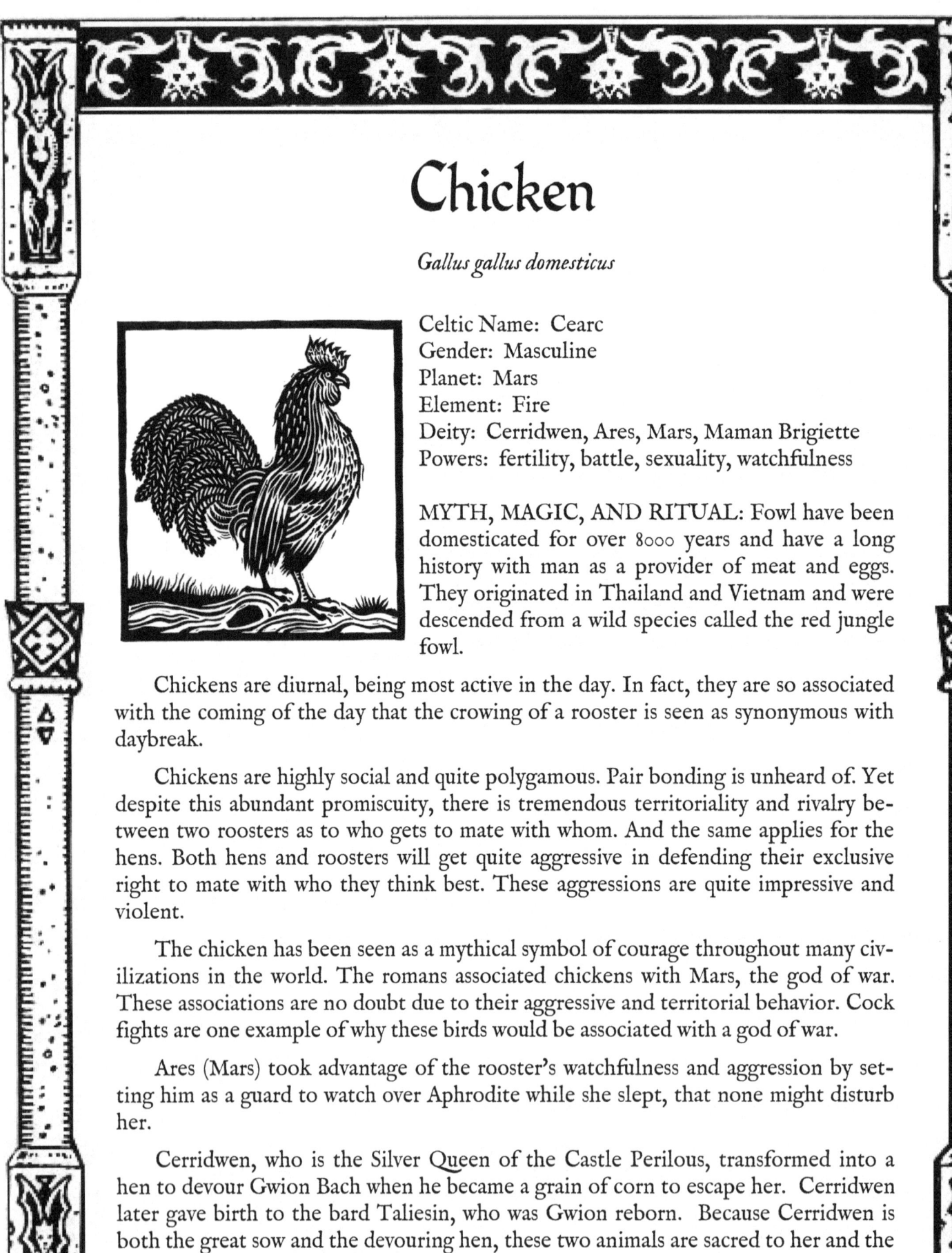

Celtic Name: Cearc
Gender: Masculine
Planet: Mars
Element: Fire
Deity: Cerridwen, Ares, Mars, Maman Brigiette
Powers: fertility, battle, sexuality, watchfulness

MYTH, MAGIC, AND RITUAL: Fowl have been domesticated for over 8000 years and have a long history with man as a provider of meat and eggs. They originated in Thailand and Vietnam and were descended from a wild species called the red jungle fowl.

Chickens are diurnal, being most active in the day. In fact, they are so associated with the coming of the day that the crowing of a rooster is seen as synonymous with daybreak.

Chickens are highly social and quite polygamous. Pair bonding is unheard of. Yet despite this abundant promiscuity, there is tremendous territoriality and rivalry between two roosters as to who gets to mate with whom. And the same applies for the hens. Both hens and roosters will get quite aggressive in defending their exclusive right to mate with who they think best. These aggressions are quite impressive and violent.

The chicken has been seen as a mythical symbol of courage throughout many civilizations in the world. The romans associated chickens with Mars, the god of war. These associations are no doubt due to their aggressive and territorial behavior. Cock fights are one example of why these birds would be associated with a god of war.

Ares (Mars) took advantage of the rooster's watchfulness and aggression by setting him as a guard to watch over Aphrodite while she slept, that none might disturb her.

Cerridwen, who is the Silver Queen of the Castle Perilous, transformed into a hen to devour Gwion Bach when he became a grain of corn to escape her. Cerridwen later gave birth to the bard Taliesin, who was Gwion reborn. Because Cerridwen is both the great sow and the devouring hen, these two animals are sacred to her and the month that she reigns over in the American Folkloric tradition (September, the time of the Fall Equinox).

Copyright Asteria Books 2020

Cougar

Puma concolor

Folk Names: Puma, Mountain lion, Panther, Painter, catamount, Mountain screamer, Ghost cat, Silver lion, Klandagi, Long Tail

Deity: Viracocha, Durga, Parvati, Moche, Bastet, Sekhmet, Kinich Ahau

Powers: Strength, leadership, protection, stealth, patience, courage, authenticity, adaptability, agility, healing

MYTH, MAGIC, AND RITUAL: In many Indigenous cultures of the Americas, the cougar is seen as a master hunter, embodying power, stealth, and leadership. The Zuni, for example, consider the cougar to be a guardian of the north and a healing fetish, believed to grant hunters success and protect travelers. Its quiet and watchful nature is seen as a lesson in patience and observation.

In magical and shamanic practices, the cougar is a potent ally for those seeking to reconnect with their inner strength and independence. Its ability to move through the wilderness unseen and unheard makes it a symbol of invisibility and the mastery of the physical world.

Rituals involving the cougar often focus on developing a sense of self-sufficiency, confidence, and courage. By working with the cougar's energy, practitioners aim to shed fear, overcome personal obstacles, and navigate life's challenges with the same quiet power and determination as the great cat itself.

Coyote

Canis latrans

Folk Names: Prairie wolf, Brush wolf, American jackal, Yote

Deity: Huehuecoyotl, Tezcatlipoca, Ma'ii, Syungmanitu

Powers: Trickster, shapeshifting, cunning, intelligence, creativity, creation, weather magick, immortality

MYTH, MAGIC, AND RITUAL: The coyote holds a prominent and often contradictory role in the myths and magic of North America. It is a quintessential trickster figure, a clever and often mischievous being who challenges established order. In many Indigenous oral traditions, Coyote is responsible for both creative and destructive acts, often bringing about significant changes to the world through his cunning and foolishness. He can be a hero, teaching humanity important skills, or a conniving thief, acting for his own self-interest.

The coyote's magic is rooted in its ability to adapt and survive. It is a master of navigating the spaces between worlds (dawn and dusk, wilderness and civilization) making it a powerful guide for those seeking to traverse liminal spaces in their own lives.

In spiritual practices, calling upon the spirit of the coyote can help practitioners become more adaptable and witty, find creative solutions to problems, or expose hidden truths.

Its howling at the moon is a ritual in itself, a call to the cosmos that symbolizes the breaking of conventions and the embrace of a wild, untamed nature.

Crane

Gruidae

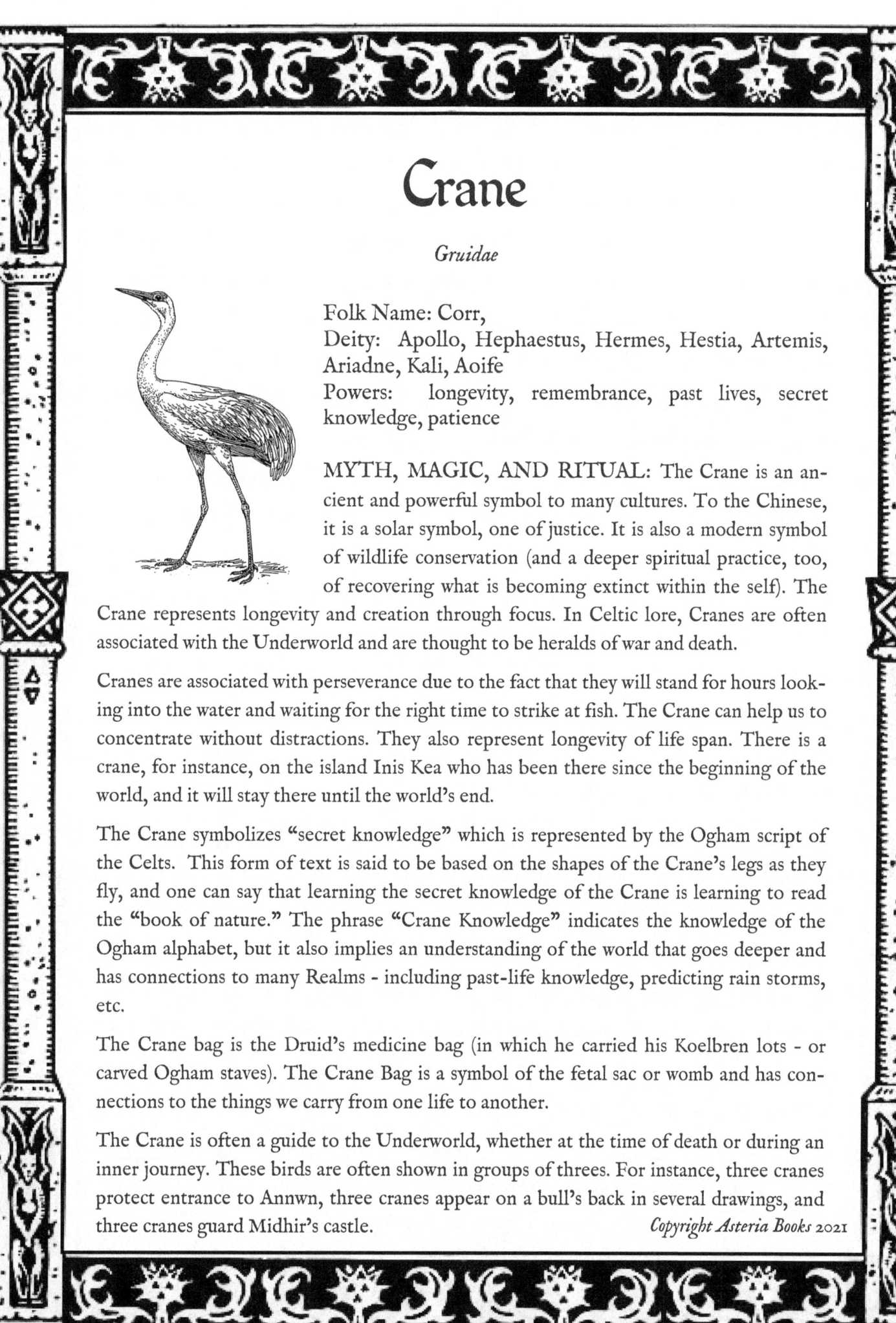

Folk Name: Corr,
Deity: Apollo, Hephaestus, Hermes, Hestia, Artemis, Ariadne, Kali, Aoife
Powers: longevity, remembrance, past lives, secret knowledge, patience

MYTH, MAGIC, AND RITUAL: The Crane is an ancient and powerful symbol to many cultures. To the Chinese, it is a solar symbol, one of justice. It is also a modern symbol of wildlife conservation (and a deeper spiritual practice, too, of recovering what is becoming extinct within the self). The Crane represents longevity and creation through focus. In Celtic lore, Cranes are often associated with the Underworld and are thought to be heralds of war and death.

Cranes are associated with perseverance due to the fact that they will stand for hours looking into the water and waiting for the right time to strike at fish. The Crane can help us to concentrate without distractions. They also represent longevity of life span. There is a crane, for instance, on the island Inis Kea who has been there since the beginning of the world, and it will stay there until the world's end.

The Crane symbolizes "secret knowledge" which is represented by the Ogham script of the Celts. This form of text is said to be based on the shapes of the Crane's legs as they fly, and one can say that learning the secret knowledge of the Crane is learning to read the "book of nature." The phrase "Crane Knowledge" indicates the knowledge of the Ogham alphabet, but it also implies an understanding of the world that goes deeper and has connections to many Realms - including past-life knowledge, predicting rain storms, etc.

The Crane bag is the Druid's medicine bag (in which he carried his Koelbren lots - or carved Ogham staves). The Crane Bag is a symbol of the fetal sac or womb and has connections to the things we carry from one life to another.

The Crane is often a guide to the Underworld, whether at the time of death or during an inner journey. These birds are often shown in groups of threes. For instance, three cranes protect entrance to Annwn, three cranes appear on a bull's back in several drawings, and three cranes guard Midhir's castle.

Copyright Asteria Books 2021

Crow

Corvus

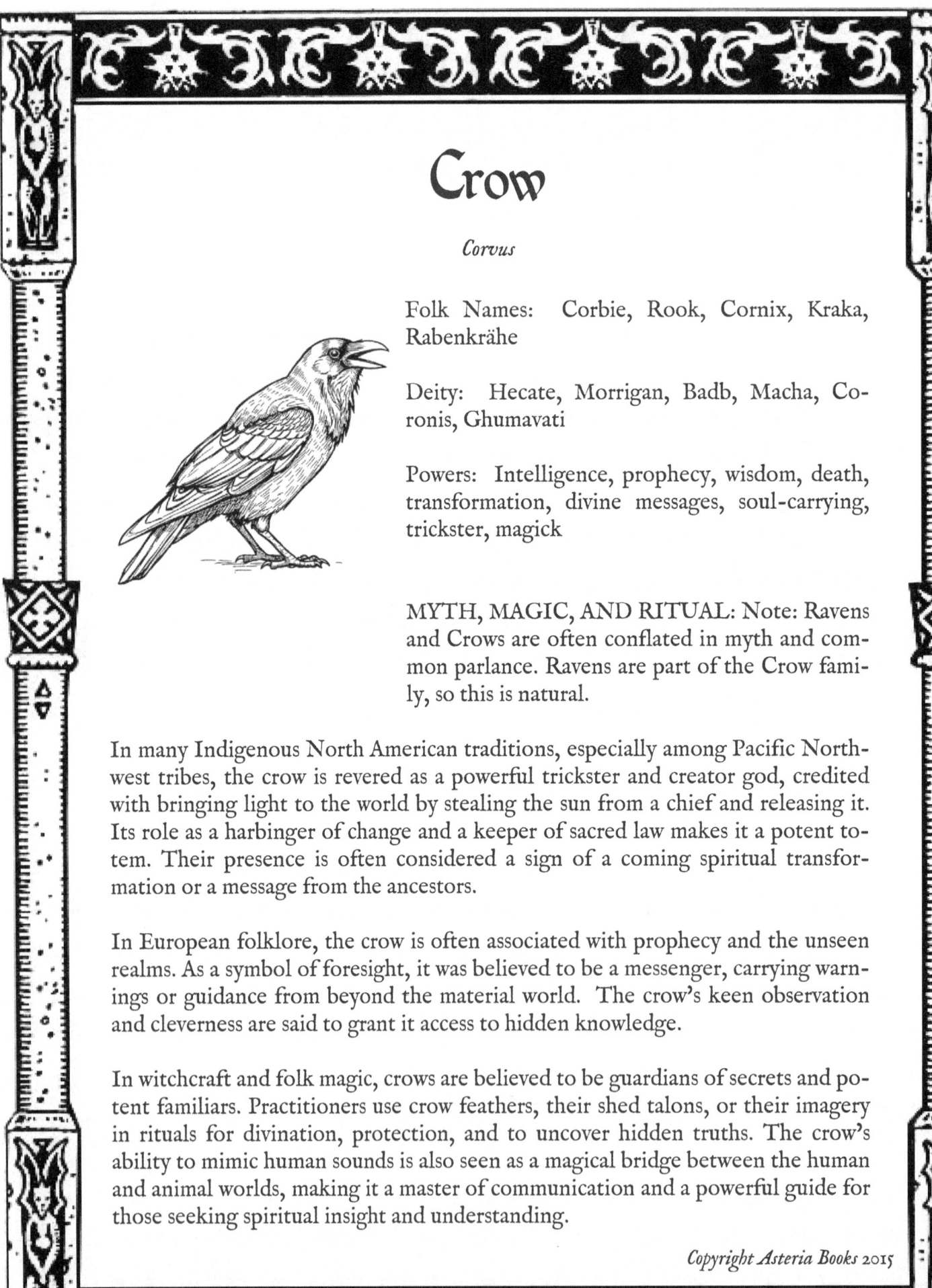

Folk Names: Corbie, Rook, Cornix, Kraka, Rabenkrähe

Deity: Hecate, Morrigan, Badb, Macha, Coronis, Ghumavati

Powers: Intelligence, prophecy, wisdom, death, transformation, divine messages, soul-carrying, trickster, magick

MYTH, MAGIC, AND RITUAL: Note: Ravens and Crows are often conflated in myth and common parlance. Ravens are part of the Crow family, so this is natural.

In many Indigenous North American traditions, especially among Pacific Northwest tribes, the crow is revered as a powerful trickster and creator god, credited with bringing light to the world by stealing the sun from a chief and releasing it. Its role as a harbinger of change and a keeper of sacred law makes it a potent totem. Their presence is often considered a sign of a coming spiritual transformation or a message from the ancestors.

In European folklore, the crow is often associated with prophecy and the unseen realms. As a symbol of foresight, it was believed to be a messenger, carrying warnings or guidance from beyond the material world. The crow's keen observation and cleverness are said to grant it access to hidden knowledge.

In witchcraft and folk magic, crows are believed to be guardians of secrets and potent familiars. Practitioners use crow feathers, their shed talons, or their imagery in rituals for divination, protection, and to uncover hidden truths. The crow's ability to mimic human sounds is also seen as a magical bridge between the human and animal worlds, making it a master of communication and a powerful guide for those seeking spiritual insight and understanding.

Copyright Asteria Books 2015

Deer

Cervidae

Celtic Name: Damh
Gender: Masculine
Planet: Jupiter
Element: Earth
Deity: Cernunnos, Herne, Gawain, Arthur
Powers: nobility, culling the herd, call to adventure, pride, grace

MYTH, MAGIC, AND RITUAL: The Stag is the male aspect of the deer, whereas the Hind is the female aspect. Deer are associated with gentleness, innocence, and a luring to new adventure. They are very adaptable, and they are native to every continent except Australia.

Many legends exist in which deer lure hunters and/or kings into the forest for adventures. One prominent example of this is the story of Gawain and the White Hart. Gawain followed the Hart willingly, though the pursuit ended in an unpleasant realization of Gawain's own shortcomings. However, by following willingly and facing his darker nature, Gawain was able to confront his rage and learn to control it, making him one of the best Knights of the Round Table.

The Stag is a symbol of pride and independence. He is an example of grace, majesty, integrity, poise, and dignity. These are indeed kingly qualities, so it is no wonder that there is a deer referred to as King Stag. In fact, this King Stag is associated in many ways with the Lord of the Wild Hunt, as both are responsible for protecting the herd and culling it of weaknesses.

The Stag is one of the five Oldest Animals in Welsh tradition. He leads a willing seeker deeper into the Mysteries and into the Otherworld. He is a guardian of the gateway between this plane and the Otherworld and delivers messages from that realm.

The Stag's antlers are made of bone and shed every year for 5 years. (In some species, both the male and female have antlers). The antlers start to grow in early summer and are fully developed by rutting time (late Autumn). The Stag sheds antlers around Imbolc (before birth of young). The antlers are protective by nature, and they also represent higher levels of attunement.

The Stag is a symbol of fertility and rampant sexuality, which is also related to the Lord of the Hunt and the Horned Gods.

Eagle

Haliaeetus and *Aquila*

Folk Names: *IOLAIR*
Deity: Zeus, Asshur
Powers: *Light, renewal, loyalty, intelligence, courage*

MYTH, MAGIC, AND RITUAL: In America, the two primary species of eagle are the Golden Eagle and the Bald Eagle. It is a symbol of freedom for Americans, and it was likewise a royal bird among Romans, Egyptian pharaohs, Greek Thebans and the Celts of Ireland and Scotland.

The eagle has a long association with sky Gods, such as Zeus and Asshur, which strengthens the bird's connections to the sun, storms, lightning and fire. Eagle is often associated with war and bravery, as well.

Native Americans hold the Eagle in highest esteem among birds, and Eagle medicine was greatly prized. Most tribes have an eagle clan, for instance, and eagle songs, dances, and ceremonies are all well-known.

Druids, as well, valued eagle magic and were said to choose this form for shapeshifting for certain ceremonies. In fact, the eagle is almost as powerful and popular a bird in Celtic myth and legend as it is in Native American lore. It is one of the four most frequently mentioned birds in the Irish and British traditions (along with the raven, swan, and crane). The eagle is particularly intertwined with the salmon at a symbolic level in Celtic myth - one representing the heights of intellect and vision; the other representing the depths of emotion and the unconscious.

Eagles are known for their swiftness, keen vision, strength, and courage.

Copyright Asteria Books 2021

Fox

Vulpes

Folk Names: *Sionnach, Reynard, tod, vixen*
Deity: Ninhursag, Dionysos, Inari,
Powers: trickster, invisibility, shape-shifting, diplomacy, wildness

MYTH, MAGIC, AND RITUAL: Fox is credited with being a "cunning one" who is "strong in council." In nature, the fox is stealthy and clever. He knows when to stay hidden and when to come out into the open. Fox can teach you the discernment to know when to speak your mind and when to keep silent. Similarly, Fox teaches invisibility.

Fox is very intelligent, diplomatic, and charming. These qualities can be seen as sly and deceitful, though, when used dishonestly. Fox is often regarded as a trickster, for this reason.

He is "quick on his feet" and can teach you to make quick decisions and put them into action right away. He can also teach you to navigate obstacles quickly and decisively.

Fox is connected to Raven in this month's totems by virtue of them both being messengers who can access all Realms. Foxes can climb into the high branches of the trees (Upperworld), are astute navigators and runners on the ground (Middleworld), and dig dens below ground (Underworld).

Names for fox in different lands have been used by chieftains, princes, and advisers. *Reynard* means "strong in council," and *Louernia* means "son of Fox."

Foxes are usually red and white (or black and white) and are therefore linked to the three sacred colors. Animals with this sort of coloring were generally seen as sacred or special by the Celts, and fox fur has been discovered in princely or religious burial sites.

Copyright Asteria Books 2021

Goat

Capra aegragus

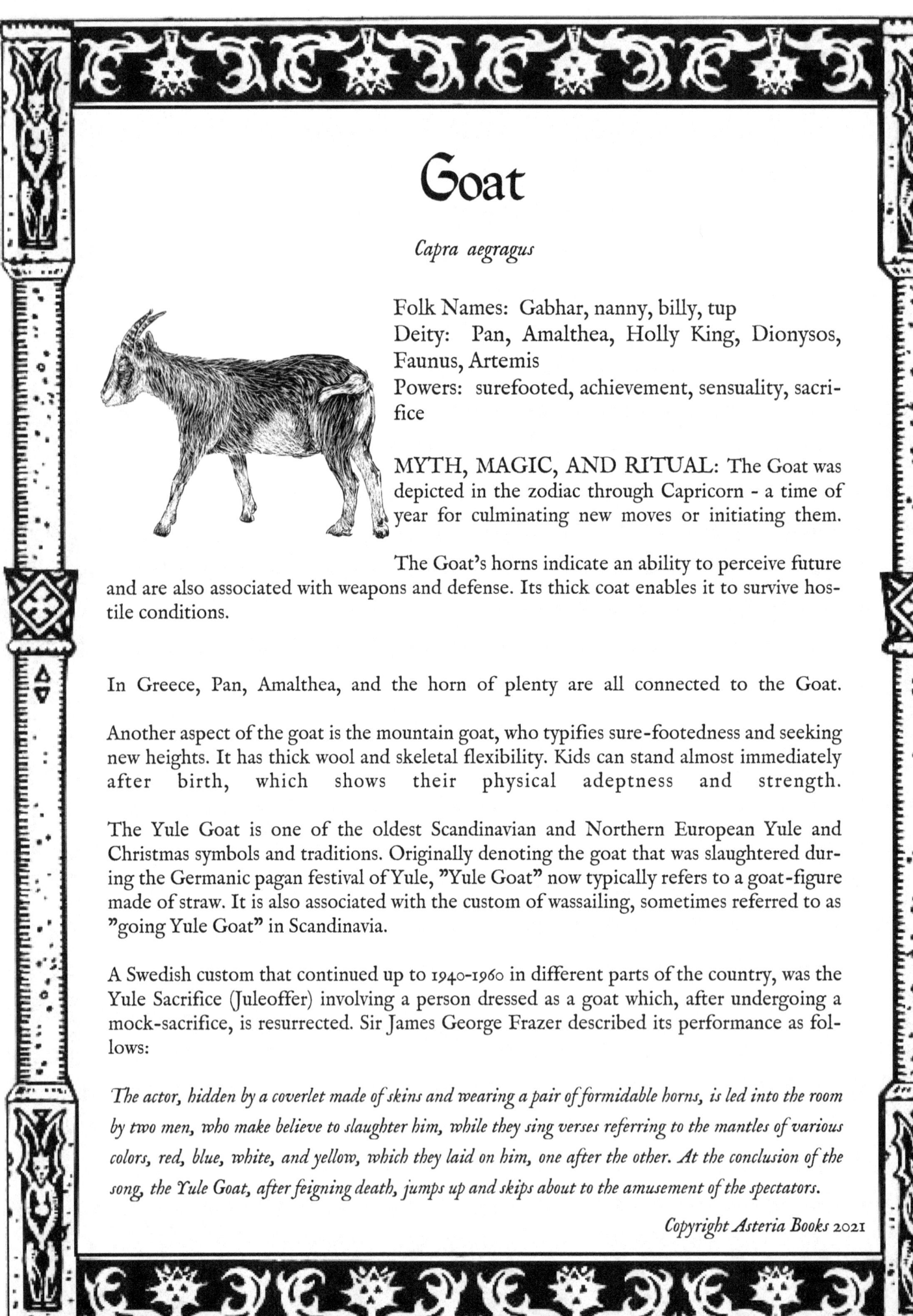

Folk Names: Gabhar, nanny, billy, tup
Deity: Pan, Amalthea, Holly King, Dionysos, Faunus, Artemis
Powers: surefooted, achievement, sensuality, sacrifice

MYTH, MAGIC, AND RITUAL: The Goat was depicted in the zodiac through Capricorn - a time of year for culminating new moves or initiating them.

The Goat's horns indicate an ability to perceive future and are also associated with weapons and defense. Its thick coat enables it to survive hostile conditions.

In Greece, Pan, Amalthea, and the horn of plenty are all connected to the Goat.

Another aspect of the goat is the mountain goat, who typifies sure-footedness and seeking new heights. It has thick wool and skeletal flexibility. Kids can stand almost immediately after birth, which shows their physical adeptness and strength.

The Yule Goat is one of the oldest Scandinavian and Northern European Yule and Christmas symbols and traditions. Originally denoting the goat that was slaughtered during the Germanic pagan festival of Yule, "Yule Goat" now typically refers to a goat-figure made of straw. It is also associated with the custom of wassailing, sometimes referred to as "going Yule Goat" in Scandinavia.

A Swedish custom that continued up to 1940-1960 in different parts of the country, was the Yule Sacrifice (Juleoffer) involving a person dressed as a goat which, after undergoing a mock-sacrifice, is resurrected. Sir James George Frazer described its performance as follows:

The actor, hidden by a coverlet made of skins and wearing a pair of formidable horns, is led into the room by two men, who make believe to slaughter him, while they sing verses referring to the mantles of various colors, red, blue, white, and yellow, which they laid on him, one after the other. At the conclusion of the song, the Yule Goat, after feigning death, jumps up and skips about to the amusement of the spectators.

Copyright Asteria Books 2021

Goose

Anatidae

Celtic Name: Geadh, gander, gosling
Deity: Hulda, Aphrodite, Artemis, Juno, Hera
Powers: feminine power, springtime, questing, vigilance

MYTH, MAGIC, AND RITUAL: The goose is the companion of that ancient and powerful goddess, Hulda, as Mother Goose. The goose is a fierce defender of its family and territory, and many ancient gates and warrior's graves have been adorned with the motif of the goose. We often speak of "a wild goose chase" as geese are notoriously difficult to capture or kill.

Several goddesses and witches of folklore have been identified by their having a goose foot (La Reine Pedauque), and thus the goose is a symbol of defensive feminine power.

The call of the goose in flight is said to be the same as the baying of the Gabriel hounds of the Wild Hunt. Hulda, whose bed is made of goose feathers, is said to lead this ride. When she shakes out her bed the snow falls from goose feathers.

The goose is a symbol of early springtime, as it denotes both snow and returning light. The goose who lays the golden egg is laying the growing sun of spring.

Geese mate for life and are associated with marital fidelity. Geese are also known for their furious mating habits, and a "goose" is sometimes used as slang for a prostitute. Their feathers are often used in bedding to bestow blessings of fertility and fidelity on the couple who sleeps there.

Geese are the symbol of migration, and therefore represent both the changing of the seasons, and the call to quest. It is unknown how geese navigate over long distances, returning year after year, but return they do. This is symbolic of the dedication of the initiate to remain true to the path.

When flying geese travel in a V formation. This way of flying makes it easier to travel long distances without fatigue, as it puts the greatest strain on the leader who "cuts" a path through the air for the followers to more easily travel behind. Thus, the goose can be a symbol of leadership.

Copyright Asteria Books 2021

Hare

Lepus

Celtic Name: Gearr
Gender: Feminine
Planet: Moon
Element: Water
Deity: Ixchel, Boudicca, Eostre, Freya, Hermes
Powers: lunar magic, fertility, sensitivity, swiftness, intuition

MYTH, MAGIC, AND RITUAL: Rabbits are notorious breeders, and are a symbol of the fertility of spring. The expression "mad as a March hare" comes from the rabbit's habit of fighting, courting, and mating during the early spring. The tradition of the "Easter bunny," or Eostre rabbit, reflects this springtime symbolism.

Rabbits have always been associated with witchcraft. They are sacred to Hecate and have the peculiar habit of gathering in a circle, the "hare's parliament." Witches are often thought to be able to transform into a rabbit.

Many cultures perceive the form of a rabbit in the full moon, and thus the rabbit is associated with lunar magic. So associated with the moon and old goddesses of Europe is the hare that it was once forbidden to eat its flesh in Britain and Ireland. In Kerry it is still said that to eat a hare is "to eat one's grandmother."

Rabbits bring great fortune to those who associate with them, due to their fecundity, and perhaps to their association with witches. Thus it became lucky to carry a rabbit's foot, especially during games of chance.

Rabbits could curse as well. It was considered very bad luck to even mention a rabbit when at sea, and pregnant women who had a rabbit cross their path were said to give birth to babies with a "hare lip."

Rabbits are most active during dawn and dusk, the liminal times, and their burrows are sometimes said to be entryways to the underworld or fairie realm. "Going down the rabbit hole" is a metaphor for entering into trance consciousness.

Rabbits have an old association with cats. They share the nicknames "pussy" (from the Latin lepus) and "malkin".

Copyright Asteria Books 2021

Hawk

Buteo

Folk Names: Peregrine, Merlin, Kestrel, Osprey, Windhover, Falcon

Deity: Horus, Gwalchmai, Ra, Vethrfolnir, Hawk of Achill, Apollo, Freyja, Indra

Powers: Divine messages, perspective, clear-vision, intuition, prophecy, wisdom, protection, transformation, new beginnings

MYTH, MAGIC, AND RITUAL: In ancient Egypt, the hawk was a sacred symbol of the god Horus, whose falcon head represented the sky and divine royalty. As a god of kingship and the heavens, Horus was believed to guide the pharaohs and protect them from harm.

Similarly, in Celtic mythology, the hawk was seen as a creature of wisdom and foresight, a messenger from the spirit world capable of seeing beyond the veil of ordinary reality.

Among many Native American tribes, the hawk is a significant totem of clear vision, focus, and leadership. It is believed to bring messages from the spiritual world, offering guidance and a higher perspective on life's challenges.

In rituals, a hawk feather is a powerful object, used to cleanse sacred spaces and carry prayers to the heavens.

Modern practitioners often call upon the spirit of the hawk to gain clarity, cut through illusions, and develop a sense of purpose. The hawk's sharp eyesight symbolizes the ability to see the truth in any situation, making it a powerful ally in divination and spiritual work.

Copyright Asteria Books 2015

Horse

Equus caballus

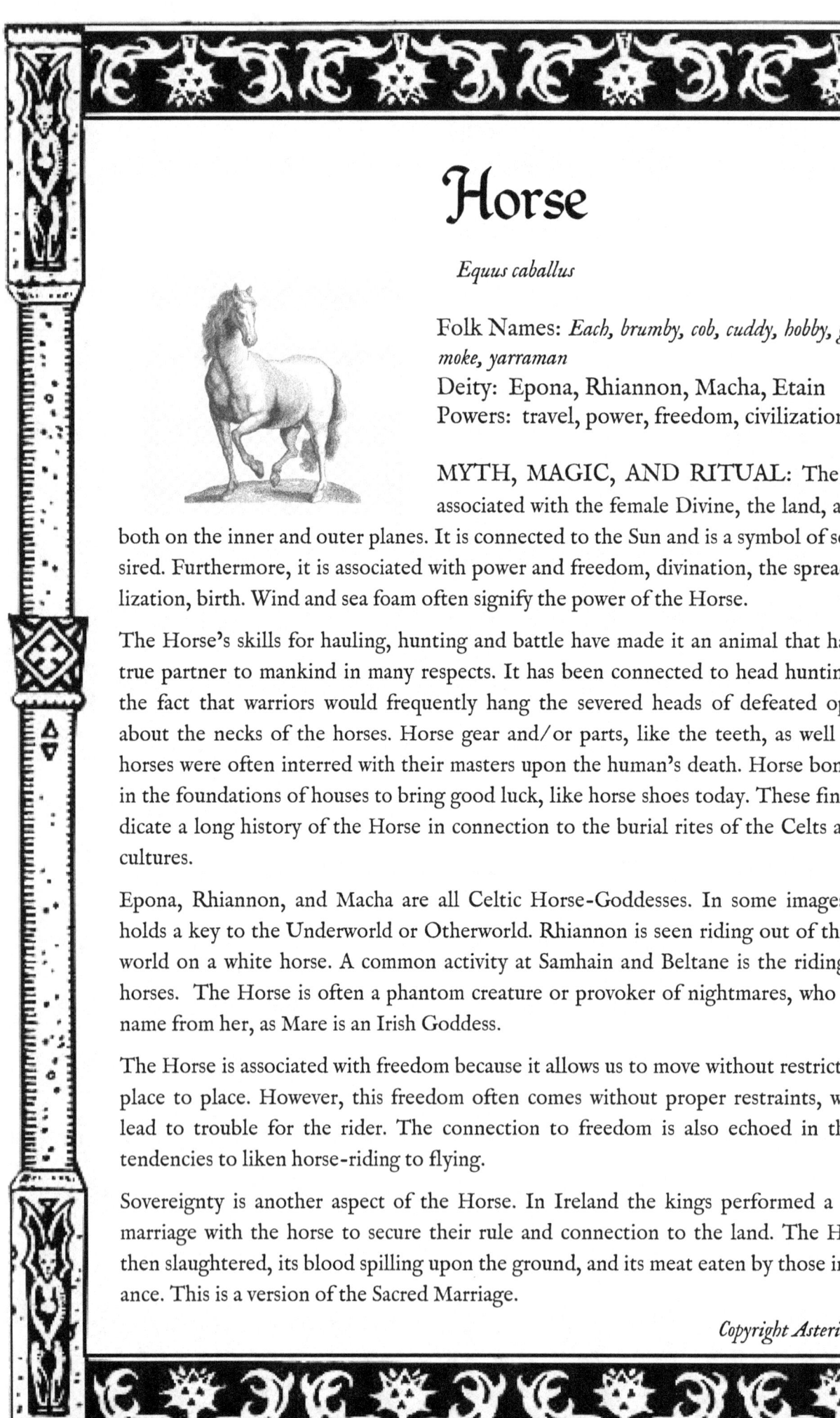

Folk Names: *Each, brumby, cob, cuddy, hobby, gee-gee, moke, yarraman*
Deity: Epona, Rhiannon, Macha, Etain
Powers: travel, power, freedom, civilization

MYTH, MAGIC, AND RITUAL: The Horse is associated with the female Divine, the land, and travel both on the inner and outer planes. It is connected to the Sun and is a symbol of sexual desired. Furthermore, it is associated with power and freedom, divination, the spread of civilization, birth. Wind and sea foam often signify the power of the Horse.

The Horse's skills for hauling, hunting and battle have made it an animal that has been a true partner to mankind in many respects. It has been connected to head hunting due to the fact that warriors would frequently hang the severed heads of defeated opponents about the necks of the horses. Horse gear and/or parts, like the teeth, as well as whole horses were often interred with their masters upon the human's death. Horse bones found in the foundations of houses to bring good luck, like horse shoes today. These findings indicate a long history of the Horse in connection to the burial rites of the Celts and other cultures.

Epona, Rhiannon, and Macha are all Celtic Horse-Goddesses. In some images a Mare holds a key to the Underworld or Otherworld. Rhiannon is seen riding out of the Otherworld on a white horse. A common activity at Samhain and Beltane is the riding hobby-horses. The Horse is often a phantom creature or provoker of nightmares, who get their name from her, as Mare is an Irish Goddess.

The Horse is associated with freedom because it allows us to move without restriction from place to place. However, this freedom often comes without proper restraints, which can lead to trouble for the rider. The connection to freedom is also echoed in the poets' tendencies to liken horse-riding to flying.

Sovereignty is another aspect of the Horse. In Ireland the kings performed a symbolic marriage with the horse to secure their rule and connection to the land. The Horse was then slaughtered, its blood spilling upon the ground, and its meat eaten by those in attendance. This is a version of the Sacred Marriage.

Copyright Asteria Books 2021

Hound

Canis lupus familiaris

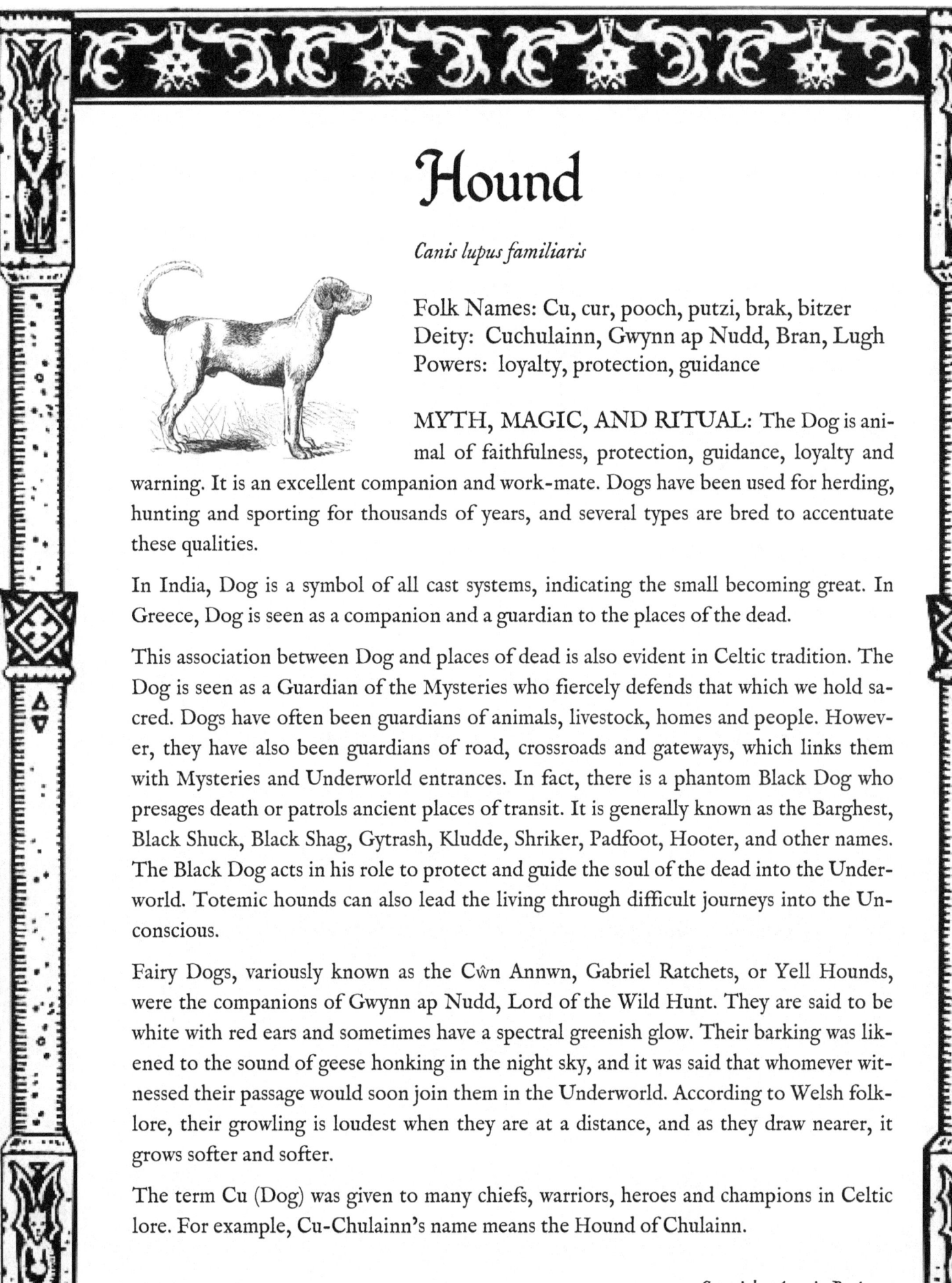

Folk Names: Cu, cur, pooch, putzi, brak, bitzer
Deity: Cuchulainn, Gwynn ap Nudd, Bran, Lugh
Powers: loyalty, protection, guidance

MYTH, MAGIC, AND RITUAL: The Dog is animal of faithfulness, protection, guidance, loyalty and warning. It is an excellent companion and work-mate. Dogs have been used for herding, hunting and sporting for thousands of years, and several types are bred to accentuate these qualities.

In India, Dog is a symbol of all cast systems, indicating the small becoming great. In Greece, Dog is seen as a companion and a guardian to the places of the dead.

This association between Dog and places of dead is also evident in Celtic tradition. The Dog is seen as a Guardian of the Mysteries who fiercely defends that which we hold sacred. Dogs have often been guardians of animals, livestock, homes and people. However, they have also been guardians of road, crossroads and gateways, which links them with Mysteries and Underworld entrances. In fact, there is a phantom Black Dog who presages death or patrols ancient places of transit. It is generally known as the Barghest, Black Shuck, Black Shag, Gytrash, Kludde, Shriker, Padfoot, Hooter, and other names. The Black Dog acts in his role to protect and guide the soul of the dead into the Underworld. Totemic hounds can also lead the living through difficult journeys into the Unconscious.

Fairy Dogs, variously known as the Cŵn Annwn, Gabriel Ratchets, or Yell Hounds, were the companions of Gwynn ap Nudd, Lord of the Wild Hunt. They are said to be white with red ears and sometimes have a spectral greenish glow. Their barking was likened to the sound of geese honking in the night sky, and it was said that whomever witnessed their passage would soon join them in the Underworld. According to Welsh folklore, their growling is loudest when they are at a distance, and as they draw nearer, it grows softer and softer.

The term Cu (Dog) was given to many chiefs, warriors, heroes and champions in Celtic lore. For example, Cu-Chulainn's name means the Hound of Chulainn.

Copyright Asteria Books 2021

Hummingbird

Trochilidae

Folk Names: Hummers, Flying Jewels, Sun Gems, Beija-Flor, Chuparosa, Picaflor

Deity: Huitzilopochtli, Iris, Eros

Powers: Rebirth, love, divine messages, reincarnation, resurrection, healing, rain-bringing, fire-bringing

MYTH, MAGIC, AND RITUAL: In Aztec cosmology, the war deity Huitzilopochtli was symbolized by the hummingbird, embodying the sun, fire, and the courage of fallen warriors who were said to be reincarnated as the tiny birds. This connection to rebirth and unstoppable power made it a sacred totem.

Among various North American Indigenous tribes, the hummingbird is a potent messenger of joy, light, and love. Its ability to drink nectar from a flower while hovering in place is seen as a magical act, symbolizing the ability to draw nourishment and beauty from life's small moments.

In certain rituals, hummingbird feathers were sought for their presumed magical properties, believed to bring good luck, healing, and happiness.

Its unique ability to fly backward is often interpreted in modern magical practices as a sign of resilience and the power to undo past hurts.

Practitioners may use its imagery in rituals to attract love, bring sweetness into their lives, and swiftly achieve their goals.

Copyright Asteria Books 2015

Lapwing

Vanellinae

Folk Names: Curracag
Deity: Ostara/Eostre
Powers: *Resourcefulness, distraction, wisdom, divination*

MYTH, MAGIC, AND RITUAL: The lapwing is one of the three guardian animals discussed by Robert Graves in his book *The White Goddess*. (The other two are Dog and Roebuck, both of which have a place in our totemic wheel). The lapwing guards the Mysteries of the Wise, he says, by "disguising the Truth." She does this by feigning injury to make herself appear helpless to predators who have come to close to her nest. This nest is on the ground in the spring, with her hatchlings inside. She flops and flails and flies in little spurts, all the time leading the predator away from her young. When she has gone far enough, she abandons the rouse and flies away.

The Greeks used the phrase "deceitful as a lapwing" because of this same behavior. Framed positively, though, we see the lapwing's great resourcefulness and cleverness.

Because Lapwing's nest rests on the ground in the spring, hares have been known to sit in them, looking like they are hatching eggs (which is where the combined association of bunnies and eggs come from for spring fertility celebrations). It is actually said in myth that the Teutonic Goddess Ostara transformed a Lapwing into a Hare. The Hare, of course, is already associated with shape-shifting, and this myth shows that Lapwing is also a shape-shifter (further adding to her ability to "disguise the Truth").

She is a Guardian of the Mysteries, and she teaches us to look beyond the superficial details, to ignore appearance and aim instead for reality.

Moose

Alces alces

Folk Names: Elk

Deity: Eiktyrne, Onhdagwija, Pamola, Cernunnos, Jenmar

Powers: Strength, resilience, wisdom, gentleness, balance, clairvoyance, intuition

MYTH, MAGIC, AND RITUAL: In many Indigenous traditions, the Moose is revered as a symbol of strength, endurance, and wisdom. The animal's ability to navigate through challenging terrain with quiet grace is seen as a lesson in resilience and self-reliance.

For some, the moose is a spiritual messenger or a guardian of the wilderness, connecting the human world with the spirit realm.

The moose's massive antlers, which are shed and regrown annually, symbolize cycles of death and rebirth, as well as protection and authority.

In the myths of some Siberian and Sámi peoples, a great moose is believed to run across the sky, its antlers holding the sun. This cosmic image represents the interconnectedness of all living things and the sun's daily journey.

Rituals often center on the hunt, with ceremonies of respect and gratitude for the animal's sacrifice. Every part of the moose, from the meat and hide to the bones and antlers, is traditionally used, reinforcing the deep reverence for the animal and its role in sustaining life.

Copyright Asteria Books 2015

Moth/Butterfly

Lepidoptera

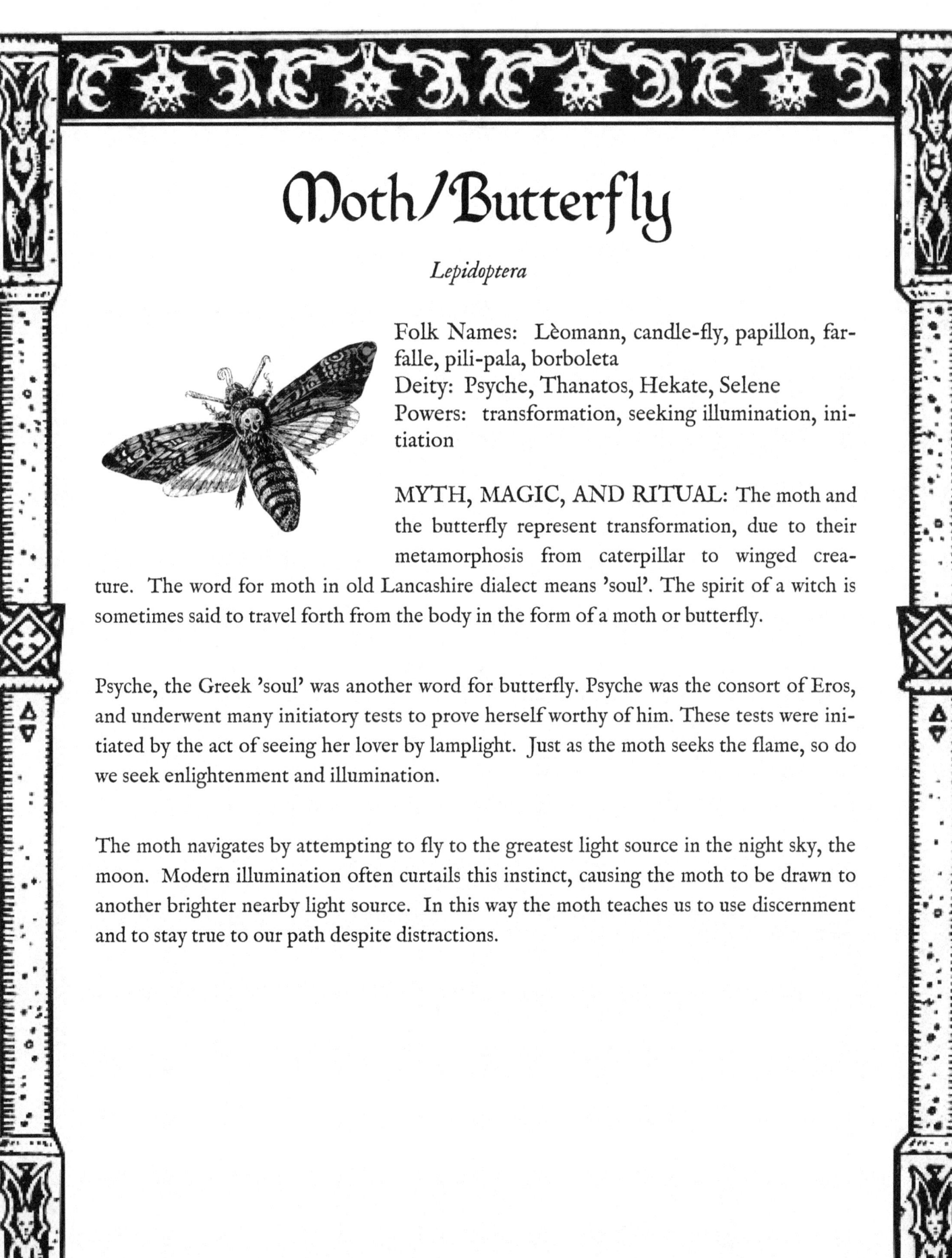

Folk Names: Lèomann, candle-fly, papillon, farfalle, pili-pala, borboleta
Deity: Psyche, Thanatos, Hekate, Selene
Powers: transformation, seeking illumination, initiation

MYTH, MAGIC, AND RITUAL: The moth and the butterfly represent transformation, due to their metamorphosis from caterpillar to winged creature. The word for moth in old Lancashire dialect means 'soul'. The spirit of a witch is sometimes said to travel forth from the body in the form of a moth or butterfly.

Psyche, the Greek 'soul' was another word for butterfly. Psyche was the consort of Eros, and underwent many initiatory tests to prove herself worthy of him. These tests were initiated by the act of seeing her lover by lamplight. Just as the moth seeks the flame, so do we seek enlightenment and illumination.

The moth navigates by attempting to fly to the greatest light source in the night sky, the moon. Modern illumination often curtails this instinct, causing the moth to be drawn to another brighter nearby light source. In this way the moth teaches us to use discernment and to stay true to our path despite distractions.

Owl

Strigiformes

Folk Names: Comhachag, strix, bubo, hooter, night-raven, owlet, howlet
Deity: Blodeuwedd, Cailleach, Lilith
Powers: Wisdom, magic, night, inner visions, change

MYTH, MAGIC, AND RITUAL: In the western tradition, Owl is inextricably associated with the quality of wisdom. This is due in part to its ancient associations with the Goddess Athena, and also with its large forward-facing eyes. In Welsh tradition, the Owl is among the most ancient of animals. It was the third animal that Culhwch asks regarding the whereabouts of Mabon. Whereas the salmon of knowledge offers a general kind of wisdom, the owl is symbolic of a more circumspect wisdom. It is objective and detached from the mundane. Owl watches and waits, in ruined castles, church towers, barns, and hollow trees. The owl is symbolic of esoteric wisdom and secrecy.

In folklore, the Owl is associated with death, night, and silence. The Owl is much noted for its unique feather and wing structure which allows it to fly silently.

Owls have acute hearing, and use a kind of echo-location to hunt their prey. The owl can be a symbol of both silence and the ability to hear those things that others might miss. An owl totem can be a sign that one would benefit from listening more.

One of the Celtic names for owl is "Cailleach-oidchce" (crone of the night), linking the owl with the Black Goddess as the Cailleach. The Black Goddess is the Lady of life-in-death and the call of the owl is seen as an omen of both the birth of a girl or the death of a man. This ability to foretell the future links the owl with clairvoyance and astral travel.

The owl is a bird set apart. She hunts at night, and is mobbed by other birds -- notably crows -- during the day. The Welsh point to the story of Blodeuwedd, the flower-bride of Lleu Llaw Gyffes, for the reason behind this. She was transformed into an owl as punishment for betraying her husband.

Copyright Asteria Books 2021

Raven

Corvus corax

Folk Names: Bran, storm petrel, Mother Carey's chicken
Deity: Odin, Morrigan, King Arthur, Apollo, Qayin
Powers: underworld messenger, shape-shifting, trickster, initiation, protection

MYTH, MAGIC, AND RITUAL: The Raven is the most sacred bird of the British Isles. Raven is a bird of magic and mysticism, shapeshifting, creation, birth and death, healing, initiation, protection and prophecy. Raven is great at vocalizations and can even be taught to speak. She can use tools, is not intimidated by others, is fast and wary, and does not make easy prey for other animals.

In the Near East, Raven is considered unclean, due to the fact that she is a scavenger. In Norse tradition, Odin had 2 Ravens as messengers (Thought and Memory). Furthermore, Odin was known to shape-shift as a Raven. In the Pacific Northwest, Raven was the bringer of life and order. She was the bringer of sunlight. Even in British tradition, Raven is seen sometimes as a bird of morning, sunlight and joy. In the tale of Beowulf, Raven helps Beowulf to victory.

Bran the Blessed, whose name means Raven, was sometimes known as the Raven King. He was beheaded in battle, and his head was buried in White Mount, which later became the hill on which the Tower of London was built. His head was placed to face the enemies and protect England from invasion. In fact, both London and Lyons had Raven totems. Furthermore, both cities were dedicated to Lugh who was warned of the approach of the Formorians by Ravens. Another legend claims that King Arthur became a Raven upon his death.

Ravens are often associated with death and the Underworld. The cries of Ravens are heard before death in battle, and Ravens are often said to bring messages from the Underworld. For this reason, they are bird of prophecy and divination. The Raven has the ability to see the past and the future, while living in the present.

In this way, the Raven is a bringer of Initiation, both little "i" and big "I" initiation is, after all, a death of one thing and the birth of another.

Raven is strongly associated with Morrigan (and one of Her particular aspects, Badb). Morrigan appears on the battlefield as Raven (or Scald-Crow), bringing havoc and fear in the enemy. Linked to their presence at or proclamation of Death, they are associated with deep healing (the kind of healing that comes from radical confrontation with the hidden), the type of healing offered by the Morrigan.

Copyright Asteria Books 2021

Robin

Turdus migratorius

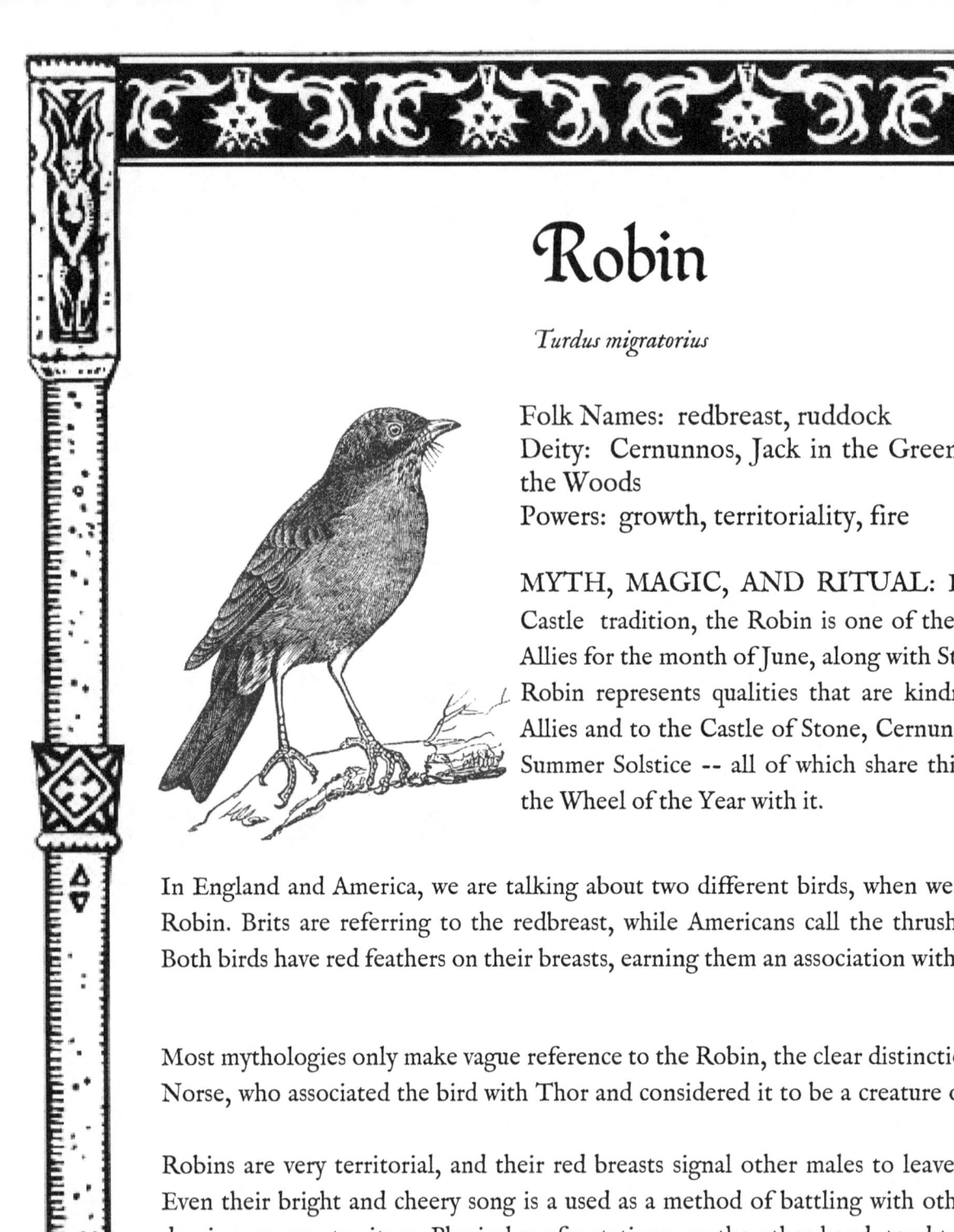

Folk Names: redbreast, ruddock
Deity: Cernunnos, Jack in the Green, Robin of the Woods
Powers: growth, territoriality, fire

MYTH, MAGIC, AND RITUAL: In the Spiral Castle tradition, the Robin is one of the three Spirit Allies for the month of June, along with Stag and Oak. Robin represents qualities that are kindred to these Allies and to the Castle of Stone, Cernunnos, and the Summer Solstice -- all of which share this portion of the Wheel of the Year with it.

In England and America, we are talking about two different birds, when we refer to the Robin. Brits are referring to the redbreast, while Americans call the thrush the Robin. Both birds have red feathers on their breasts, earning them an association with fire.

Most mythologies only make vague reference to the Robin, the clear distinction being the Norse, who associated the bird with Thor and considered it to be a creature of the storm.

Robins are very territorial, and their red breasts signal other males to leave their space. Even their bright and cheery song is a used as a method of battling with other males for dominance over territory. Physical confrontations, on the other hand, tend to be symbolic. Male robins don't seek to hurt each other physically.

The Robin's bright blue egg is distinctive in color. Both male and female Robins share in the feeding of the young, which is a very active process for these birds. Hatchlings are born with no feathers at all, and feedings occur at an average of every twelve minutes. Even so, Robins manage to hatch more than one brood each year. This is a testament to their growth and incredible vitality.

Copyright Asteria Books 2021

Salmon

Salmo salar

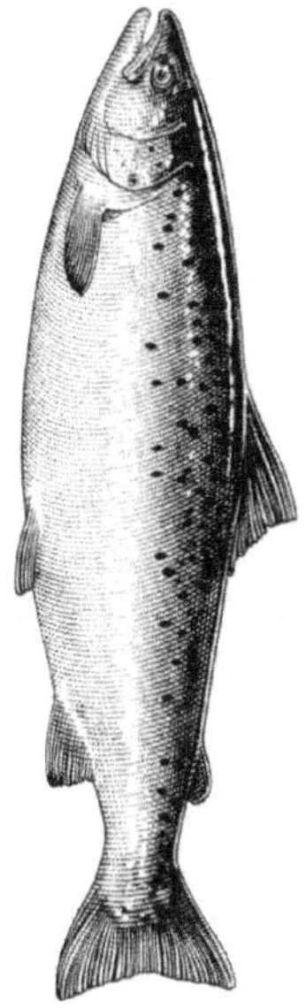

Celtic Name: Bradan
Gender: Masculine
Planet: Mercury
Element: Water
Deity: Cuchulainn, Fionn MacCumhaill
Powers: *wisdom, knowledge, inspiration*

MYTH, MAGIC, AND RITUAL: The Salmon is the "Oldest Animal" in Welsh mythology and is critical in the search for Mabon. Salmon is a symbol of wisdom, inspiration, and rejuvenation.

The Salmon will return to the place of its own birth to mate (often with great difficulty) and is, therefore, a reminder that we need to journey back to our own beginnings to find wisdom. The Druid quest is for wisdom and knowledge, leading eventually to the Oldest Animal.

It swims in the Well of Wisdom (Connla's Well) at the source of all life, a sacred pool that has nine hazel trees growing around it. Fionn MacCumhaill received the wisdom of the Salmon when he was cooking the fish for his teacher. The grease splashed on his hand, and he got the knowledge of the fish when he sucked the burned spot. This is a reminder to us all that the one who does the work (catches, cleans, and cooks the fish) is the one who reaps the rewards of wisdom.

Wisdom is a blessing that comes from experience. There are no shortcuts. Time, pain, and hardship are very effective teachers, though they are not the only ones by which we learn. Still, it is our OWN experience by which we gain true wisdom, and not merely insightful observation.

Seal

Pinnipedia

Folk Names: Sea lion, Sea wolf, Sea bear, Sea calf, Sea dog

Deity: Sedna, Proteus, Selkies, Psamanthe, Komokwa

Powers: Shapeshifting, seduction, creation, abundance, wealth, wisdom, prophecy

MYTH, MAGIC, AND RITUAL: In folklore, seals and sea lions are often seen as liminal beings, existing between the land and the sea.

Across Celtic and Norse traditions, the Selkie is a prominent myth — a creature that can shed its seal skin to become human. These stories often involve love, loss, and the call of the ocean, symbolizing the deep, often tragic, connection between humanity and the wild.

Among coastal Indigenous peoples of North America, seals and sea lions are considered sacred. They are powerful hunting totems and are revered for their spirit, which is believed to be generous and wise.

Rituals of gratitude and respect are performed to honor the animals and ensure their continued abundance. For these communities, seals represent both a physical and spiritual gift from the ocean.

In magical traditions, a seal's image or found parts, such as whiskers or bones, are used for spells related to communication, intuition, and navigating emotional depths.

The seal's ability to thrive in both water and on land makes it a symbol of balancing two different worlds (the conscious and the unconscious, or the earthly and the spiritual) and a powerful guide for those seeking to understand their dreams or hidden truths.

Copyright Asteria Books 2015

Sheep

Ovis aries

Folk Names: Jumbuck, Woolies, Shornies, Fuzzball, Lamb, Ewe, Ram, Tup, Wether

Deity: Lahar, Duttur, Pan, Faunus, Pales, Khnum, Biroba, Kurwaichin, Jesus

Powers: Restful sleep, dream magic, astral projection, healing, prophecy, guidance, wisdom, inner peace, protection, sacrifice

MYTH, MAGIC, AND RITUAL: In Abrahamic religions, the lamb is a potent symbol of purity and divine redemption, a representation of both vulnerability and unwavering faith. The shepherd and his flock are a recurring motif, signifying protection, guidance, and the relationship between a leader and their people.

In Celtic folklore, sheep were considered to be messengers of the Otherworld, and their fleece was thought to hold magical properties for protection and warmth.

Rituals would involve offerings of wool to spirits of the land to ensure the health of the flock.

Similarly, in ancient Greek tradition, the Golden Fleece of the ram was a symbol of authority and kingship, sought after by the hero Jason and his Argonauts. The quest for this powerful artifact represents a journey of transformation and the acquisition of a sacred, almost divine, power.

In magical practices today, sheep's wool is used in knot magic to bind intentions or create protective charms for the home, drawing on the animal's ancient associations with innocence and security.

Copyright Asteria Books 2015

Snake

Serpentes

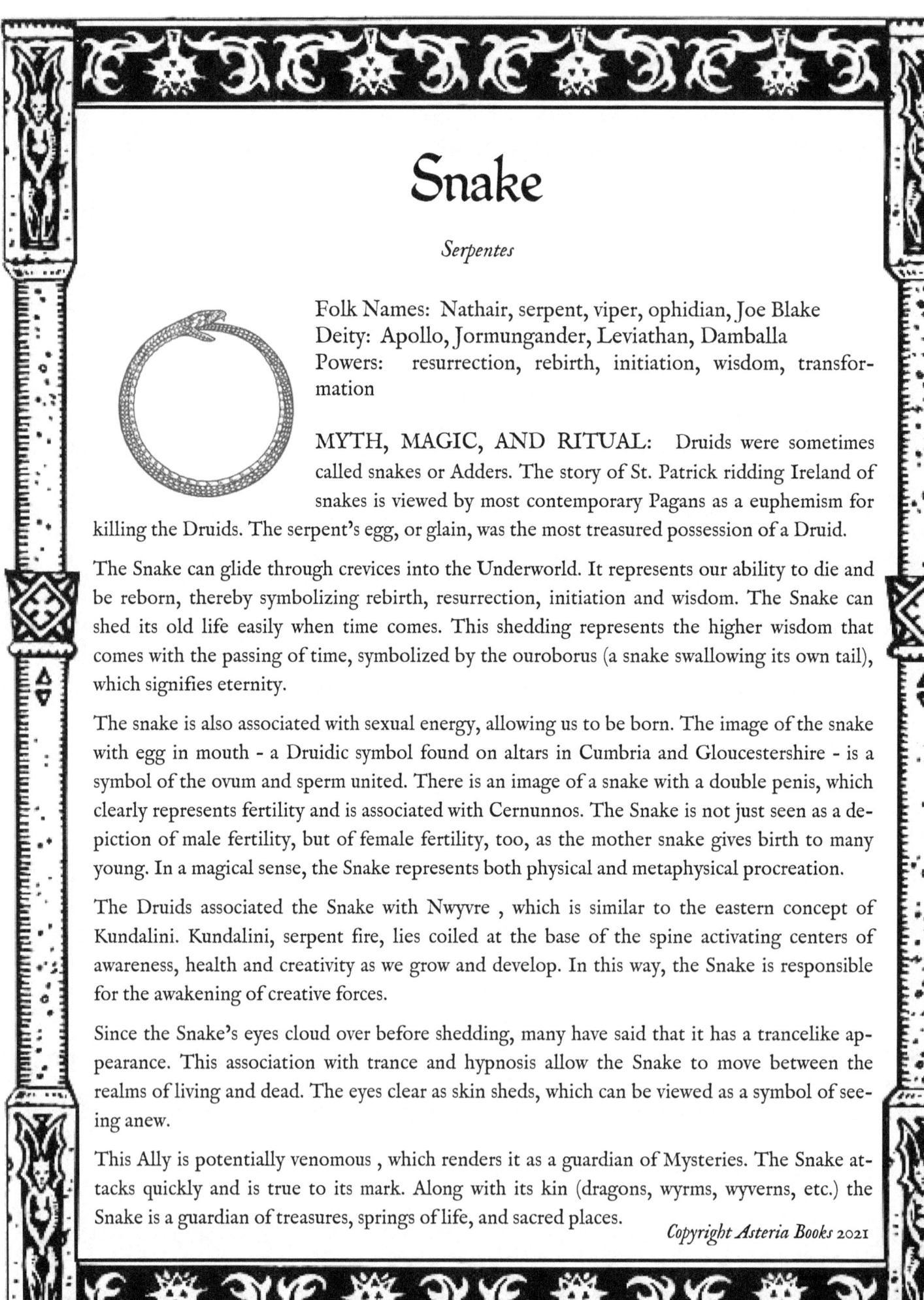

Folk Names: Nathair, serpent, viper, ophidian, Joe Blake
Deity: Apollo, Jormungander, Leviathan, Damballa
Powers: resurrection, rebirth, initiation, wisdom, transformation

MYTH, MAGIC, AND RITUAL: Druids were sometimes called snakes or Adders. The story of St. Patrick ridding Ireland of snakes is viewed by most contemporary Pagans as a euphemism for killing the Druids. The serpent's egg, or glain, was the most treasured possession of a Druid.

The Snake can glide through crevices into the Underworld. It represents our ability to die and be reborn, thereby symbolizing rebirth, resurrection, initiation and wisdom. The Snake can shed its old life easily when time comes. This shedding represents the higher wisdom that comes with the passing of time, symbolized by the ouroborus (a snake swallowing its own tail), which signifies eternity.

The snake is also associated with sexual energy, allowing us to be born. The image of the snake with egg in mouth - a Druidic symbol found on altars in Cumbria and Gloucestershire - is a symbol of the ovum and sperm united. There is an image of a snake with a double penis, which clearly represents fertility and is associated with Cernunnos. The Snake is not just seen as a depiction of male fertility, but of female fertility, too, as the mother snake gives birth to many young. In a magical sense, the Snake represents both physical and metaphysical procreation.

The Druids associated the Snake with Nwyvre , which is similar to the eastern concept of Kundalini. Kundalini, serpent fire, lies coiled at the base of the spine activating centers of awareness, health and creativity as we grow and develop. In this way, the Snake is responsible for the awakening of creative forces.

Since the Snake's eyes cloud over before shedding, many have said that it has a trancelike appearance. This association with trance and hypnosis allow the Snake to move between the realms of living and dead. The eyes clear as skin sheds, which can be viewed as a symbol of seeing anew.

This Ally is potentially venomous , which renders it as a guardian of Mysteries. The Snake attacks quickly and is true to its mark. Along with its kin (dragons, wyrms, wyverns, etc.) the Snake is a guardian of treasures, springs of life, and sacred places.

Copyright Asteria Books 2021

Spider

Aranae

Folk Names: Weaver, Spinner, Jumper, Skitters, Attercop, Lobbe, Gangewifre, Arachnid

Deity: Athena, Arachne, Anansi, Neith, Grandmother Spider, Uttu, Areop-Enap, Iktomi

Powers: Creation, patience, wisdom, storytelling, communication, cunning, interconnectedness and networking

MYTH, MAGIC, AND RITUAL: In many mythologies, the spider is a primordial weaver, spinning the cosmos into existence. The goddess Neith in ancient Egypt and the Ashanti spider-god Anansi both wove the world from their own silk, representing cosmic order and the power of storytelling.

In many Native American traditions, the spider is a teacher of wisdom and patience, with Spider Woman creating the stars, moon, and sun. Her webs symbolize the delicate interconnectedness of all life.

In ritual, spider imagery and the act of weaving are used to manifest intentions and bind spells, drawing parallels between the creation of a web and the construction of one's own reality.

Modern magical practitioners often work with the spider's energy for creative projects, intricate spellwork, and to gain insight into the complex patterns of destiny.

It is seen as a creature of shadow and light, teaching the balance between creation and destruction, as its web is both a home and a trap.

Copyright Asteria Books 2015

Swan

Cygnus

Folk Names: *Eala*
Deity: Goda, Oenghus, Lyr, Cuchulain, Aphrodite and Apollo
Powers: shape-shifting, love, grace, beauty

MYTH, MAGIC, AND RITUAL: The Swan is often depicted with a silver or gold chain around the neck in Celtic legends -- possibly a carry-over from the Aphrodite tradition of the golden sash. Aphrodite was a waterbird Goddess in early Proto-Indo European practice, and the Swan is heavily associated with her in Greek tradition. This is hardly a surprising connection, given that the Swan is very prominent in love stories in Celtic lands, including the tale of Oenghus and Yewberry (who is a Swan Maiden).

In Celtic lore, Swan is associated with Otherworldly travel and migration of the Soul. The "swan song" speaks of both grace and beauty (because Swan's final song is said to be strikingly beautiful) and also of death and transition. Swan is often the poetic representation of the Soul itself in Celtic lore.

This bird's skin and feathers were used to make the bard's ceremonial cloak, according to Philip and Stephanie Carr-Gomm's Druid Animal Oracle. This is another sign of grace and beauty -- the grace and beauty of word and song, which the celts understood to be very important to both art and magic.

Swans are intimately linked with shape-shifting in celtic lore, as well. Several tales speak of children and maidens who are changed (or can change themselves) into swans for one reason or another. Because of these shape-shifting characteristics, Swan is also further linked to Elphame and the realm of Faerie.

Swan, Horse and Apple are a very potent feminine, Faerie Totemic set in relation to the White Goddess (known/shown to members of the Spiral Castle Tradition as Goda).

Copyright Asteria Books 2021

Swine

Sus

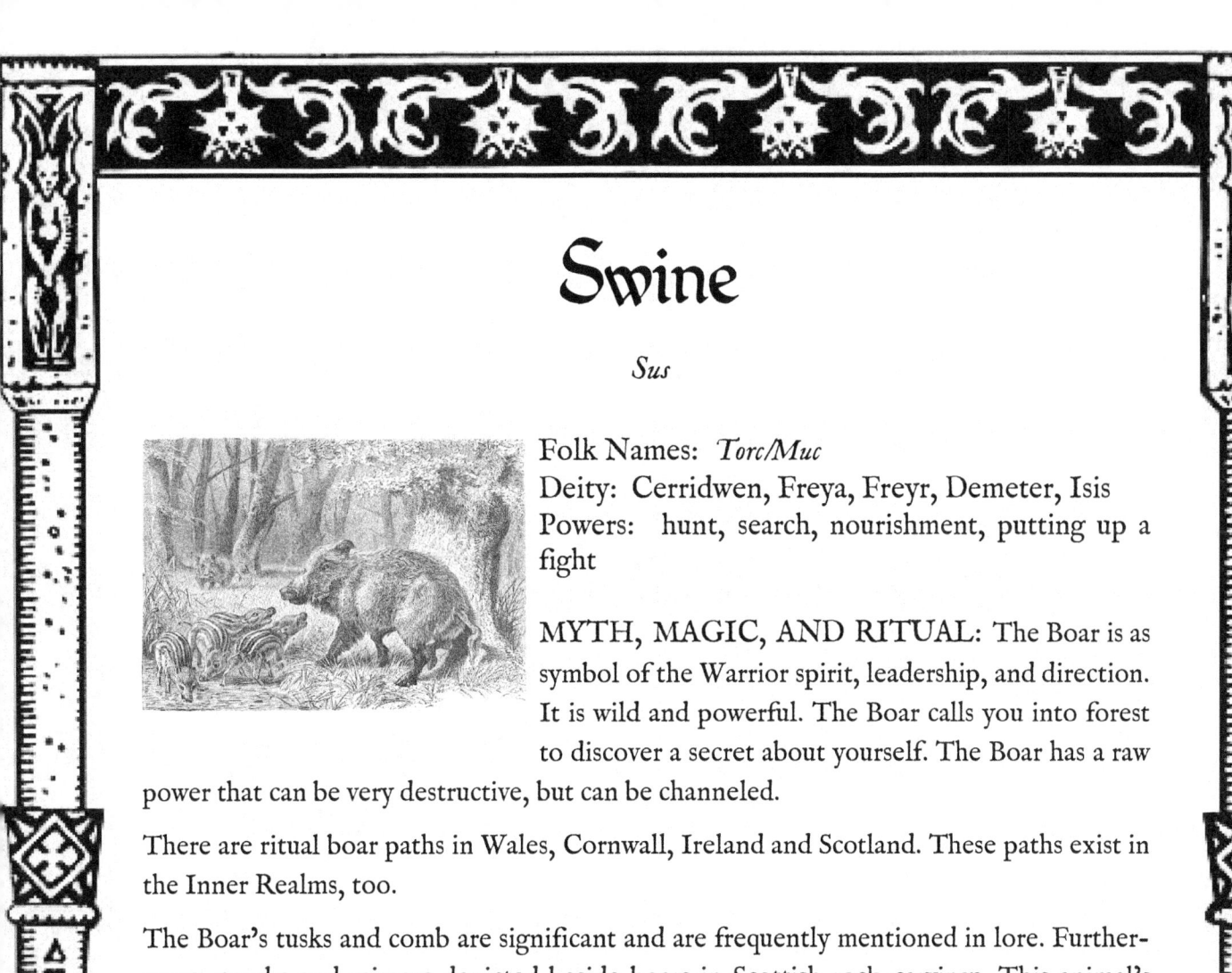

Folk Names: *Torc/Muc*
Deity: Cerridwen, Freya, Freyr, Demeter, Isis
Powers: hunt, search, nourishment, putting up a fight

MYTH, MAGIC, AND RITUAL: The Boar is as symbol of the Warrior spirit, leadership, and direction. It is wild and powerful. The Boar calls you into forest to discover a secret about yourself. The Boar has a raw power that can be very destructive, but can be channeled.

There are ritual boar paths in Wales, Cornwall, Ireland and Scotland. These paths exist in the Inner Realms, too.

The Boar's tusks and comb are significant and are frequently mentioned in lore. Furthermore, combs and mirrors depicted beside boars in Scottish rock-carvings. This animal's image was often used as emblem on helmets and mouthpiece of battle-horns to terrify enemies and on swords and bronze shields to protect the warrior.

It is a secretly (inwardly) feminine symbol that is connected with healing as well as destruction. In Scotland, women would give birth at the Boar Stone, with their bare feet on the stone to absorb its power. In Celtic terms, hunting and healing seen as connected.

The sow is a symbol of nourishment, as swine are a particularly potent food source. Indeed, it is said that "everything but the oink" is used as food. Just as the sow gives life as food, so does she take life away. Any pig farmer can attest to the practice of sows eating their own piglets after birth. The sow is therefore symbolic of the Goddess who is death-in-life and life-in-death.

The sow is especially associated with Cerridwen, whose name is sometimes translated as "white sow," making her association with September (in the Spiral Castle Trad) particularly potent.

Copyright Asteria Books 2021

Toad

Bufonidae

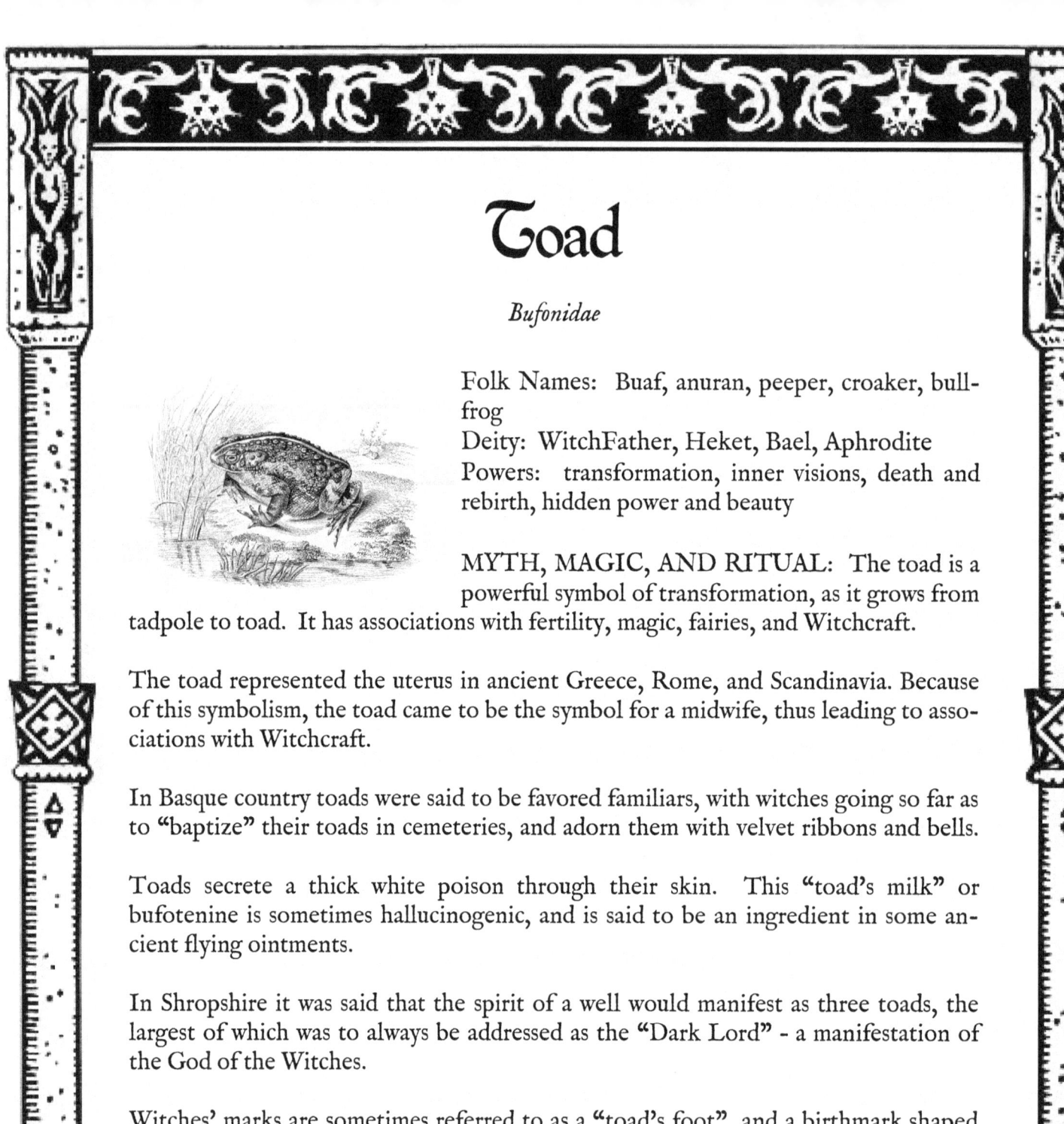

Folk Names: Buaf, anuran, peeper, croaker, bullfrog
Deity: WitchFather, Heket, Bael, Aphrodite
Powers: transformation, inner visions, death and rebirth, hidden power and beauty

MYTH, MAGIC, AND RITUAL: The toad is a powerful symbol of transformation, as it grows from tadpole to toad. It has associations with fertility, magic, fairies, and Witchcraft.

The toad represented the uterus in ancient Greece, Rome, and Scandinavia. Because of this symbolism, the toad came to be the symbol for a midwife, thus leading to associations with Witchcraft.

In Basque country toads were said to be favored familiars, with witches going so far as to "baptize" their toads in cemeteries, and adorn them with velvet ribbons and bells.

Toads secrete a thick white poison through their skin. This "toad's milk" or bufotenine is sometimes hallucinogenic, and is said to be an ingredient in some ancient flying ointments.

In Shropshire it was said that the spirit of a well would manifest as three toads, the largest of which was to always be addressed as the "Dark Lord" - a manifestation of the God of the Witches.

Witches' marks are sometimes referred to as a "toad's foot", and a birthmark shaped like a toad is a sure sign of witch power.

Toadstools are so named due to the toad's associations with fairyland, and with their hallucinogenic properties.

Doreen Valiente was a fan of the natterjack toad, and recommended them as pets and excellent familiars. The natterjack toad has associations with the "yellow ringed" toad which produced the legendary Toad Bone amulet, which was said to confer many strange magical powers on those who carried it. It is related to the toadstone, a stone said to rest in the head of a toad.

Copyright Asteria Books 2021

Wolf

Canis lupus

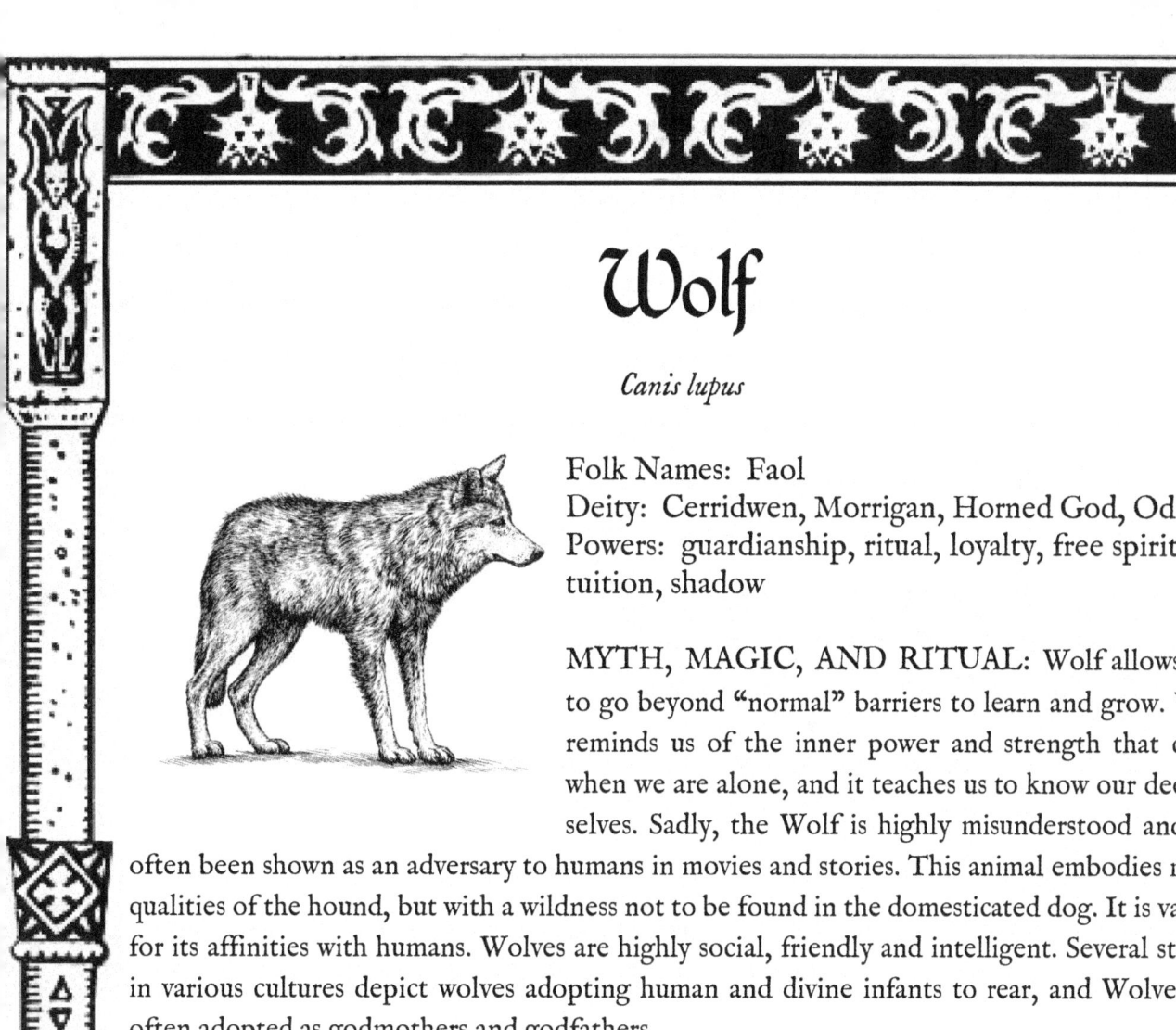

Folk Names: Faol
Deity: Cerridwen, Morrigan, Horned God, Odin
Powers: guardianship, ritual, loyalty, free spirit, intuition, shadow

MYTH, MAGIC, AND RITUAL: Wolf allows you to go beyond "normal" barriers to learn and grow. Wolf reminds us of the inner power and strength that come when we are alone, and it teaches us to know our deepest selves. Sadly, the Wolf is highly misunderstood and has often been shown as an adversary to humans in movies and stories. This animal embodies many qualities of the hound, but with a wildness not to be found in the domesticated dog. It is valued for its affinities with humans. Wolves are highly social, friendly and intelligent. Several stories in various cultures depict wolves adopting human and divine infants to rear, and Wolves are often adopted as godmothers and godfathers.

The Celts would cross-breed hounds with wolves for a powerful battle dog. In the area of fighting, it is important to know that the Wolf does not fight unnecessarily. In fact, it will avoid fights if it can. Like a true Warrior, it does not have to demonstrate dominance, but can when called upon.

The Morrigan takes the form of a She-wolf and attacks Cu-Chulainn for spurning her amorous advances, and one of Cerridwen's gifts as Henwen was a wolf-cub. The Wolf is an ally of the Horned One on Gundestrap cauldron. (And in many images, there is a powerful connection between the Wolf and the Raven.)

In magic and medicine, people have believed that a Wolf's hide provided protection from epilepsy, and the teeth were considered lucky - rubbed on teething baby's gums and worn as charms and amulets.

In the Americas, the Wolf is seen as the spirit of free and unspoiled wilderness. There are several types of Wolves in this part of the World - the Red Wolf, the Mexican Wolf, the Timber Wolf (or Gray Wolf), and the Arctic Wolf. In size, they are smaller than people imagine (about like a good-sized German Shepherd).

Copyright Asteria Books 2021

Wren

Troglodytidae

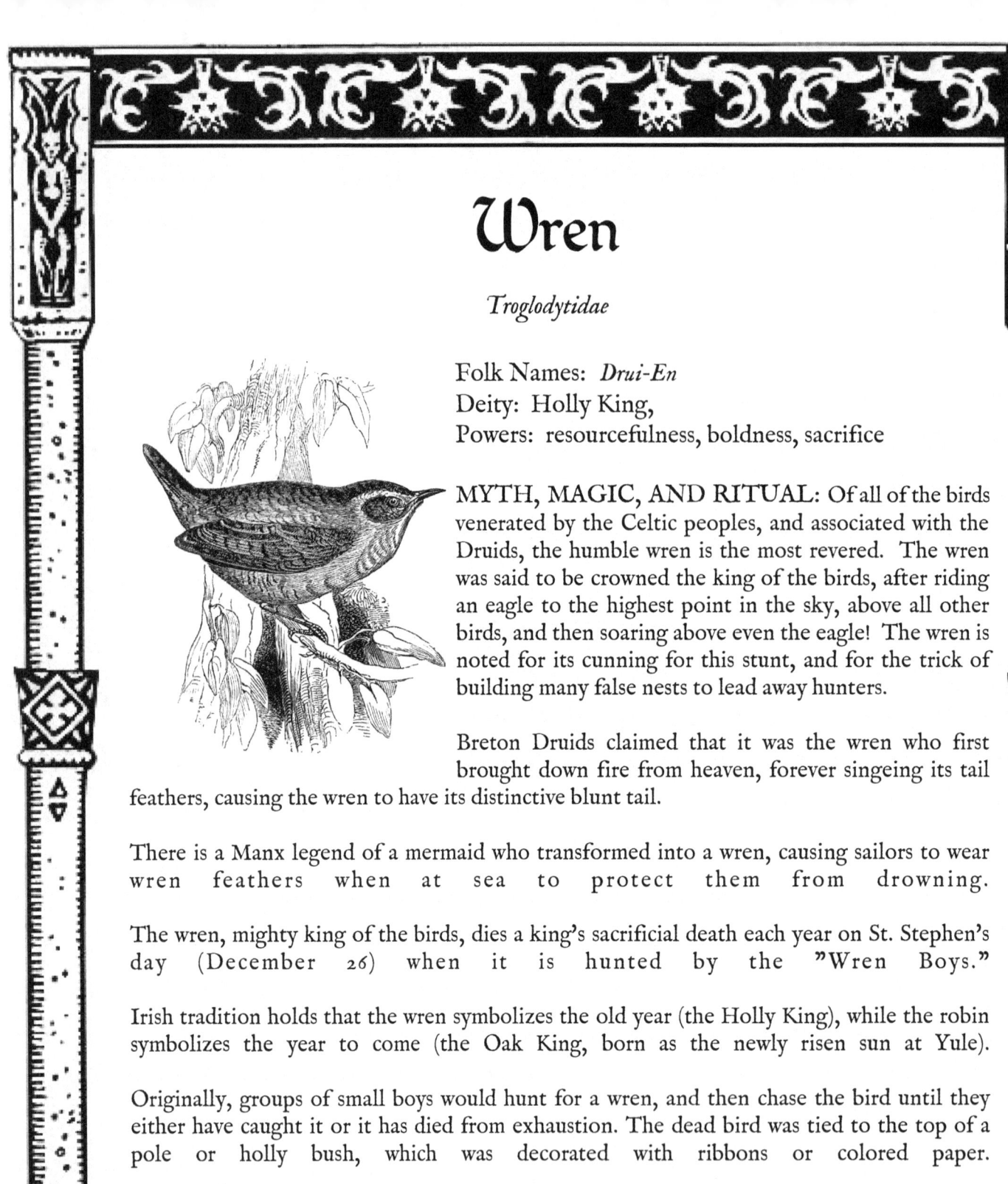

Folk Names: *Drui-En*
Deity: Holly King,
Powers: resourcefulness, boldness, sacrifice

MYTH, MAGIC, AND RITUAL: Of all of the birds venerated by the Celtic peoples, and associated with the Druids, the humble wren is the most revered. The wren was said to be crowned the king of the birds, after riding an eagle to the highest point in the sky, above all other birds, and then soaring above even the eagle! The wren is noted for its cunning for this stunt, and for the trick of building many false nests to lead away hunters.

Breton Druids claimed that it was the wren who first brought down fire from heaven, forever singeing its tail feathers, causing the wren to have its distinctive blunt tail.

There is a Manx legend of a mermaid who transformed into a wren, causing sailors to wear wren feathers when at sea to protect them from drowning.

The wren, mighty king of the birds, dies a king's sacrificial death each year on St. Stephen's day (December 26) when it is hunted by the "Wren Boys."

Irish tradition holds that the wren symbolizes the old year (the Holly King), while the robin symbolizes the year to come (the Oak King, born as the newly risen sun at Yule).

Originally, groups of small boys would hunt for a wren, and then chase the bird until they either have caught it or it has died from exhaustion. The dead bird was tied to the top of a pole or holly bush, which was decorated with ribbons or colored paper.

Early in the morning of St. Stephen's Day, the wren was carried from house to house by the boys, who wore straw masks or blackened their faces with burnt cork, and dressed in old clothes. At each house, the boys sing the Wren Boys' song. Such as:

The wren, the wren, the king of all birds,
On St. Stephen's Day was caught in the furze;
Up with the kettle and down with the pan,
Pray give us a penny to bury the wren.

Copyright Asteria Books 2021

www.ingramcontent.com/pod-product-compliance
Lightning Source LLC
Chambersburg PA
CBHW081157230426
43666CB00016B/2843